Colloquial

Hindi

The Colloquial Series

The following languages are available in the Colloquial series:

Afrikaans
Albanian
Amharic
Arabic (Levantine)
Arabic of Egypt
Arabic of the Gulf and Saudi Arabia
Basque
Breton
Bulgarian
Cambodian
Cantonese
Catalan
Chinese
Croatian
Czech
Danish
Dutch
English
Estonian
Finnish
French
German
Greek
Gujarati
Hebrew
Hindi
Hungarian
Icelandic
Indonesian
Irish (forthcoming)
Italian
Japanese
Korean
Latvian
Lithuanian
Malay
Mongolian
Norwegian
Panjabi
Persian
Polish
Portuguese
Portuguese of Brazil
Romanian
Russian
Scottish Gaelic
Serbian
Slovak
Slovene
Somali
Spanish
Spanish of Latin America
Swahili
Swedish
Tamil
Thai
Turkish
Ukrainian
Urdu
Vietnamese
Welsh
Yoruba

COLLOQUIAL 2s Series

The Next Step in Language Learning

Chinese
Dutch
French
German (forthcoming)
Italian
Portuguese of Brazil (forthcoming)
Russian
Spanish
Spanish of Latin America

All these Colloquials are available in book and CD packs, or sold separately. You can order them from http://www.routledge.com or from your bookseller.

Colloquial
Hindi

The Complete Course for Beginners

Tej K. Bhatia

LONDON AND NEW YORK

First published 1996
by Routledge

Reprinted 1999, 2001, 2002, 2003, 2004
Transferred to Digital Printing 2006

This edition first published 2008
by Routledge
2 Park Square, Milton Park, Abingdon, Oxon OX14 4RN

Simultaneously published in the USA and Canada
by Routledge
270 Madison Ave, New York, NY 10016

Reprinted 2010

Routledge is an imprint of the Taylor & Francis Group, an informa business

Typeset in 10/12 pt Times by Graphicraft Limited, Hong Kong
Printed and bound in Great Britain by
TJ International Ltd, Padstow, Cornwall

British Library Cataloguing in Publication Data
A catalogue record for this book is available from the British Library

Library of Congress Cataloging-in-Publication Data
Bhatia, Tej K.
Colloquial Hindi : a complete course for beginners / Tej K. Bhatia. – [2nd, rev. ed.].
p. cm.
Previously published: 1996.
Includes index.
1. Hindi language – Textbooks for foreign speakers – English. 2. Hindi language – Conversation and phrase books – English. 3. Hindi language – Grammar. I. Title.
PK1935.B525 2007
491′. 4382421–dc22 2007001478

ISBN10: 0–415–41956–5 (pbk)
ISBN10: 0–415–39528–3 (audio CDs)
ISBN10: 0–415–39527–5 (pack)

ISBN13: 978–0–415–41956–7 (pbk)
ISBN13: 978–0–415–39528–1 (audio CDs)
ISBN13: 978–0–415–39527–4 (pack)

In memory of
my mother, Shrimati Krishna Wanti Bhatia
and
my father, Shri Parma Nand Bhatia

Contents

Preface

Since the publication of this book over a decade ago, it has undergone several reprints. Nothing is more gratifying for an author than to hear from his/her readers. I consider myself privileged to be the beneficiary of my readers' reactions, suggestions, compliments and wish-lists which poured in from a highly diverse cross-section of readers around the globe. This encouraged me to create a revised and expanded version of the book. Based on the input that I have received, I know it is not the ideal solution to the multitudes of topics (ranging from the treatment of the Hindi script, grammatical details and cross-cultural insights) that one wishes to address; however, it is a modest step toward that goal.

Many changes have occurred since the first publication of the book. India is fast becoming a major global power. The dynamics of communicative situations further call for changes to reflect new situations and realities. Readers will find the following new changes and additions in this book:

- Facts and figures have been updated.
- The section dealing with the script has been beefed up considerably.
- Dialogues and prose texts integrate the Roman as well as the Devanagari in a way that reflects a mutually-feeding relationship between the two. As one of the anonymous reviewers of the book rightly noted, the execution of the Devanagari version of conversations and prose texts was cumbersome in the first edition. This limitation has been addressed.
- Roman is a non-syllabic script whereas Devanagari is syllabic. Whenever relevant, the complementary strengths of the two writing systems are exploited, particularly in explanations of grammar.
- While the new guidelines issued by the Government of India have been followed throughout the book (e.g. the letter **j^{h}a**; preference for ***e*** instead of ***ye*** in words such as **cāhie**; not separating the postpositions with the pronouns), readers are also exposed to

variation (e.g. two ways of writing the third person singular, polite imperative forms and the past tense).
- Whenever relevant, the content has been modernized.
- New topics of cross-cultural communication have been introduced in the cultural notes (e.g. how to say 'no' in socially sensitive situations, linguistic attitudes and hyper-politeness, etiquettes of gift-giving).
- Another innovation is the Online Resource Guide and the Internet links.
- Old errors and misprints have been corrected.

In spite of this, I am acutely aware that this work is not free from limitations. Therefore, I would be grateful for any comments, criticisms or suggestions that perceptive scholars may have on this book. Please send them to me at the following address: Linguistic Studies Program, 312 HBC, Syracuse University, Syracuse, New York-13244-1160, USA or send an email to: tkbhatia@syr.edu.

Acknowledgements

I am especially indebted to Sophie Oliver, Senior Editor, Language Learning, for agreeing to consider and produce the new and revised version of this book and for her commendable patience and encouragement. I am equally indebted to three anonymous reviewers for their constructive and insightful input.

I have contracted many debts in the process of writing this book and its earlier edition. I am also grateful to my teachers and colleagues, Yamuna and Braj Kachru who have taught me and influenced me since my graduate school. I am also indebted to my friends and colleagues Rajeshwari Pandharipande, James W. Gair, Hans Hock, Meena and S.N. Sridhar, Rakesh Bhatt, Rajesh Kumar, William C. Ritchie, Jaklin Kornfilt, Jennifer L. Smith, Vasu Reganathan, Afroz Taj, Amer Bridger, Cassidy Perraeault and Dr Mangat R. Bhardwaj, the author of the companion volume on Punjabi, for their valuable discussions on matters of Hindi teaching and linguistics. Finally, I also owe my thanks to Dr P.R. Mehandiratta (Director General, American Institute of Indian Studies, New Delhi) and to my colleagues at the South Asia Center, Ann Gold, Jishnu Shankar and Susan Wadley, for their comments, support and encouragement.

My mother passed away before the first edition of this book became a reality. This has left a permanent vacuum in my life. My family migrated from the North West Frontier province close to the Pakistan and Afghanistan border, so Hindi was my mother's third language and according to the value system of that time she never had any formal schooling. During the writing of this book I remembered how at the insistence of her children she learned to sign her name in Hindi instead of using a thumb print as a signature. It is still a mystery to me how and when she learned to read the *Gita* in Hindi. I had thought there would still be a lot of time for us and that these questions were not urgent. I was wrong. This work is especially dedicated to her memory.

I owe special thanks to my wife, Shobha, for her encouragement and support and to my daughter, Kanika, and my son, Ankit, who first inspired me to write this book so that they could learn Hindi. My special thanks are also due to my niece, Nandita. No words can express my deepest appreciation of my brothers in India for their constant support during my entire career.

The pictures produced in this book were taken by the author as part of the ongoing collaborative project, Hindi OnLine, between Syracuse University and the University of Illinois at Urbana-Champaign and the University of Texas at Austin. The project is funded by a grant from the South Asia Research Center (SALRC), the University of Chicago and the US Department of Education. I gratefully acknowledge the support of Dr Steven M. Poulos, Director, SALRC, for making this work possible.

My heartfelt thanks are also due to: Professor Omkar Koul for his technical assistance in the preparation of the manuscript and his perceptive comments; and to the College of Arts and Sciences' Dean Cathryn R. Newton, Associate Dean Dr Gerold Greeenberg and Dr Ben Ware, Vice President, Research and Computing, for their support of this work.

भूमिका
b^{h}umikā
Introduction

A word to the learner

Welcome to *Colloquial Hindi*. Very often at social get-togethers in the West, I am asked with utmost sincerity whether or not I speak Hindu. Although I have no difficulty in understanding the real intent of the question, unwittingly I find myself in an embarrassing situation. This is particularly true if this inquiry happens to come directly from my host. You see, *Hindu* is the name of the predominant religion in India and Nepal; *Hindi* is the name of the language that is the *lingua franca* of South Asia.

About the language

Hindi is a modern Indo-Aryan language spoken in South Asian countries (India, Pakistan, Nepal) and also in other countries outside Asia (Mauritius, Trinidad, Fiji, Surinam, Guyana, South Africa and other countries). Approximately eight hundred million people speak Hindi, as either a first (480 million) or second language. It is the second most widely spoken language in the world. Along with English, it is the official language of India. In addition, it is the state language of Bihar, Chattisgarh, Delhi, Haryana, Himachal Pradesh, Jarkhand, Madhya Pradesh, Rajasthan and Uttar Pradesh. Also, I should point out that Hindi is the language of Agra (the city of the Taj Mahal).

Hindi, which is a descendant of the Sanskrit language, is not strictly the name of any chief dialect of the area but is an adjective, Persian in origin, meaning Indian. Historically, it was synonymous with Hindui, Hindawi, Rexta and Rexti. The terms Urdu and Hindustani are also used to refer to this language. All these labels denote a mixed speech spoken around the area of Delhi, North India, which gained currency during the twelfth and thirteenth century as a contact language between the Arabs, Afghans, Persian and Turks, and native residents.

Hindi is written in the Devanagari script which is ranked as the most scientific writing system among the existing writing systems of the world. The Devanagari script is written from left to right and is a descendant of the Brahmi script which was well established in India before 500 BC. The script is phonetic in nature and there is a fairly regular correspondence between the letters and their pronunciation. For more details see the section on the Hindi writing system and pronunciation.

The literary history of Hindi goes back to the twelfth century. Some notable literary figures of Hindi are Kabir, Surdas and Tulsidas. The two notable linguistic features of the language are as follows: (1) Hindi still retains the original Indo-European (1500 BC) distinction between aspirated and unaspirated consonants which results in a four-way contrast as shown by the following examples: ***kāl***, 'time', ***k^{h}āl***, 'skin', ***gāl***, 'cheek' and ***g^{h}āl***, 'to put into'; (2) it has the feature of retroflexion in its consonant inventory, cf. ***Tāl***, 'to put off' and ***tāl***, 'pond'. The retroflex consonant is transcribed as the capital **T**. For more details see the section on the Hindi writing system and pronunciation.

Hindi has an approximately three-century-old, well-attested and rich grammatical tradition of its own. It is a by-product of the colonial era and was born shortly after the arrival of Europeans in India. For a detailed treatment of this topic in general and the grammatical tradition in particular, see Bhatia (1987).

About this book

This book is designed as a complete first-year language course, keeping in mind the proficiency guidelines of the American Council on the Teaching of Foreign Languages (ACTFL) and the European Language Community. Every attempt is made to optimize this goal by integrating the linguistic content with the culture of South Asia in general and India in particular. In fact, while teaching the language I have attempted to answer those questions that are often asked about the culture of India.

In my professional life I have often witnessed the fact that the teaching of non-Western languages, including Hindi, is more challenging in the West than the teaching of Western languages. If you have experienced any of the following problems, this book will enable you to achieve the goals described above:

- You sweat at the mere thought of learning a foreign language and/or foreign script.
- You think Hindi is a very difficult language to learn, so why try?
- You have some serious business, research interests or not-so-serious interests (such as travel) in India but you have been led to believe that everybody in India speaks English.
- You have learned Hindi from tools and settings which make native speakers laugh secretly or openly at your language use.
- India is culturally and linguistically so distant from the West that one cannot help but shy away from it.
- You haven't heard of Bollywood movies.
- You consider French the only language fit for romance.

If you subscribe to one or all of the above, you are in for a surprise. First, you might discover in the process of learning the language that learning about Hindi is learning about one's own roots. The only difference is that European migration to India is perhaps the oldest of all migrations from Europe, or vice versa as shown by recent DNA research. For this reason, you will still find some striking similarities between Hindi and English. For example, the Hindi word for English 'name' is **nām**. The list goes on and on. The important thing to know is that Hindi belongs to the Indo-European language family and is similar to English in a number of ways. Learning to note these similarities will make the process of learning this language full of pleasant surprises.

The book is grounded in the *current theories of language acquisition, learnability* and *language use*. Unlike other books (even some of the latest ones), it never loses sight of the social–psychological aspects of language use. In this book, I have not attempted to act like a protector or saviour of language by engaging in linguistic prescriptivism and puritanism. What you will find in this book is how Hindi speakers use Hindi and communicate with each other in meaningful ways. No attempt is made to translate the English word artificially into Hindi if Hindi speakers treat the English word like any other Hindi word. I was outraged when I noticed in a widely circulated course on Hindi in which the waiter asks his customers for their order, the word 'order' translated using the same verb as the English 'obey my order!' For more details see the section entitled 'English Prohibition?' in Unit 2.

Beware . . .

These prescriptivist tendencies defeat the real goal of learning a language in order to communicate with native speakers. Even some of the latest books on Hindi suffer from such problems and unwittingly do a disservice to their learners because of their authors' lack of familiarity with the social–psychological dimensions of language use. I came across some examples in one of the most recent books on Hindi which teaches learners how to introduce themselves to native speakers. The sentences are grammatically correct but the author(s) fail to take into account the invisible dimension of the phenomenon of 'turn taking'. For example, it is acceptable for English speakers to introduce themselves with a string of two clauses following the word 'Hi' (e.g. 'Hi, my name is John and what is yours?'). However, the Hindi speaker will pause after the Hindi equivalent of 'Hi' and wait for the listener to respond with a greeting, and only after that will the Hindi speaker perform the task of telling his name and asking about his listener's name. The failure to teach learners about 'turn taking' through naturalistic conversations makes them run the risk of being seen as 'pushy' or 'impatient' by native speakers. This book is particularly aware of such 'non-linguistic' or invisible dimensions of language use. Therefore, this book never loses sight of *cross-cultural communication* while teaching *linguistic communication.*

This book deals with the four main linguistic skills:

	receptive	*productive*
Aural–oral	listening comprehension	speaking comprehension
Visual	reading comprehension	writing comprehension

These skills are introduced in a manner consistent with the insights of modern Chomskyan linguistics. The learners are exposed to rules and discovery procedures, similar to those employed by native speakers, which enable them to generate an infinite number of sentences in their native language. Not only that, these rules enable native speakers to generate new sentences they have never encountered before (see Bhatia and Ritchie 2006 for details). This is the conceptual framework, combined with my twenty-five years of classroom experience, which has gone into the makeup of this book. Unlike other phrasebooks which emphasize parroting sentences without gaining insight into the linguistic system, this book emphasizes and serves as a catalyst to promote linguistic creativity and optimization. This goal is achieved in a simple and unpretentious way avoiding system overload.

How this book is organized

This book attempts to accommodate two types of learners: (1) those who want to learn the language through the Hindi script called the Devanagari script; and (2) those who wish to learn the language in a relatively short period of time without the aid of the Devanagari writing system (henceforth, Hindi script). Such pragmatic considerations are an important feature of this book.

The book begins with Hindi script and pronunciation. The main body deals with ten conversational units which consist of the following parts: (1) vocabulary; (2) dialogues with English translation; (3) notes detailing pronunciation, grammar and usage relating to the unit; and (4) exercises. The dialogues with 'Tell me why?' and humour columns together with the notes explicitly deal with those aspects of Indian culture about which I am most often asked. The vocabulary or the new words used in the dialogues are given in English and Devanagari script. You may wish to consult the vocabulary sections while doing exercises.

The grammar summary gives an overview of the Hindi grammatical tradition with full paradigms. This section complements the section 'Notes and grammar' given in each lesson.

The vocabulary section gives all the Hindi words used in the dialogues. The words are listed alphabetically both in Hindi and English. The basic vocabulary section classifies Hindi words into different semantic groups.

How to use this book

This book focuses on two types of track: (1) for those learners who want to adopt the English script path; and (2) for those who want to learn the Hindi script. Although learning Hindi script is highly recommended, if you decide to choose the first track, you can bypass the lessons on the writing system. For every learner, on both tracks, the lesson on the 'Hindi writing system and pronunciation' is a must and familiarity with the salient phonetic features of Hindi together with the 'Transcription table' is imperative. Please make sure that you learn the transcription of conversations, which differs from media convention. As shown in the transcription table, media convention is often broad and unsystematic. Examples of pronunciation are also recorded on the CD. The exercises with the audio icon are recorded on the CD. If you wish, you can refer to the listening exercises transcripts at the end of the book.

If you are on the Hindi script track, you should start from script unit 1: you will learn Devanagari script in its printed as well as its handwritten form. Conversations and keys are given in Roman as well as in Hindi script. While working on the script units, you can make a start on the conversation units. There is an added incentive to consult the script units: their exercise sections give some of the most common expressions any visitor to India may need. They deal with situations such as customs and immigration, baggage, reading weather charts, making reservations, sending mail, gift-giving, annoying and cautionary settings, shopping, food, entertainment and renting.

Naturally, you will need to memorize the vocabulary. The notes sections give you help on pronunciation, grammar and usage. Reading and learning these notes will stimulate your linguistic creativity.

The reference grammar goes hand in hand with the grammatical notes given at the end of each dialogue. Answers to the exercises can be found in the key to exercises, in both Hindi and English scripts.

Icons used in this book

Icons are used throughout this book for several reasons, the most important of which is to draw attention to those sections that require careful reading.

Audio Symbol

This symbol means that the corresponding exercise requires the use of the CD that accompanies this course.

Magic Key

Information next to this icon is critical for creativity and is worth memorizing.

Sherlock Holmes

This icon appears next to important examples of regular usage, the understanding of which is a primary source of creativity for the native speakers.

Remember

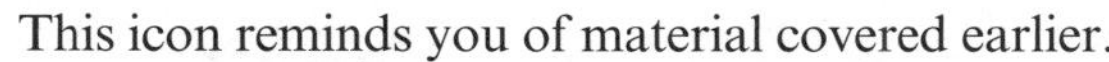

This icon reminds you of material covered earlier.

Caution

The material marked by this icon deserves special attention. It warns you about common mistakes and sources of misunderstanding.

Web links

For additional practice or materials, web links are provided.

The other icons used in the book are thematic in nature and should prove self-explanatory.

Where to go from here

Of course, I do not pretend to teach you everything that needs to be known about Hindi. Language learning can be a life-long venture if you set your goals very high. Your next step is to look for books offering the intermediate and advanced Hindi courses listed at the end of the book. I give this information to alleviate the misconception, quite widespread in the West, that there is a lack of intermediate and advanced-level courses in Asian and African languages. There is no shortage of material, in print or on the web, at these levels. The only difficulty you might face is that this material will invariably be in Hindi script. If that poses a problem for you, there are still many ways you can continue to sharpen your linguistic skills, the most important of which is Hindi films. India is the world's largest producer of films which are widely accessible in the East and the West on video and DVD. To develop a taste for Hindi films is most important in taking you to advanced Hindi language learning.

Readers will find the following web resources useful. Please remember, however, that the links may not always be active and that the content may change. The following links were active at the time of writing:

http://www.latrobe.edu.au/indiangallery/hin11.htm
http://www.ncsu.edu/project/hindi_lessons/

Due to limitations of space, detailed descriptions of monuments such as the Taj Mahal could not be included in this book; for the sight and sounds of Indian monuments, lessons 2 and 9 from the www.ncsu.edu website are particularly recommended.

For intermediate and advance readings, the following sites deserve attention:

http://ccat.sas.upenn.edu/plc/hindi/video/
http://lrrc3.sas.upenn.edu/hindi_unicode/
http://philae.sas.upenn.edu/Hindi/hindi.html
http://munshi-premchand.blogspot.com/
http://www.abhivyakti-hindi.org/
http://www.anubhuti-hindi.org/

Newspaper and media sites:

http://www.bbc.co.uk/hindi/
http://www.naidunia.com/

Collection of Indian Newspaper sites:

http://www.indiapress.org/index.php/Hindi/400x60

Best wishes.

Reference

Bhatia, Tej K. 1987. *A History of the Hindi Grammatical Tradition*. Leiden: E.J. Brill.

Bhatia, Tej K. and William C. Ritchie. 2006. *Handbook of Bilingualism*. Oxford: Blackwell Publishing.

हिन्दी लेखन और उच्चारण
hindī lek^{h}an aur uccāraN

Hindi writing system and pronunciation

Introduction (CD 1; 2)

This chapter briefly outlines the salient properties of Devanagari script and Hindi pronunciation. Hindi is written in Devanagari script. Even if you are not learning the script, this chapter is indispensable because you need to know the pronunciation values of the Roman/English letters used in the conversational units. Also, one or two unfamiliar symbols are drawn from the International Phonetic Alphabet (IPA). The transcription scheme followed here is widely used in the teaching of Hindi and in Hindi language, literature and linguistics. As I have said, the best way to learn Hindi is to learn the script as well. However, if this is not possible due to consideration of time, you will still need to refer to the transcription table until you have mastered the letters and their pronunciation value.

Listen to and repeat the pronunciation of Hindi vowels and consonants together with their minimal pairs, recorded on the CD accompanying this book.

Devanagari script

A number of languages are written in Devanagari script. Besides Hindi, Nepali, Marathi and Sanskrit are also written in this script. Other languages such as Punjabi, Bengali, Gujarati use a slight variation of this script. This means that roughly *half of humanity* use either this script or its close variant which follows the same underlying organizational system.

All scripts of Indic origin, including Devanagari script, are descendants of the Brahmi script which was well established some time before 500 BC in India. These scripts are considered the most scientific among the existing writing systems of the world for a number of reasons. (1) The arrangement and classification of the letters or symbols follow a system based on physiological or phonetic principles, namely the point and manner of articulation. Other writing systems, including the Roman system, employ arbitrary, random criteria to arrange and categorize the letters. (2) Each letter represents one sound only (at least in most cases). For example, in English the [k] sound can be represented by the letters **k**, **q**, **c** and **ch**. This does not happen in Devanagari. Because of its scientific and phonetic nature, this script has become the foundation of modern speech science and the International Phonetic Alphabet (IPA.) The IPA is basically the romanized version of Devanagari script. As a result there is fairly regular correspondence between script and pronunciation. In other words, the words are pronounced as they are written, and that is good news for our learners.

Devanagari script is written from left to right and from the top of the page down, like Roman script. It does not distinguish between upper-case and the lower-case letters. It is syllabic in nature, i.e. every consonant letter/symbol represents the consonant plus the inherent vowel अ **a**. The pronunciation of the inherent vowel is the major exception to the rule of correspondence between script and pronunciation. These exceptions are detailed in script unit 1 and script unit 4. Other minor exceptions are indicated by angular brackets < > with the words listed in the vocabulary of each unit.

Below you will find Hindi vowel and consonant charts. In Devanagari vowels and consonants are listed separately because they involve distinct articulations.

Hindi vowels

Independent forms

अ	आ	इ	ई	उ	ऊ	ए	ऐ	ओ	औ	ऋ
a	ā	i	ī	u	ū	e	ɛ	o	au	ri

Dependent forms: following a consonant

ø	ा	ि	ी	ु	ू	े	ै	ो	ौ	ृ
a	ā	i	ī	u	ū	e	ɛ	o	au	ri

Notes on Hindi vowels

Hindi vowels do not distinguish between capital and non-capital. However, they do distinguish between independent and dependent forms. The independent forms are often called 'the main' or 'full' vowels, whereas the corresponding dependent forms are called 'matra' vowels and are connected to the preceding consonant.

Nasalization

In the production of a nasal vowel, a vowel is pronounced through the mouth and the nose at the same time. Using either the symbol ँ or ं with the vowel indicates nasalization in Hindi. Long vowels are usually nasalized in Hindi. In our transcription, the tilde symbol ˜ is used to indicate vowel nasalization, as in

आँ ã   ऊँ ũ   एँ ɛ̃

The symbol ं is used to indicate vowel nasalization when any stroke of the vowel crosses the top horizontal line, as in ऐं.

Diphthongs

ऐ **ɛ** and औ **au** are pronounced as *a* + *i* and *a* + *u* in the Eastern variety of Hindi, but are pronounced as single vowels in Standard Hindi. They receive dipthongal pronunciation only if they are followed by *y* and *w*/*v*, respectively.

ऋ **ri** does not occur in Hindi. It is used in the writing of a handful of words which are borrowed by Hindi from Sanskrit.

Hindi consonants

	Voiceless unaspirated	*Voiceless aspirated*	*Voiced unaspirated*	*Voiced aspirated*	*Nasal*
k-group	क **ka**	ख **k^{h}a**	ग **ga**	घ **g^{h}a**	ङ **ŋa**
c-group	च **ca**	छ **c^{h}a**	ज **ja**	झ **j^{h}a**	ञ **ña**
T-group	ट **Ta**	ठ **T^{h}a**	ड **Da**	ढ **D^{h}a**	ण **Na**
t-group	त **ta**	थ **t^{h}a**	द **da**	ध **d^{h}a**	न **na**
p-group	प **pa**	फ **P^{h}a**	ब **ba**	भ **b^{h}a**	म **ma**
Others	य **ya**	र **ra**	ल **la**	व **wa/va**	श **sha**
	ष **SHa**	स **sa**	ह **ha**		
	ड़ **Ra**	ढ़ **R^{h}a**			

Sanskrit letters used infrequently: क्ष **ksha** त्र **tra** ज्ञ **gya**

Notes on Hindi consonants

The first five groups of consonants are called stops because they are pronounced by stopping outgoing air from the mouth. The fifth column of these five groups of consonants is called nasal because the air is released through the nose while it is stopped from the mouth. The nasal consonants of the first two groups, i.e. ङ **ŋa** and ञ **ña** are *never* used in their syllabic form in Hindi, so you will not find them in this book. They are included here because they are part of the traditional Devanagari consonant chart.

Place of articulation

All consonants arranged within each of the five groups share the same place of articulation, as described below:

क-वर्ग *k-group*

These consonants are also called 'velar' because the back of the tongue touches the back of the soft palate, called the velum. They are similar to the English *k* and *g*.

क	ख	ग	घ	ङ
ka	k^{h}a	ga	g^{h}a	ŋa

च-वर्ग *c-group*

These sounds are the closest equivalent to the English sound **ch** in 'church.' The main body of the tongue touches the hard palate in the articulation of these sounds.

च	छ	ज	झ	ञ
ca	c^{h}a	ja	j^{h}a	ña

ट-वर्ग *T-group* (the 'capital T group')

ट	ठ	ड	ढ	ण
Ta	T^{h}a	Da	D^{h}a	Na

These consonants represent the most colourful features of the languages of the Indian subcontinent. They are also called 'retroflex' consonants. There is no equivalent of these sounds in English. In the articulation of these sounds, the tip of the tongue is curled back and the *underside* of the tongue touches the hard palate. The following diagram can help in the production of these sounds:

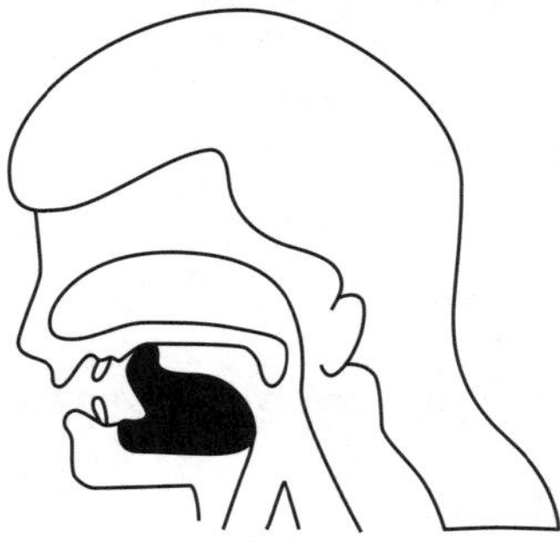

Note that ड़ *R* and ढ़ R^h are also pronounced with the same point of articulation.

त-वर्ग *t-group*

The tip of the tongue touches the back of the teeth, and not the gum ridge behind the teeth as is the case in the pronunciation of the English **t** or **d**.

त	थ	द	ध	न
ta	t^ha	da	d^ha	na

Study the following diagrams carefully in order to distinguish Hindi *t*-group of sounds from the English *t*-group of sounds.

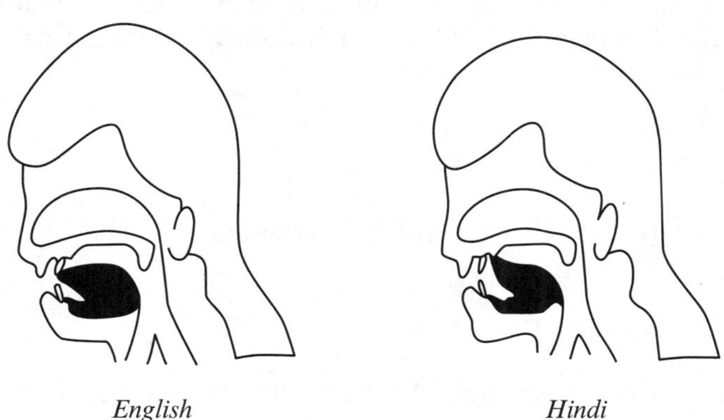

English *Hindi*

प-वर्ग *p-group*

These sounds are similar to English **p** or **b** sounds. They are pronounced by closing or nearly closing the lips.

प	फ	ब	भ	म
pa	p^ha	ba	b^ha	ma

Manner of articulation

All columns in the five groups involve the same *manner of articulation.*

Voiceless unaspirated

क	च	ट	त	प
ka	ca	Ta	ta	pa

These sounds are like the English **k** (as in 'skin' but not as in 'kin'), **p** (as in 'spin' but not as in 'pin'). In 'kin' and 'pin', the English sounds **k** and **p** are slightly aspirated, i.e. they are followed by a slight 'puff of air'. In order to pronounce the corresponding Hindi **k** and **p**, you need to reduce the flow of breath.

Voiceless aspirated

ख	छ	ठ	थ	फ
k^ha	c^ha	T^ha	t^ha	p^ha

The superscripted ^{h} means that these sounds are pronounced with a strong 'puff of air'. All you have to do is to increase the air flow slightly in the pronunciation of the English **k** and **p** sounds.

Voiced unaspirated

ग	ज	ड	द	ब
ga	ja	Da	da	ba

In the production of these sounds the vocal cords vibrate and produce a buzzing sound, like that of a bee. You should have no difficulty producing these sounds as they are like English **g** and **b**.

Voiced aspirated (breathy voiced)

If you pronounce voiced unaspirated consonants with a 'puff of air', you will produce voiced aspirated sounds. The superscripted ^{h} indicates the presence of the 'puff of air'. If this seems difficult, try pronouncing the voiced unaspirated consonants with an *h* (as in ho*g*-*h*og). If you pronounce the words fast enough, you will obtain the voiced aspirate g^h at the end of the first break between the two words.

घ	झ	ढ	ध	भ
g^ha	j^ha	D^ha	d^ha	b^ha

Nasal

ङ	ञ	ण	न	म
ŋa	ña	Na	na	ma

These sounds are similar to English nasal consonants such as **n** and **m**. The velar and palatal nasals are similar to the nasal consonants in the English words 'king' and 'bunch', respectively.

य-ह वर्ग Other consonants (miscellaneous)

The following consonants grouped together as 'others' are very similar to English sounds, so do not call for detailed phonetic description. The English transcription is sufficient to give you information about their pronunciation.

य	र	ल	व	श	स	ह
ya	ra	la	wa/va	sha	sa	ha

As mentioned above, the following two consonants are pronounced with a curled tongue. However, the underside of the tongue is flapped forward quickly, touching the hard palate slightly, instead of articulating the stop with the hard palate. ढ़ **R^h^a** is the aspirated counterpart of ड़ **Ra**.

ड़	ढ़
Ra	R^ha

Sanskrit letters

The following four consonants are from Sanskrit. They do not exist in Hindi except in the handful of words borrowed from Sanskrit.

ष SHa   क्ष ksha   त्र tra   ज्ञ gya

ष **SHa** is pronounced like श **sha**, and the other three letters represent consonant clusters in Hindi.

Borrowed Perso-Arabic and English sounds

By placing a dot under the following five consonant symbols, the five Perso-Arabic sounds are represented:

फ़	ज़	ख़	क़	ग़
fa	za	xa	qa	Ga

Out of these five, the first two are used quite frequently in Hindi. The reason for this is that **fa** and **za** are also found in English. The other three consonants are usually pronounced as **k^{h}a**, **ka** and **ga**, respectively. Even the first two sounds **fa** and **za** can be pronounced as **p^{h}a** and **ja**, respectively.

It should be noted that English alveolar sounds **t** and **d** are usually perceived and written as **T** and **D**, respectively. So the **t** and **d** in the proper name 'Todd' are written with the letters ट and ड, respectively.

Pronunciation practice

Minimal pair practice  (CD 1; 3)

Vowels

Oral vowels

Vowel		*Pronunciation cue (English near-equivalent)*	*Hindi words*		
अ	**a**	*a*bout	कल	**kal**	yesterday/tomorrow
आ	**ā**	f*a*ther	काल	**kāl**	time, tense
इ	**i**	s*i*t	दिन	**din**	day
ई	**ī**	s*ea*t	दीन	**dīn**	poor
उ	**u**	b*oo*k	कुल	**kul**	total, family
ऊ	**ū**	b*oo*t, l*oo*t	कूल	**kūl**	shore
ए	**e**	l*a*te, d*a*te (without a glide)	हे	**he**	hey
ऐ	**ɛ**	b*e*t	है	**hɛ**	is
ओ	**o**	b*oa*t (without a glide)	ओर	**or**	side, towards
औ	**au**	b*ou*ght	और	**aur**	and

Nasalized vowels ँ ं

Nasalized vowels (long)		*Hindi words*		
आँ	**ā̃**	माँ	**mā̃**	mother
ईं	**ī̃**	कहीं	**kahī̃**	somewhere
ऊँ	**ū̃**	हूँ	**hū̃**	am
एँ	**ẽ**	में	**mẽ**	in
ऐं	**ɛ̃**	मैं	**mɛ̃**	I
ओं	**õ**	गोंद	**gõd**	gum
औं	**ãũ**	चौंक	**cãũk**	be alarmed, be startled

Minimal pair practice: words with oral and nasalized vowels

Oral vowels				*Nasalized vowels*			
आ	**ā**	कहा	**kahā** said (m.sg)	आँ	**ā̃**	कहाँ	**kahā̃** where
ई	**ī**	कही	**kahī** said (f.sg)	ईं	**ī̃**	कहीं	**kahī̃** somewhere
ऊ	**ū**	पूछ	**pūc^h** ask	ऊँ	**ū̃**	पूँछ	**pū̃c^h** a tail
ए	**e**	ले	**le** take	एँ	**ẽ**	लें	**lẽ** take (optative)
ऐ	**ɛ**	है	**hɛ** is	ऐं	**ɛ̃**	हैं	**hɛ̃** are
ओ	**o**	गोद	**god** the lap	ओं	**õ**	गोंद	**gõd** gum
औ	**au**	चौक	**cauk** a crossing	औं	**ãũ**	चौंक	**cãũk** be alarmed, be startled

Consonants  (CD 1; 4)

Listen to the recording and repeat the words.

Remember, the contrasts shown below are very critical in Hindi. Failing to maintain such contrasts will result in a breakdown of communication. If you want to ask for food, खाना **k^hānā** failing to aspirate will result in saying काना **kānā** and you will end up asking for a one-eyed person. Similarly, if you do not distinguish the *T*-group of consonants from the *t*-group of consonants, rather than asking for रोटी **roTī**, 'bread', you will end up reporting that the girl is crying (i.e. रोती **rotī**).

Minimal pair practice: words with unvoiced unaspirated stops and unvoiced aspirated stops

Unvoiced unaspirated				*Unvoiced aspirated*			
क	**ka**	काल	**kāl** time	ख	**k^ha**	खाल	**k^hāl** skin
च	**ca**	चल	**cal** walk	छ	**c^ha**	छल	**c^hal** cheat
ट	**Ta**	टाल	**Tāl** postpone	ठ	**T^ha**	ठाल	**T^hāl** sit idle
त	**ta**	तान	**tān** tune	थ	**t^ha**	थाल	**t^hāl** plate
प	**pa**	पल	**pal** moment	फ	**p^ha**	फल	**p^hal** fruit

Minimal pair practice: words with voiced unaspirated stops and voiced aspirated stops

Voiced unaspirated			*Voiced aspirated*		
ग **ga**	गा **gā**	sing	घ **g^{h}a**	घा **g^{h}ā**	the fourth letter of the *k*-series
ज **ja**	जल **jal**	water	झ **j^{h}a**	झल **j^{h}al**	fan
ड **Da**	डाल **Dāl**	a branch	ढ **D^{h}a**	ढाल **D^{h}āl**	shield
द **da**	दान **dān**	charity	ध **d^{h}a**	धान **d^{h}ān**	paddy
ब **ba**	बाल **bāl**	hair	भ **b^{h}a**	भाल **b^{h}āl**	forehead

Minimal pair practice: words with unvoiced aspirated stops and voiced aspirated stops

Unvoiced aspirated			*Voiced aspirated*		
ख **k^{h}a**	खाना **k^{h}ānā**	food	घ **g^{h}a**	घाना **g^{h}ānā**	Ghana, the name of a country
छ **c^{h}a**	छल **c^{h}al**	cheat	झ **j^{h}a**	झल **j^{h}al**	fan
ठ **T^{h}a**	ठक **T^{h}ak**	tapping sound	ढ **D^{h}a**	ढक **D^{h}ak**	cover
थ **t^{h}a**	थान **t^{h}ān**	roll of cloth	ध **d^{h}a**	धान **d^{h}ān**	paddy
फ **p^{h}a**	फूल **p^{h}ūl**	flower	भ **b^{h}a**	भूल **b^{h}ūl**	mistake

Minimal pair practice: words with the *T*-group (retroflex) stops and the *t*-group (dental) stops

ट-वर्ग *T-group*			त-वर्ग *t-group*		
ट **Ta**	टाल **Tāl**	postpone	त **ta**	ताल **tāl**	pond
ढ **T^{h}a**	ठक **T^{h}ak**	tapping (sound)	थ **t^{h}a**	थक **t^{h}ak**	be tired
ड **Da**	डाल **Dāl**	branch	द **da**	दाल **dāl**	lentil
ढ **D^{h}a**	ढक **D^{h}ak**	cover	ध **d^{h}a**	धक **d^{h}ak**	palpitation, excitement

Listen to the following:

Nasal consonants

Nasal consonant	*Hindi word*		
ङ **ŋa**	अंग	**aŋg**	body, limb
ञ **ña**	अंजू	**añjū**	female name
ण **Na**	बाण	**bāN**	arrow
न **na**	नान	**nān**	bread
म **ma**	मान	**mān**	respect

Other consonants

Listen to the following words:

Consonant	*Hindi word*		
य **ya**	यार	**yār**	friend
र **ma**	राजा	**rājā**	king
ल **la**	लाल	**lāl**	red
व **wa/va**	वार	**vār**	an attack
श **sha**	शाल	**shāl**	shawl
स **sa**	साल	**sāl**	year
ह **ha**	हाल	**hāl**	condition, state

Minimal pair practice: words with **r**, **R** and **R^h**

Consonant	*Hindi word*		
र **ra**	पर	**par**	on, at
ड़ **Ra**	पड़	**paR**	lie, fall
ढ़ **R^{h}a**	पढ़	**paR^h**	read, study

Borrowed consonants

फ़	ज़	ख़	क़	ग़
fa	**za**	**xa**	**qa**	**Ga**

As pointed out earlier, these consonants were not present in Hindi originally. Many speakers of Hindi still substitute the closest corresponding Hindi consonant for them, as shown below:

फ़	**fa**	becomes	फ	**p^{h}a**
ज़	**za**	becomes	ज	**ja**
ख़	**xa**	becomes	ख	**k^{h}a**
क़	**qa**	becomes	क	**ka**
ग़	**Ga**	becomes	ग	**ga**

In other words, the dots are added to the native symbols to represent the borrowed sounds.

Now listen to the two possible pronunciations of the following words.

Consonant	*Word*			*Consonant*	*Word*	
फ़ **fa**	फ़ीस	**fīs**	tuition, fee	फ **p^{h}a**	फीस	**p^{h}īs**
ज़ **za**	ज़रा	**zarā**	just, a little	ज **ja**	जरा	**jarā**
ख़ **xa**	ख़रीद	**xarīd**	buy	ख **k^{h}a**	खरीद	**k^{h}arīd**
क़ **qa**	क़लम	**qalam**	pen	क **ka**	कलम	**kalam**
ग़ **Ga**	ग़रीब	**Garīb**	poor	ग **ga**	गरीब	**garīb**

Syllables, **stress** and intonation: see Script Unit 5.

Punctuation marks

With the exception of the full stop, which is represented by the sign ।, Hindi uses the same punctuation marks as English. For abbreviation purposes, a small circle • is used after the first syllable. For example, पं• stands for Pandit. Sometimes the sign ˘ is used over the vowel आ **ā** to represent the English sound **o**, as in जॉन 'John' and यॉर्क 'York'.

Numerals

१	२	३	४	५	६	७	८	९	०
1	2	3	4	5	6	7	8	9	0

If you do not have the recording, either skip the following section or seek the assistance of a native speaker.

अभ्यास **ab^{h}yās** Exercises

Exercise 1 (CD 1; 5)

Listen to each group of three words and circle the word that is different.

	A	B	C
	कर	खर	कर
Example: you hear	kar	k^{h}ar	kar
Answer:		B	

1	A	B	C
2	A	B	C
3	A	B	C
4	A	B	C
5	A	B	C

Exercise 2 (CD 1; 6)

Listen to each group of four words and circle the aspirated words.

	A	B	C	D
	कर	खर	गर	घर
Example: you hear:	kar	k^{h}ar	gar	g^{h}ar
Answer:		B, D		

1	A	B	C	D
2	A	B	C	D
3	A	B	C	D
4	A	B	C	D
5	A	B	C	D

Exercise 3 (CD 1; 7)

Listen to pairs of words contrasting the *T*-group (retroflex) and the *t*-group of consonants.

A		B	
टिक	**Tik**	तिक	**tik**

After each pair has been pronounced, you will hear either 'A' or 'B' again. Underline the word that you hear this time.

Example: you hear टिक **Tik**, then underline **Tik**.

1	ताक	**tāk**	टाक	**Tāk**
2	थक	**t^{h}ak**	ठक	**T^{h}ak**
3	दाग	**dāg**	डाग	**Dāg**
4	धक	**d^{h}ak**	ढक	**D^{h}ak**
5	पर	**par**	पड़	**paR**
6	सर	**sar**	सड़	**saR**
7	करी	**karī**	कढ़ी	**kaR^{h}ī**
8	थीक	**t^{h}īk**	ठीक	**T^{h}īk**

Exercise 4 (CD 1; 8)

Listen to pairs of words with constrasting vowel sounds.

A		*B*	
दिन	**din**	दीन	**dīn**

After each pair has been pronounced, you will hear either 'A' or 'B' again. Underline the word that you hear this time.

Example: you hear दीन **dīn**, then underline **dīn**.

	A		B	
1	काल	**kāl**	कल	**kal**
2	दिन	**din**	दीन	**dīn**
3	मिल	**mil**	मील	**mīl**
4	चुक	**cuk**	चूक	**cūk**
5	मेल	**mel**	मैल	**mɛl**
6	सेर	**ser**	सैर	**sɛr**
7	बिन	**bin**	बीन	**bīn**
8	बाल	**bāl**	बल	**bal**

Transcription table

If you wish to learn Hindi principally via the Roman/English path or if you are used to seeing Hindi words in the English or Bollywood media, you might find the transcription of Hindi words a little odd or unfamiliar at first. However, a quick glance will reveal that media transcription is usually very broad, ambiguous and inconsistent. English–Hindi bilinguals/native speakers can cope with such transcription because they know the target word. Foreign learners do not have this advantage.

It is imperative that learners make themselves familiar with the scientific transcription used in this book – SALT, the transcription system widely used in South Asian language and literature. Such familiarity is critical to avoiding mishaps in communication and to increase learning efficiency: see the section entitled 'Hindi writing system and pronunciation' for details. The table below provides you with a convenient source of reference for Hindi sounds.

Letter (Devanagari)	*SALT (South Asian Language Transcription)*	*Media*	*As in* English *words*
Vowels			
अ	**a**	**uh/a**	*a*bout
आ	**ā**	**aa/ah/a**	f*a*ther
इ	**i**	**i/e**	s*i*t
ई	**ī**	**ee**	s*ea*t
उ	**u**	**u**	b*oo*k
ऊ	**ū**	**oo/u**	b*oo*t, l*oo*t
ए	**e**	**ay/e**	l*a*te, d*a*te (without a glide)
ऐ	**ɛ (ai)**	**ai/aye**	b*e*t
ओ	**o**	**o**	b*oa*t (without a glide)
औ	**au**	**au**	b*ou*ght
Nasal vowels	(e.g. **ã, ĩ, ā̃, ī̃** . . .); see 'Hindi writing system and pronunciation'	vowel + **n/m**	

Letter (Devanagari)	SALT (South Asian Language Transcription)	Media	As in English words
Consonants			
क	**ka**	**ka/ca**	ba*ck*
ख	**k^{h}a**	**kha/ka**	*c*at
ग	**ga**	**ga**	*g*ate
घ	**g^{h}a**	**gha**	ho*g-h*og
ङ	**ŋa**	**na**	ki*ng*
च	**ca**	**cha**	*ch*urch
छ	**c^{h}a**	**chha**	*ch*urch (with slight puff of air)
ज	**ja**	**ja**	*j*ug
झ	**j^{h}a**	**jha/ja**	hed*ge-h*og
ञ	**ña**	**na**	bu*n*ch
ट	**Ta**	**ta**	Not in English: see 'Hindi writing system and pronunciation'
ठ	**T^{h}a**	**t^{h}a**	
ड/ड़	**Da/Ra**	**da/da**	
ढ/ढ़	**D^{h}a/R^{h}a**	**dha/da**	
ण	**Na**	**na**	
त	**ta**	**ta**	ca*t*
थ	**t^{h}a**	**t^{h}a**	*t*in
द	**da**	**da**	*d*og
ध	**d^{h}a**	**dha**	*dh*arma
न	**na**	**na**	*n*ab
प	**pa**	**pa**	zi*p*
फ/फ़	**p^{h}a**	**pha**	*P*at
ब	**ba**	**ba**	*b*at
भ	**b^{h}a**	**bha**	ta*b-l*et
म	**ma**	**ma**	*m*at
य	**ya**	**ya**	*y*es
र	**ra**	**ra**	*r*at
ल	**la**	**la**	*l*ate
व	**wa/va**	**wa/va**	*v*at
श	**sha**	**sha**	*sh*e
ष	**SHa**	**SHa**	Like retroflex; not in English
स	**sa**	**sa**	*s*it
ह	**ha**	**ha**	*h*at

Source: Adapted from Bhatia, Tej K. (2000). *Advertising in Rural India: Language, Marketing Communication and Consumerism*. Tokyo: Institute for the Study of Languages and Cultures of Asia and Africa, Tokyo University of Foreign Studies.

A sample of transcriptional variation

Media	*SALT*
Mahabharat	**Mahābhārata** 'Sanskrit epic'
Ramayan	**ramāyaNa** 'Sanskrit epic'
gharana	**g^{h}arānā** 'lineage'
akashvani	**ākāshvāNī** 'radio'
doordarshan	**dūrdharshan** 'television'
beedi, beeri	**bīRī** 'native cigarette'
Chaay	**cāy** 'tea'
Chaarpay	**cārpāī** 'a string bed with four wooden legs'
Amitabh Bachhan	**Amitāb^{h} Baccan** (famous actor)

लिपि और लेखन
lipi aur lek^han
Script and handwriting

1 पहला पाठ – लिपि pɛhlā pāT^h – lipi

Script unit 1

The first letter of the Devanagari script is अ **a**.

When the preceding sound is a consonant, it is inherent in the consonant, so it is not written separately (as in the Hindi word पर **par** 'on/at'). In all other situations, however, it is written separately (e.g. अब **ab** 'now').

Look at the following combinations of consonants with the vowel अ **a** and try to read them aloud first. You may need to refer to the consonant chart in the transcription table.

Letters				*Word*		*Pronunciation*
प	+	र	=	पर		
pa	+	**ra**	=	**para**	on/at	**par**
अ	+	ब	=	अब		
a	+	**ba**	=	**aba**	now	**ab**
क	+	ल	=	कल		
ka	+	**la**	=	**kala**	yesterday/tomorrow	**kal**

Note that with a preceding **p**, **r**, **b**, **k** or **l** the independent shape of the vowel अ is not used. In such cases the vowel is absorbed into the consonant. It is for this reason that Hindi script is called a 'syllabic' script, i.e. a consonant letter such as क stands for **k** + **a**. Each consonant letter is not written separately, as is the case with the Roman script. So, **k** + **a** *cannot* be written as क + अ. Of course, there are ways to write a consonant without a vowel; we will learn to do this at a later stage.

If you thought that the vowel **-a** at the end of a word is absorbed into the preceding consonant, but is *not* pronounced (i.e. silent) in Standard Hindi speech, you would be right. So, a word written as

पर **para** ‘on/at’ is actually pronounced as **par**. Some dialects of Hindi do not drop the word-final **a** in pronunciation.

Combinations of three or more consonants follow the same pattern.

Letters						*Word*		*Pronunciation*
स	+	ड़	+	क	=	सड़क		
sa	+	**Ra**	+	**ka**	=	**saRakx**	road	**saRak**
म	+	ग	+	र	=	मगर		
ma	+	**ga**	+	**ra**	=	**magarx**	but	**magar**
अ	+	ग	+	र	=	अगर		
a	+	**ga**	+	**ra**	=	**agarx**	if	**agar**

Handwriting

Stroke order

Letter/ Pronunciation	*Stroke order*	*Head stroke/ Head bar*	*Handwriting*
क – वर्ग			
क **ka**	क	क	क
ख **kʰa**	ख	ख	ख
ग **ga**	ग	ग	ग
घ **gʰa**	घ	घ	घ
च – वर्ग			
च **ca**	च	च	च
छ **cʰa**	छ	छ	छ
ज **ja**	ज	ज	ज
झ **jʰa**	झ	झ	झ

Letter/ Pronunciation	*Stroke order*	*Head stroke/ Head bar*	*Handwriting*
ट – वर्ग			
ट **Ta**			
ठ **T^{h}a**			
ड **Da**			
ढ **D^{h}a**			
ण **Na**			
त – वर्ग			
त **ta**			
थ **t^{h}a**			
द **da**			
ध **d^{h}a**			
न **na**			
प – वर्ग			
प **pa**			
फ **p^{h}a**			
ब **ba**			
भ **b^{h}a**			
म **ma**			
य – ह वर्ग			
य **ya**			
र **ra**			
ल **la**			
व **va**			
श **sha**			
ष **SHa**			

Letter/ Pronunciation	*Stroke order*	*Head stroke/ Head bar*	*Handwriting*
स **sa**		स	स
ह **ha**		ह	ह
संस्कृत			
क्ष **ksha**		क्ष	क्ष
त्र **tra**		त्र	त्र
ज्ञ **gya/jya**		ज्ञ	ज्ञ
अन्य *Other retroflex letters*			
ड़ **Ra**		ड़	ड़
ढ़ **R^h^a**		ढ़	ढ़

Observation exercise

Similar-looking characters

घ	**g^h^a**	ध	**d^h^a**						
ख	**k^h^a**	र	**ra**	व	**wa/va**				
ब	**ba**	व	**wa/va**						
भ	**b^h^a**	म	**ma**						
द	**da**	ड	**Da**	ढ	**D^h^a**	ड़	**Ra**	ढ़	**R^h^a**
थ	**t^h^a**	य	**ya**						

अभ्यास ab^h^yās Exercises

Exercise 1

Read aloud the Hindi words given below. Feel free to consult the consonant chart in the transcription table. However, resist the temptation to transcribe and write every letter before you pronounce the word. Treat this as an exercise in simple arithmetic addition. The difference is that you have words rather than numbers here.

You can compare your pronunciation against the recording, if you have it.

1 अमन **2** असल **3** जलन **4** कलम **5** कमल **6** गरम **7** जब **8** कब **9** तब **10** सब

Exercise 2

Identify and transcribe the following letters. Also, observe some similarities between these letters.

क य थ त घ ध भ म व ब

Exercise 3

Write the following in the Devanagari alphabet.

1 k^ha, ra, wa/va
2 Ta, ta, T^ha, tha
3 da, Da, d^ha, D^ha
4 pa, p^ha, ba, ya
5 ra, Ra, R^ha

Exercise 4

Write the following words in Hindi script. Assume that the word-final vowel **a** is dropped.

1 kaT **2** gal **3** cal **4** namak **5** sabak **6** $parak^h$
7 sadar **8** calan **9** man **10** pal **11** garam

Web resources

For the dynamics of stroke order, see Syracuse University's Hindi web page:

http://faculty.maxwell.syr.edu/jishnu/101/alphabet/default.asp?section=0

The following link is also recommended:

http://www.avashy.com/hindiscripttutor.htm

2 दूसरा पाठ – लिपि dūsrā pāT^h – lipi

Script unit 2

In Script Unit 1, we learnt how to use the independent form of short अ **a** and about its absorption into the preceding consonant.

Now, let us learn to combine dependent forms of more vowel symbols. The independent and dependent forms (मात्रा **mātrā**) of Hindi vowels are given below:

Independent	*Dependent (मात्रा **mātrā**)* *'Following a consonant'*	*Position*
अ **a**	0 (zero)	
आ **ā**	ा	after a consonant
इ **i**	ि	before a consonant
ई **ī**	ी	after a consonant
उ **u**	ु	under a consonant
ऊ **ū**	ू	under a consonant
ए **e**	े	top of a consonant
ऐ **ɛ**	ै	top of a consonant
ओ **o**	ो	after a consonant
औ **au**	ौ	after a consonant

Now let us consider the following three dependent vowel symbols:

ा	long	**ā**
ि	short	**i**
ी	long	**ī**

As mentioned above, ा and ी are placed after a consonant, whereas ि is placed before a consonant, as shown below:

ग + ा	क + ी	क + ि
ga + **ā**	**ka** + **ī**	**ka** + **i**
गा **gā**	की **kī**	कि **ki**

Notice when a dependent form of the vowel is adjoined to a consonant, the invisible short अ **a** is actually absorbed. As mentioned in script unit 1, the word-final short **a** is silent.

बा + त	ब + ता	ती + न
bā + **ta**	**ba** + **tā**	**tī** + **na**
बात **bāt**	बता **batā**	तीन **tīn**
thing, matter	tell	three

Now look at the following examples:

बा + री	च + ना	गि + रा
bā + **rī**	**ca** + **nā**	**gi** + **rā**
बारी	चना	गिरा
turn	chick pea	fell

Observe the following three-syllable words:

क + हा + नी   कहानी story
ka + **hā** + **nī**

म + सा + ला   मसाला spice
ma + **sā** + **lā**

कि + ध + र   किधर where, which direction
ki + **d^{h}a** + **ra**

की + म + त   कीमत price
kī + **ma** + **ta**

Now let us turn our attention to the next four dependent vowel forms.

ु	ू	े	ै
u	**ū**	**e**	**ɛ**

These vowel symbols are either placed above or below a consonant symbol, as shown here:

तु	तू	ते	तै
tu	**tū**	**te**	**tɛ**

Read the following words. (In what follows the absence of the word-final short **a** is assumed.)

चु	+	क	=	चुक	finish
cu	+	**ka**		**cuk**	
पू	+	छ	=	पूछ	ask
pū	+	**c^ha**	=	**pūc^h**	
जे	+	ल	=	जेल	jail
je	+	**la**	=	**jel**	
पै	+	सा	=	पैसा	money
pɛ	+	**sā**	=	**pɛsā**	

Exceptions

When ु and ू are joined to र **ra**, they are joined to the middle joint of the र, as shown below:

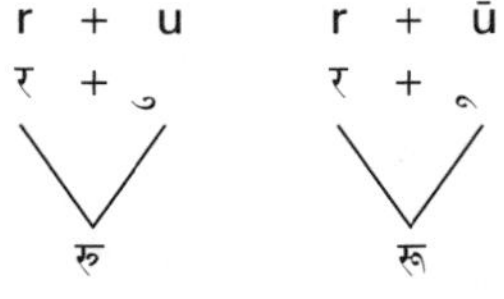

It is incorrect to place ु and ू below the र as in रु **ru** and रू **rū**.

Also, notice the difference in the shape of ु. With र the symbol of the dependent vowel **u** becomes ु.

Now here are the last two dependent vowel forms:

ो	ौ
o	**au**

They are placed to the right of a consonant like **ā** and **ī**, as shown below:

छो	+	टा	=	छोटा	small
c^ho	+	**Tā**			

चौ + क = चौक crossing
cau + k

Observe some more examples of the vowels in question:

प + ड़ौ + सी = पड़ौसी neighbour
pa + **rau** + **sī**

हौ + स + ला = हौसला courage
hau + **sa** + **lā**

पौ + शा + क = पौशाक dress
pao + **shā** + **k**

नि + चो + ड़ = निचोड़ squeeze, essence
ni + **co** + **R**

The use of मात्रा **mātrā** vowels with preceding consonants is shown below. The consonants that never occur with mātrā vowels are not listed here.

क	का	कि	की	कु	कू	के	कै	को	कौ
ka	**kā**	**ki**	**kī**	**ku**	**kū**	**ke**	**kɛ**	**ko**	**kau**
ख	खा	खि	खी	खु	खू	खे	खै	खो	खौ
k^{h}a	**k^{h}ā**	**k^{h}i**	**k^{h}ī**	**k^{h}u**	**k^{h}ū**	**k^{h}e**	**k^{h}ɛ**	**k^{h}o**	**k^{h}au**
ग	गा	गि	गी	गु	गू	गे	गै	गो	गौ
ga	**gā**	**gi**	**gī**	**gu**	**gū**	**ge**	**gɛ**	**go**	**gau**
घ	घा	घि	घी	घु	घू	घे	घै	घो	घौ
g^{h}a	**g^{h}ā**	**g^{h}i**	**g^{h}ī**	**g^{h}u**	**g^{h}ū**	**g^{h}e**	**g^{h}ɛ**	**g^{h}o**	**g^{h}au**
च	चा	चि	ची	चु	चू	चे	चै	चो	चौ
ca	**cā**	**ci**	**cī**	**cu**	**cū**	**ce**	**cɛ**	**co**	**cau**
छ	छा	छि	छी	छु	छू	छे	छै	छो	छौ
c^{h}a	**c^{h}ā**	**c^{h}i**	**c^{h}ī**	**c^{h}u**	**c^{h}ū**	**c^{h}e**	**c^{h}ɛ**	**c^{h}o**	**c^{h}au**
ज	जा	जि	जी	जु	जू	जे	जै	जो	जौ
ja	**jā**	**ji**	**jī**	**ju**	**jū**	**je**	**jɛ**	**jo**	**jau**
झ	झा	झि	झी	झु	झू	झे	झै	झो	झौ
j^{h}a	**j^{h}ā**	**j^{h}i**	**j^{h}ī**	**j^{h}u**	**j^{h}ū**	**j^{h}e**	**j^{h}ɛ**	**j^{h}o**	**j^{h}au**
ट	टा	टि	टी	टु	टू	टे	टै	टो	टौ
Ta	**Tā**	**Ti**	**Tī**	**Tu**	**Tū**	**Te**	**Tɛ**	**To**	**Tau**
ठ	ठा	ठि	ठी	ठु	ठू	ठे	ठै	ठो	ठौ
T^{h}a	**T^{h}ā**	**T^{h}i**	**T^{h}ī**	**T^{h}u**	**T^{h}ū**	**T^{h}e**	**T^{h}ɛ**	**T^{h}o**	**T^{h}au**

ड	डा	डि	डी	डु	डू	डे	डै	डो	डौ
Da	**Dā**	**Di**	**Dī**	**Du**	**Dū**	**De**	**Dɛ**	**Do**	**Dau**
ढ	ढा	ढि	ढी	ढु	ढू	ढे	ढै	ढो	ढौ
D^{h}a	**D^{h}ā**	**D^{h}i**	**D^{h}ī**	**D^{h}u**	**D^{h}ū**	**D^{h}e**	**D^{h}ɛ**	**D^{h}o**	**D^{h}au**
ण	णा	णि	णी	णु	णू	णे	णै	णो	णौ
Na	**Nā**	**Ni**	**Nī**	**Nu**	**Nū**	**Ne**	**Nɛ**	**No**	**Nau**
त	ता	ति	ती	तु	तू	ते	तै	तो	तौ
ta	**tā**	**ti**	**tī**	**tu**	**tū**	**te**	**tɛ**	**to**	**tau**
थ	था	थि	थी	थु	थू	थे	थै	थो	थौ
t^{h}a	**t^{h}ā**	**t^{h}i**	**t^{h}ī**	**t^{h}u**	**t^{h}ū**	**t^{h}e**	**t^{h}ɛ**	**t^{h}o**	**t^{h}au**
द	दा	दि	दी	दु	दू	दे	दै	दो	दौ
da	**dā**	**di**	**dī**	**du**	**dū**	**de**	**dɛ**	**do**	**dau**
ध	धा	धि	धी	धु	धू	धे	धै	धो	धौ
d^{h}a	**d^{h}ā**	**d^{h}i**	**d^{h}ī**	**d^{h}u**	**d^{h}ū**	**d^{h}e**	**d^{h}ɛ**	**d^{h}o**	**d^{h}au**
न	ना	नि	नी	नु	नू	ने	नै	नो	नौ
na	**nā**	**ni**	**nī**	**nu**	**nū**	**ne**	**nɛ**	**no**	**nau**
प	पा	पि	पी	पु	पू	पे	पै	पो	पौ
pa	**pā**	**pi**	**pī**	**pu**	**pū**	**pe**	**pɛ**	**po**	**pau**
फ	फा	फि	फी	फु	फू	फे	फै	फो	फौ
p^{h}a	**p^{h}ā**	**p^{h}i**	**p^{h}ī**	**p^{h}u**	**p^{h}ū**	**p^{h}e**	**p^{h}ɛ**	**p^{h}o**	**p^{h}au**
ब	बा	बि	बी	बु	बू	बे	बै	बो	बौ
ba	**bā**	**bi**	**bī**	**bu**	**bū**	**be**	**bɛ**	**bo**	**bau**
भ	भा	भि	भी	भु	भू	भे	भै	भो	भौ
b^{h}a	**b^{h}ā**	**b^{h}i**	**b^{h}ī**	**b^{h}u**	**b^{h}ū**	**b^{h}e**	**b^{h}ɛ**	**b^{h}o**	**b^{h}au**
म	मा	मि	मी	मु	मू	मे	मै	मो	मौ
ma	**mā**	**mi**	**mī**	**mu**	**mū**	**me**	**mɛ**	**mo**	**mau**
य	या	यि	यी	यु	यू	ये	यै	यो	यौ
ya	**yā**	**yi**	**yī**	**yu**	**yū**	**ye**	**yɛ**	**yo**	**yau**
र	रा	रि	री	रु	रू	रे	रै	रो	रौ
ra	**rā**	**ri**	**rī**	**ru**	**rū**	**re**	**rɛ**	**ro**	**rau**
ल	ला	लि	ली	लु	लू	ले	लै	लो	लौ
la	**lā**	**li**	**lī**	**lu**	**lū**	**le**	**lɛ**	**lo**	**lau**
व	वा	वि	वी	वु	वू	वे	वै	वो	वौ
va	**vā**	**vi**	**vī**	**vu**	**vū**	**ve**	**vɛ**	**vo**	**vau**
श	शा	शि	शी	शु	शू	शे	शै	शो	शौ
sha	**shā**	**shi**	**shī**	**shu**	**shū**	**she**	**shɛ**	**sho**	**shau**
ष	षा	षि	षी	षु	षू	षे	षै	षो	षौ
SHa	**SHā**	**SHi**	**SHī**	**SHu**	**SHū**	**She**	**SHɛ**	**SHo**	**SHau**
स	सा	सि	सी	सु	सू	से	सै	सो	सौ
sa	**sā**	**si**	**sī**	**su**	**sū**	**se**	**sɛ**	**so**	**sau**
ह	हा	हि	ही	हु	हू	हे	है	हो	हौ
ha	**hā**	**hi**	**hī**	**hu**	**hū**	**he**	**hɛ**	**ho**	**hau**

The horizontal bar/head stroke and words

The horizontal bar is placed on a word. Thus **kām** क ा म = काम but not का म.

अभ्यास ab^{h}yās Exercises

Exercise 1

Read the following Hindi words aloud and transcribe them. Note that your transcription should take into account the word-final absence of the short vowel अ **a**.

1 भारी **2** बड़ा **3** कितना **4** काला **5** भारत **6** गाड़ी **7** किनारा
8 गीत **9** गायब **10** चावल **11** चाहना **12** चिड़ियाघर **13** ज़रा **14** जीवन
15 जापान **16** चोर **17** मोर **18** फल **19** भूत **20** चौथा **21** डौल
22 पुलिस **23** हाथी **24** सितार **25** शाम

Exercise 2

Write the following words in Devanagari script:

1 jabki **2** kī **3** bāzār **4** rājā **5** rānī **6** pahacān
7 naī **8** banāras **9** kānapur **10** mātā **11** pitā **12** kab^{h}ī
13 milan **14** zamīn **15** kār **16** mahīnā **17** sāl **18** din
19 cār **20** sāt **21** saverā **22** cāy **23** pānī **24** pati
25 b^{h}ālū **26** rāt **27** dopahar **28** k^{h}ol **29** sau **30** sonā

Exercise 3

Practise writing the following names:

1 Richard **2** Bill **3** Sarah (seyra) **4** Jennifer **5** Don

Exercise 4

The following words are written incorrectly in Hindi. Look at their transcription and write their correct form in Hindi:

Correct	*Incorrect*	*Correct*	*Correct*	*Incorrect*	*Correct*
rupayā	ुपया		Dar	दर	
rūk^{h}ā	ूखा		nām	नाभ	
kar	कअर		t^{h}ān	धान	
ki	कि		g^{h}ar	धर	
aur	आर		Dāl	ड़ाल	

3 तीसरा पाठ – लिपि
tīsrā pāT^h – lipi
Script unit 3

Independent vowels

In this unit we will learn how to use independent vowel forms and nasalized vowels. In the last unit we showed that dependent counterparts are used with a preceding consonant. In all other cases, the independent form is used. Here is the list of the independent vowels again. These vowels are also called 'main' vowels.

अ	आ	इ	ई	उ	ऊ	ए	ऐ	ओ	औ
a	**ā**	**i**	**ī**	**u**	**ū**	**e**	**ɛ**	**o**	**au**

When the word begins with a vowel, the independent form of the vowel is used, as in

आ + म = आम mango, common
ā + **m** = **ām**

*but **not** the dependent form*

ा + म = ाम

Similarly:

इ + ध + र = इधर in this direction, here
i + **d^{h}a** + **r**

*but **not***

ि + ध + र = धिर

Also, observe in the following example:

औ	+	र	=	और	and
au	+	**r**			

but ***not***

ौ	+	र	=	ौर

If the *preceding* sound is a vowel, the independent form of a vowel is used, e.g.:

ā	+	**i**	+	**e**			
आ	+	इ	+	ए	=	आइए	please come

but ***not*** *any of the following ways:*

ा	+	ि	+	ए	=	ािए
ा	+	ि	+	े	=	ािे
आ	+	ि	+	े	=	आिे

Now you should be able to distinguish between the following two words:

k + **ī** → की of

ka + **ī** → कई several

Notice that the independent form of ई **ī** is used in कई **kaī** because its preceding sound is the vowel **a** अ.

Nasalized vowels

In our transcription, vowel nasalization is indicated by a tilde ~ over the transliterated vowel.

In Hindi, the two symbols which are used to mark vowel nasalization are: **candrabindu** (moon dot) ँ and **bindu** (dot) ं. The former is used either over the head stroke of the vowel itself or over the head stroke of the consonant to which the vowel is attached. If any part of the vowel is written above the head stroke, then the dot is used rather than the moon dot. Note the following examples:

moon dot ँ dot ं

Nasalized vowel	*Independent vowel*	*Dependent vowel* (matra)
ā̃	आँ	ाँ
ī̃	ईं	ीं
ū̃	ऊँ	ुँ ूँ
ẽ	एँ	ें
ɛ̃	ऐं	ैं
õ	ओं	ों
ãũ	औं	ौं

Now examine the usage of the nasalized vowels in the following words:

ह	+	ाँ	=	हाँ	yes		ह	+	ूँ	=	हूँ	am
h	+	**ā̃**					**h**	+	**ū̃**			
आँ	+	ख	=	आँख	eye		म	+	ाँ	=	माँ	mother
ā̃	+	**k^h^**	=	**ā̃k^h^**			**m**	+	**ā̃**	=	**mā̃**	
ऊँ	+	ट	=	ऊँट	camel		म	+	ें	=	में	in
ū̃	+	**T**	=	**ū̃T**			**m**	+	**ẽ**	=	**mẽ**	
औं	+	धा	=	औंधा	overturned		म	+	ैं	=	मैं	I
ãũ	+	**d^h^ā**	=	**ãũd^h^ā**			**m**	+	**ɛ̃**	=	**mɛ̃**	

लेखन **lek^{h}an** Writing

Letter/ pronunciation	*Stroke order*	*Head stroke/ Head bar*	*Handwriting*
अ a	अ	अ	अ
आ ā	आ	आ	आ
इ i	इ	इ	इ
ई ī	ई	ई	ई
उ u	उ	उ	उ
ऊ ū	ऊ	ऊ	ऊ
ए e	ए	ए	ए

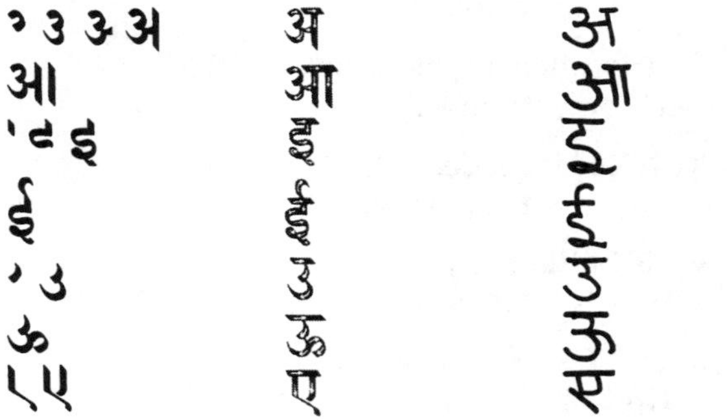

Letter/ pronunciation	*Stroke order*	*Head stroke/ Head bar*	*Handwriting*
ऐ ε	ऐ	ऐ	ऐ
ओ o	आ ओ	ओ	ओ
औ au	औ	औ	औ

अभ्यास ab^{h}yās Exercises

Exercise 1

Write the following expressions in Devanagari script. Since they are useful, their English translation is also provided.

1 **t^{h}ānā vahī̃ hɛ**.
The police station is right there.

2 **āp merī madad kar sakte hɛ̃**?
Can you help me?

3 **mɛ̃ vahā̃ kɛse jāū̃**?
How shall I get there?

4 **ye merī galatī nahī̃**.
This is not my mistake.

5 **yahā̃ xatrā hɛ**.
There is danger here.

6 **bacāo**!
Save! (or help!)

7 **ye** (written as **yah**) **bahut zarūrī hɛ**.
This is very urgent.

8 **Dāk-k^{h}ānā kahā̃ hɛ**?
Where is the post office?

9 **kis k^{h}iRkī par jāū̃**?
Which window should I go to?

10 **TikaT** (ticket) **kitnā lagegā**?
How much postage will (it) need?

11 **e-mail amrīkā** (America) **b^{h}ejanā cāhatā hū̃**.
(I) want to send an e-mail to America.

12 **mujhe cintā/fikr hɛ**.
I am worried.

Exercise 2

If you have the recording, listen to the above expressions while silently reading them.

Exercise 3

Write the following words in Devanagari script:

1 āie **2 āo** **3 k^{h}āie** **4 k^{h}āo** **5 k^{h}ā lo** **6 māika** (Mike)

Exercise 4

Oral vs nasal vowels

1	हा exclamatory sound	vs	हाँ yes
2	हू a sound		हूँ am
3	है is		हैं are
4	मे May		में in

Now transcribe the above words into Roman.

4 चौथा पाठ – लिपि caut^{h}ā pāT^{h} – lipi

Script unit 4

Conjunct letters

In script unit 1 I mentioned that since Devanagari script is syllabic, every consonant symbol contains an invisible अ **a** in it. Now let us learn to write consonants without this vowel. Such consonants are also called 'half' consonants.

The simplest way to drop the अ **a** is to use the sign ् called 'hal' or 'halant'. For example, if you want to write the word **kyā**, just put the halant sign under क and then go on to write the next syllable. However, Hindi speakers, particularly in handwriting, tend to prefer special conjunct symbols over the halant sign. The halant is more prevalent in word processing and the Internet. These special conjuncts are described in this section.

If the consonant has a right vertical stroke ा, the vertical line is dropped, as in:

Consonant	*Conjunct form (half consonant)*	*Word with a conjunct*		
ख़ **xa**	ख़्‍ **x**	सख़्त	**saxt**	hard
ग **ga**	ग्‍ **g**	अग्नि	**agni**	fire
च **ca**	च्‍ **c**	अच्छा	**acc^{h}ā**	good
ज **ja**	ज्‍ **j**	ज्यों	**jyõ**	as
ण **Na**	ण्‍ **N**	ठण्डा	**ThaNDā**	cold
त **ta**	त्‍ **t**	त्यौहार	**tyauhār**	festival
न **na**	न्‍ **n**	अन्धा	**and^{h}ā**	blind
स **sa**	स्‍ **s**	सस्ता	**sastā**	cheap

Notice the placement of the dependent form of the vowel ि **i** which is placed before the conjunct letter ग्‍ **g** but is pronounced after the न्‍ **n**.

Consonants which contain the stroke ा in their *middle* have the following forms:

क **ka**	क् **k**	क्या **kyā**	what
फ़ **fa**	फ़् **f**	हफ़्ता **haftā**	week

For all other letters, either the halant sign is used or the conjunct letter sits on the top of the full consonant letter, as in:

ट् **T** + ट **Ta**	ट् + ट	**T** + **Ta**	*or*	ट्ट
	पट्टी	**paTTī**	*or*	पट्टी bandage
ड् **D** + ड **Da**	ड् + ड	**D** + **Da**	*or*	ड्ड
	अड्डा	**aDDā**	*or*	अड्डा station (bus)

With the emergence of new printing technology, the halant form is gaining more prominence.

Exceptions

Once again र **ra** is notorious and it needs special attention. The symbol for the conjunct र is र्, as in

क	+	र्	+	म	=	कर्म	*but not*	र्कम
ka	+	**r**	+	**ma**	=	**karma**	fate	

The conjunct **r** is placed at the very end of the syllable it precedes, e.g.

व	+	र्	+	मा	=	वर्मा	*but not*	र्वमा
va	+	**r**	+	**mā**	=	**Varma**	a last name	

When र is the second member of the conjunct, it is realized as ्र. Note the following clusters with **r**.

प्	+	्र	=	प्र
p	+	**ra**	=	**pra**
त्	+	्र	=	त्र
t	+	**ra**	=	**tra**

श् + ् = श्र
sh + **ra** = **shra**

With ट **Ta** and ड **Da**, ् is added rather than ्.

ट् + ् = ट्र
T + **ra** = **Tra**

ड् + ् = ड्र
D + **ra** = **Dra**

Long consonants

With the exception of **tta**, the long consonants follow the conjunct formation rules described above.

त् + त = त्त *but not* त्‍त
t + **ta** = **tta**

Nasal consonants

In Script Unit 3 we saw that the *moon dot* and the simple *dot* can express vowel nasalization. However, the dot has yet another function. When it appears over either a short vowel or a consonant, it shows the presence of a homorganic nasal consonant. 'Homorganic' means the sound is produced by the same speech organ. The consonants listed in each of the five groups in the consonant chart are homorganic. For example, the five consonant sounds listed in the fifth column – ङ **ŋ**, ञ **ñ**, ण **N**, न **n** and म **m** are homorganic to the rest of the velar, palatal, retroflex, dental and labial consonants, respectively.

When a dot is placed either over a short vowel or a consonant, it indicates the corresponding homorganic conjunct nasal consonant of the following consonant. So the dot can also be written with a conjunct nasal consonant, as in

अंग	=	अङ्ग	**aŋg**	limb
पंच	=	पञ्च	**pañc**	juror
ठंड	=	ठण्ड	**T^{h}aND**	cold
हिंदी	=	हिन्दी	**hindī**	the Hindi language
खंबा	=	खम्बा	**k^{h}ambā**	pole

Web resources

For more details, see Syracuse University's Hindi web page:

http://faculty.maxwell.syr.edu/jishnu/101/alphabet/default.asp?section=0

For more on consonant clusters:

http://www.avashy.com/hindiscripttutor.htm
http://acharya.iitm.ac.in/sanskrit/lessons/Devan/conj_1.html

The hide and seek game of अ a

I mentioned in the chapter on the Hindi writing system and pronunciation that the Devanagari script is a phonetic script and that the words are primarily written in the way they are pronounced. However, one should keep in mind that language is a living thing; it keeps changing and even the most scientific script cannot keep up with all the changes. We have already discussed the case of the word-final silence of अ **a** in Script Units 1 and 2. Now do some detective work and see another situation in which अ **a** is *written but not pronounced.*

Word	*Written*	*Pronounced*	*Word*	*Written*	*Pronounced*
सड़क road	**saRak**	**saR*a*k**	सड़कें road	**saR*a*k+ẽ**	**saRkẽ**
औरत woman	**aurat**	**aur*a*t**	औरतें women	**aur*a*t+ẽ**	**aurtẽ**
लड़क child (*not used alone*)	**laRak**	**laR*a*k**	लड़का boy	**laR*a*k+ā**	**laRkā**
लड़क child (*not used alone*)	**laRak**	**laR*a*k**	लड़की girl	**laR*a*k+ī**	**laRkī**
समझ understand	**samaj**^{h}	**sam*a*j**^{h}	समझा understood	**sam*a*j**^{h}**+ā**	**samj**^{h}**ā**

If you noticed that the penultimate (second to last) vowel **a** is dropped before a suffix, then your observation is correct. Now examine the following words:

Word	*Written*	*Pronounced*	*Word*	*Written*	*Pronounced*
सड़क road	**saRak**	**saR*a*k**	सड़कपन roadlike	**saR*a*k+pan**	**saR*a*kpan**
औरत woman	**aurat**	**aur*a*t**	औरतपन womanhood	**aur*a*t+pan**	**aur*a*tpan**
लड़क child	**laRak**	**laR*a*k**	लड़कपन childhood	**laR*a*k+pan**	**laR*a*kpan**
समझ understand	**samaj^h**	**sam*a*j^h**	समझदार intelligent	**sam*a*j^h+dār**	**sam*a*j^{h}dār**

The data presented above show that the penultimate **a** is dropped in pronunciation if the suffix begins with a vowel. Othewise it is retained.

अभ्यास ab^{h}yās Exercises

Exercise 1

Write the following expressions in Hindi. These are very useful expressions, so their meaning is also given.

1 **pūc^h-tāc^h kā daftar**
Inquiry office

2 **mẽ rāstā b^{h}ūl gayī hū̃**.
I (f.) am lost. (lit. I have lost my way.)

3 **mẽ rāstā b^{h}ūl gayā hū̃**.
I (m.) am lost. (lit. I have lost my way.)

4 **taŋg mat karo**.
Do not bother me.

5 **mẽ kuñjī D^{h}ū̃R^h rahā hū̃**.
I am looking for my key.

6 **nahī̃ mil rahī**.
(I) can't find (it).

7 **ciTT^{h}ī havāī Dākse b^{h}ejiye**.
Please send (this) letter by air mail.

8 **kyā āp yah sāmān sīd^{h}e mumbaī b^{h}ej sakte hẽ**?
Can you send this baggage straight to Mumbai?

9 **sāmān ke liye rasīd dījiye**.
Please give (me) a receipt for this baggage.

10 **merā sāmān nahī̃ āyā**.
My baggage did not arrive (by this flight).

Exercise 2

Transcribe the following sentences. Some words used in these expressions are from English but they have been written in the way they are pronounced by Hindi speakers. If you have the recording, listen to their pronunciation. Otherwise after transcribing the sentences, read the sentences and practise their pronunciation on your own.

1 हम एक हफ़्ता दिल्ली में रहेंगे।
We will stay in Delhi for a week.

2 मैं यहाँ छुट्टी पर हूँ।
I am here on holiday.

3 हम यहाँ काम से आये हैं।
We (m.) came here on a business trip. (lit. We have come here with work.)

4 यह मेरा पासपोर्ट है।
This is my passport.

5 क्या इस सामान पर ड्यूटी लगेगी?
Will this baggage (*or* things) require duty?

6 ये चीज़ें मेरे अपने इस्तेमाल के लिए हैं।
These things are for my own (personal) use.

7 मेरे पास ड्यूटी वाला सामान नहीं है।
I have nothing to declare. (lit. I do not have anything that requires duty).

8 मेरे पास कुछ गिफट्स हैं।
I have some gifts.

9 इसमें सिर्फ कपड़े और किताबें हैं।
There are only clothes and books in this (bag).

10 इस के अलावा और कोई चीज़ नहीं है।
Besides this (I) have nothing else (to declare for duty.)

Exercise 3

Note that the presence or absence of the word-medial **a** in the following words. Take a lead from the Roman transcription and practise the pronunciation.

1	सड़क	saR*a*k	सड़कें	saRkẽ
2	औरत	aur*a*t	औरतें	aurtẽ
3	लड़क	laR*a*k	लड़का	laRkā
4	लड़कपन	laR*a*kpan	लड़की	laRkī
5	समझ	sam*a*j^{h}	समझा	samj^{h}ā
6	समझदार	sam*a*j^{h}dār	समझी	samj^{h}ī

Exercise 4

Read and transliterate the the following information about the functions of a Nokia cell phone into Roman text:

नोकिया फोन की दुनिया में आपका स्वागत है।
You are welcome in the Nokia world.

हिन्दी में टेक्ट सन्देश भेजिए
Send a text message in Hindi.

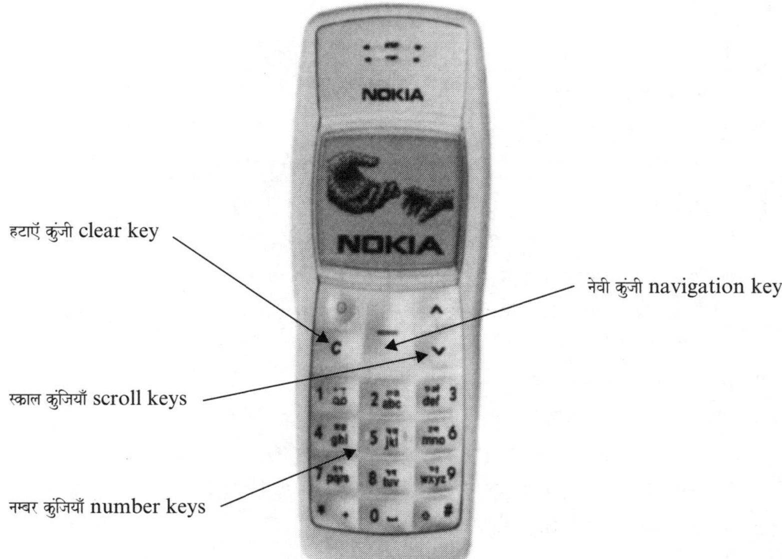

5 पाँचवाँ पाठ – लिपि
pā̃cvā̃ pāT^{h} – lipi
Script unit 5

You must have heard the expression 'It is not what you say that matters but how you say it.' In this chapter we will consider some 'how to' aspects of script and pronunciation together with some other questions, such as significant and insignificant variations.

Syllables

The vowel and consonant segments can be combined into units which are called syllables. Syllables are the smaller units which make up a word. The syllable boundary is indicated by the symbol #, as follows:

Between successive vowels

Word		*Syllabification*	
जाओ	**jāo**	जा # ओ	**jā # o**
आइए	**āie**	आ # इ # ए	**ā # e # o**
नई	**naī**	न # ई	**na # ī**
खाए	**k^{h}āe**	खा # ए	**khā # e**

Between vowels and consonants

Word		*Syllabification*	
जाता	**jātā**	जा # ता	**jā # tā**
सोना	**nā**	सो # ना	**so # nā**
पता	**patā**	प # ता	**pa # tā**

Between consonants

Word		*Syllabification*	
इच्छा	**icc^{h}ā**	इच # छा	**ic # c^{h}ā**
सड़कें	**saRkẽ**	सड़ # कें	**saR # kẽ**
आदमी	**ādmī**	आद # मी	**ād # mī**

Stress

Stress means loudness, a change in volume to express a wide variety of meanings such as emotions, contrast, focus and change in grammatical categories. This term is interchangeably used with 'accent' by some linguists. It refers to the most prominent part of a syllable or word. As in English, stress distinguishes some nouns from verbs in Hindi, as in

Noun			*Verb*		
*ग*ला	***ga*lā**	neck	ग*ला*	**ga*lā***	cause to melt
*त*ला	***ta*lā**	sole	त*ला*	**ta*lā***	cause to fry

The stressed syllable is in italics. However, stress is usually indistinct in Hindi. So, whether one places stress on the first syllable or the second, the meaning will not be affected, nor will the quality of the pronunciation of the vowel:

*सु*ना   सु*ना*
su*nā**   **su*nā

This is different from English, where the vowel in the non-stressed syllable is reduced, such as in **A*la*ska**, where one witnesses a difference between the pronunciation of the *a* in the middle position (i.e. stressed syllable) and in the word-initial and final position (i.e. unstressed syllables). This is why stress is not as distinctive and crucial in Hindi as in English. Therefore, Hindi is often characterized as a 'syllable-timed' language like French, where the syllables are pronounced in a steady flow, resulting in a 'machine-gun' effect.

The predominant pattern in Hindi is to stress the penultimate syllable, as in

किराया	**ki*rā*yā**	rent
जाना	***jā*nā**	to go
चीता	***cī*tā**	leopard
इन्दु	***in*du**	a name
रुचि	***ru*ci**	interest
कनिका	**ka*ni*kā**	a female name

Since short vowels are not stressed in English, chances are you will not hear stress on the Hindi syllables with short vowels.

The long vowel receives stress and thus takes precedence over the penultimate syllable rule, e.g.:

तारिणी	***tā*riNī**	a female name
सिरका	**sir*kā***	vinegar

Also, notice that if there is more than one long syllable, the stress falls on the first syllable. The other intricate aspects of the stress system in Hindi are beyond the scope of this introductory book. At the level of word-compounding, the stress is usually placed on the second word, as in

बात-चीत	**bāt-*cīt***	conversation
बोल-चाल	**bol-*cāl***	colloquial

In information-type questions, the question-word is usually stressed.

आप *क्या* करेंगे?
āp ***kyā*** **karẽge**?
you what do-will
What will you do?

आप ये *क्यों* करेंगे?
āp ye ***kyõ*** **karẽge**?
you this why do-will
Why would you do this?

आप *कहाँ* जायेंगे?
āp ***kahā̃*** **jāẽge**?
you where go-will
Where will you go?

Intonation pattern

Take for example, the word अच्छा **acc^hā** 'good, ok'. It can be pronounced with different intonation in different contexts. When अच्छा **acc^hā** is uttered in the different contexts – in response to an inquiry, 'What kind of person is x?'; in a statement expressing surprise, 'Is that so?'; as an expression of agreement, disagreement or detachment – it will be produced with different intonation. Intonation is the rise and fall of the pitch of the voice. Hindi exhibits the following four main intonation patterns:

rising ↗
falling ↘
rising, falling and rising ⁀‿↗
neutral or level —

Rising intonation

As in English, the intonation rises towards the end of the sentence in a yes-no type of question.

क्या आप वहाँ जायेंगे?
kyā āp vahā̃ jāẽge?
what you there go-will
Will you go there?

In exclamatory sentences the intonation rises sharply:

वो पास हो गया!
vo pās ho gayā!
he pass be went
He passed (the exam!)

Falling intonation

Statements, prohibitives and information questions show this intonation pattern:

लड़का अच्छा है।
laRkā acc^hā hɛ.
boy good is
The boy is good.

सिगरेट पीना मना है।
cigreT pīnā manā hɛ.
cigarette drinking prohibited is
Smoking is prohibited.

आप कहाँ जायेंगे?
āp kahā̃ jāyẽge?
you where go-will
Where will you go?

Rising-falling and rising intonation

In tag-questions intonation rises at the beginning of the verb and falls at the end of the verb, and then rises slightly again while the tag marker is pronounced.

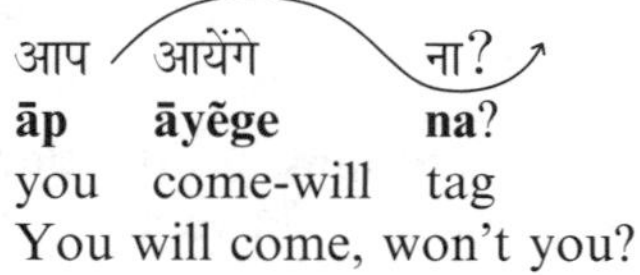

आप आयेंगे ना?
āp āyẽge na?
you come-will tag
You will come, won't you?

Neutral or level intonation

Ordinary imperative sentences are uttered with a neutral or level intonation.

तुम जाओ
tum jāo.
You go.

Linguistic variation

As mentioned in the section on the Hindi writing system and pronunciation, Hindi is spoken in a vast area both inside and outside South Asia. It is natural to expect linguistic variation in the regions. Some regional pronunciation differences have already been pointed out in the description of Hindi vowels and borrowed consonant sounds. One example of variation is the pronunciation of the word-final and medial **a**. In the eastern and southern varieties of Hindi, the vowel **a** is retained in both positions. However, the **a** is optional in many words of Perso-Arabic origin, even in Standard Hindi, as shown here:

कुरसी	**kur*a*sī**	**kursī**	कुर्सी	chair
सरदी	**sar*a*dī**	**sardī**	सर्दी	winter, cold
गरमी	**gar*a*mī**	**garmī**	गर्मी	summer, hot
नज़दीक	**naz*a*dīk**	**nazdīk**	नज़्दीक	near
कतल	**qat*a*l**	**qatl**	कत्ल	murder

Another important source of variation is the consonant **h**. The preceding stressed vowel **a** becomes ɛ if **h** is followed by a non-vowel sound. For example:

कह	**k*a*h**	but pronounced	कैह	**kɛh**
रहना	**r*a*hnā**	but pronounced	रैह	**rɛhnaa**
वह	**v*a*h**	but pronounced	वो	**vo**
यह	**y*a*h**	but pronounced	ये	**ye**

The stressed vowel is in italics. The only exceptions are the third-person singular pronouns which are pronounced as वो **vo** and ये **ye**, respectively.

When the preceding vowel is unstressed, the ह **h** is dropped but the vowel becomes long, as in

वजह	**vajah**	but pronounced	वजा	**vajā**
तरह	**tarah**	but pronounced	तरा	**tarā**

If the **h** is preceded by **a** and followed by **u**, the **h** is dropped and the merger of the two vowels either results in **au** (as in 'caught') or **o**. For example, **bahut** is pronounced either as **baut** or **bot**.

In many dialects, the **h** follows the script pronunciation (i.e. is pronounced the way it is written).

Verb forms: more than one spelling

Some verb forms ending in **aa** and **e** can be written with more than one spelling. For example, the subjunctive, past and imperative forms of the verb can be written using the following variations:

Verb	*Past*	*Subjunctive*	*Imperative*
जा **jā** to go	गए **gaye** गये **gaye**	जाए **jāe** जाये **jāye** जाय **jāy**	जाओ **jāo** जाइए **jāiye** जावो **jāvo** जाइये **jāiye**

Phonetic considerations are primarily responsible for variations in traditional spellings.

अभ्यास **ab^hyās** Exercises

Exercise 1

Mark the syllable boundary in the following words using the symbol #.

1 आइये **āiye**
2 औरतें **aurtẽ**
3 पढ़ता **paR^hṭā**
4 सुनो **suno**
5 नमस्ते **namaste**
6 मिलेंगे **milẽge**
7 सुनकर **sunkar**
8 आदमी **ādmī**

Exercise 2

Read through the following question and answers, and try to imagine the intonation patterns involved. It would be helpful to seek the assistance of a native speaker.

1 Yes–no type
Q: क्या वो पास हो गया?
kyā vo *pās* ho gayā? Did he pass (the exam)?
Ans: हाँ
hā̃

2 Information question
Q: कौन सा ग्रेड मिला?
kaun sā *grade* milā? What grade did he get?
Ans: A ग्रेड ।
'A' grade

3 Statement
वो अच्छा लड़का है।
vo acc^{h}ā laRkā hɛ.
He is a good boy.

4 Surprise
Statement: वो पास हो गया।
vo pās ho gayā. He passed the exam.
reply: अच्छा!
acc^{h}ā! (with surprised intonation) implying 'Is that so? I do not believe you.'

5 Agreement
आओ, फिल्म देखने चलें।
Suggestion: **āo, *film* dek^{h}ne calẽ**. Come on, let's go and see a film.
Agreement: अच्छा।
acc^{h}ā. Okay.

6 Detached
Suggestion: आओ, फिल्म देखने चलें।
āo, *film* dek^{h}ne calẽ. Come on, let's go and see a film.
Agreement: अच्छा।
acc^{h}ā. Okay.

7 Normal commands
दरवाजा बंद करो।
darvāzā band karo. Close the door.

Exercise 3

Read the following weather forecast for India and transcribe the Hindi words into Roman. For numerals, consult the English–Hindi vocabulary section. Assume that the word-final **a** is dropped.

मौसम weather	दिल्ली Delhi	मुम्बई Mumbai	कोलकता Kolkata
तापमान temperature	10 डिग्री सी 10°C	15 डिग्री सी 15°C	16 डिग्री सी 16°C
बरसात rain, precipitation	बारिश rain	बादल cloud	धूप sunny
हवा wind	तेज़ strong	हल्की light	मन्द light

पाठ
pāT^h
Units

1 नमस्ते/नमस्कार । namaste/ namaskār

Greetings and social etiquette

By the end of this unit you should be able to:

- use simple greetings
- learn expressions of social etiquette
- use expressions for leave-taking
- ask simple questions
- make simple requests
- use personal pronouns (e.g., 'I', 'we', 'you', etc.)
- use some nouns and adjectives

बातचीत **bātcīt Dialogue 1** (CD 1; 9)

नमस्ते ***namaste greetings***

Hindu–Sikh greetings and other social etiquette

Hindi greetings vary according to the religion of the speaker, but not according to the time of the day. In some cases, the speaker may choose to greet according to the religion of his/her listener. Such a choice is socially more appealing to the listener and you can easily win the hearts of your listeners by being sensitive to their way of greeting.

Mohan goes to see Sarita in her office. They know each other but are not close friends.

मोहन: नमस्ते जी।
MOHAN: namaste jī.
सरिता: नमस्ते। क्या हाल है?
SARITA: namaste. kyā hāl hɛ?
मोहन: ठीक है और आप?
MOHAN: Tʰīk hɛ, aur āp?
सरिता: मैं भी ठीक हूँ। हुकम कीजिये।
SARITA: mɛ̃ bʰī Tʰīk hū̃. hukam kījie.
मोहन: हुकम नहीं, विनती है।
MOHAN: hukam nahī̃, vintī hɛ.
(The conversation continues for some time.)
मोहन: अच्छा, नमस्ते।
MOHAN: accʰā, namaste.
सरिता: नमस्ते।
SARITA: namaste.

MOHAN: *Greetings.*
SARITA: *Greetings. How are you?*
MOHAN: *Fine. And you?*
SARITA: *I am fine too. What can I do for you?* [lit. do order]
MOHAN: *(It is) not an order, (but) a request.*
(The conversation continues for some time.)
MOHAN: *Okay. Goodbye.*
SARITA: *Goodbye.*

शब्दावली **shabdāvalī** **Vocabulary**  (CD 1; 10)

*(Note: It is standard convention to transliterate Hindi words in lower case and this convention is used here. Therefore, the first letter of the first word is not capitalized. The only exceptions are upper case **T**, **D**, **N** and **R** which represent the retroflex sounds.)*

नमस्ते	**namaste**	Hindu greeting and reply to the greeting; may be used by other religions too
जी	**jī**	honorific word (optional with greetings)
क्या	**kyā**	what
हाल	**hāl** (m.)	condition
है	**hɛ**	is
ठीक	**T^{h}īk**	fine; okay
और	**aur**	and
आप	**āp**	you (honorific)
मैं	**mɛ̃**	I
भी	**b^{h}ī**	also
हूँ	**hū̃**	am
हुकम	**hukam** (m.)	order
कीजिए	**kījie**	please do
नहीं	**nahī̃**	not
विनती	**vintī** (f.)	request

Pronunciation

In the eastern Hindi-speaking area (e.g. in the city of Banaras), the vowel **ɛ** in the words, मैं **mɛ̃** and है **hɛ**, is pronounced as a diphthong, a combination of two vowels, i.e. [**ai** = **a** + **i**]. However, in the western Hindi-speaking area (e.g. in Delhi), it is pronounced as a vowel **ɛ**, as in English words such as **cat**. Since this vowel pronunciation is considered to be the standard, this is given in the recordings. The word given in angular brackets < > shows that its pronunciation differs from that suggested by the script. This is shown only when the word is introduced for the first time.

The verb form कीजिए [**kījie**] can also be pronounced as [**kījiye**]. The semivowel [**y**] can intervene between the last two vowels. This word can be written with the semivowel too: कीजिये **kījiye**.

Notes

Hindu–Sikh greetings and their regional variants

नमस्ते **namaste** (lit. 'I bow in your respect'.) is the most common greeting used by Hindus and even by non-Hindus. It is expressed with the hands folded in front of the chest. It may be optionally followed by जी **jī** to show respect and politeness. A more formal alternative to नमस्ते **namaste** is नमस्कार **namaskār**. In the rural areas many other variants such as राम-राम **rām-rām** and जय **jɛ rām jī kī** (pronounced जै) राम जी की are found. Sikhs prefer सत श्री अकाल **sat srī akāl** instead of नमस्ते **namaste**. The gesture of folding hands, however, remains the same. Hindi greetings do not vary at different times of day.

namaste नमस्ते (or **sat srī akāl** सत श्री अकाल by Sikhs) and its variants are used for both 'hello' and 'goodbye'.

Word-for-word translation

Where a Hindi expression differs literally from its English translational equivalent, we show this difference in the notes by giving a word-for-word translation. Observe the word-for-word translation of the Hindi equivalent of the English 'How are you?':

क्या हाल है?
kyā hāl hɛ?
what condition is?

and its reply

ठीक है।
T^{h}īk hɛ
fine is

Honorific pronoun

The honorific pronoun आप **āp** 'you' is grammatically plural, even if it refers to one person. Grammatically, it is the same as the English 'you'. For example, in Standard English one will never say 'you is'.

The politeness bug

Politeness can be quite infectious. If the speaker is being very polite in his/her speech, the listener is obligated either to match or outperform the speaker. The expression

हुकम कीजिए।
hukam kījie.
order please do
Please (give me) an order. = What can I do for you?

is a very formal and cultured way of asking 'What can I do for you?' The listener appropriately uses an equally polite expression:

हुकम नहीं विनती है।
hukam nahī̃ vintī hɛ
order not request is
It is not an order (but) a request.

Word order

Note the difference between the word order of Hindi and that of English. In Hindi, the verb (e.g. 'is', 'am', 'are', etc.) usually appears at the end of the sentence. The object (e.g. 'order') appears before the verb.

बातचीत bātcīt Dialogue 2 (CD 1; 12)

सलाम salām salam

Muslim greetings and social etiquette

Muslims tend to use more Persian and Arabic words and phrases. They may refer to their language as 'Urdu' or 'Hindustani'. However, Hindi, Urdu and Hindustani are mutually intelligible (for details see the Introduction).

Tahsin Siddiqui and Razia Arif run into each other in a car park (parking lot).

तहसीन: सलाम, रजिया जी।
TAHSIN: salām, raziā jī.
रजिया: सलाम, सब ख़ैरियत है?
RAZIA: salām. sab xɛriyat hɛ?
तहसीन: मेहरबानी है, और आपके मिज़ाज कैसे हैं?
TAHSIN: meharbānī hɛ, aur āpke mizāj kɛse hɛ̃?
रजिया: अल्लाह का शुक्र है।
RAZIA: allāh kā shukra hɛ.
(The conversation continues for some time.)

तहसीन: अच्छा, ख़ुदा हाफ़िज़।
TAHSIN: acc^{h}ā, xudā hāfiz.
रज़िया: ख़ुदा हाफ़िज़।
RAZIA: xudā hāfiz.

TAHSIN: *Greetings Razia.*
RAZIA: *Greetings. How are you?*
TAHSIN: *Fine. And, how are you?*
(The conversation continues for some time.)
RAZIA: *I am fine.*
TAHSIN: *Okay. Goodbye.*
RAZIA: *Goodbye.*

शब्दावली **shabdāvalī Vocabulary**

सलाम	**salām**	Muslim greeting and reply to the greeting
सब	**sab**	all
ख़ैरियत	**xɛriyat** (f.)	safety, welfare
मेहरबानी	**meharbānī** (f.)	kindness
आपके	**āpke**	your
मिज़ाज	**mizāj** (m.)	temperament, nature
कैसे	**kɛse**	how
हैं	**hɛ̃**	are
अल्लाह का शुक्र	**allāh kā shukra**	fine
ख़ुदा हाफ़िज़	**xudā hāfiz**	goodbye

Pronunciation

ख़ैरियत **xɛriyat** and ख़ुदा **xudā** are often pronounced as **k^{h}ɛriyat** and **k^{h}udā** by non-Muslims, respectively. In short, **x** may be pronounced as [**k^{h}**]. (See Script Unit 1.)

मिज़ाज **mizāj** and हाफ़िज़ **hāfiz** are often pronounced as [**mijāj**] and [**hāp^{h}ij**] respectively by non-Muslims. In other words, **z** may be pronounced as [**j**].

Notes

Muslim greeting and leave taking

सलाम **salām** (an abbreviated form of **salām alɛkum**) is used for 'hello' by Muslims instead of नमस्ते **namaste**. It is expressed by raising the right hand to the forehead. The word for 'goodbye' is ख़ुदा हाफ़िज़ **xudā hāfiz**.

Other ways of saying 'How are you?'

Another way of saying 'How are you?' is 'Is everything fine?' or 'Is all well (with you)?' The expression for this is

सब	ख़ैरियत	है?
sab	**xɛriyat**	**hɛ**?
all	welfare	is

How are you? (lit. 'Is everything fine [with you]?')

which is followed by an answer:

मेहरबानी	है।
meharbānī	**hɛ**
kindness	is

(It is your) kindness, i.e. because of your kindness, everything is fine with me.

Yet another interchangeable way of asking 'How are you?' is something like 'How are your habits?', as in the following sentence:

आपके	मिज़ाज	कैसे	हैं?
āpke	**mizāj**	**kɛse**	**hɛ̃**?
you-of	habits	how	are

This question is followed by the answer 'With God's grace, everything is fine.' The Hindi expression for this is:

अल्लाह	का	शुक्र	है।
allāh	**kā**	**shukra**	**hɛ**
God	of	thank	is

The above exchange is considered super-polite. Such an exchange is usually used more often by Muslims. Nevertheless, Hindus and others may also use it, depending upon their regional (e.g. in the city of Lucknow) and social background (e.g. inter-ethnic dealings).

What to do when speakers of different religions meet

When speakers of different religions greet each other, it is considered polite for the person who speaks first to greet the listener according to his or her religion. Respecting the religious feelings of others is the rule of politeness. Nowadays the English word 'hello' can be used to stress neutrality and modernity at the same time. However, the English word 'hello' is usually followed by the respectful and polite denoting word जी **jī**.

व्याकरण vyākaraNa Grammar

Word order in Hindi

The order of words in a Hindi sentence is not as rigidly fixed as it is thought to be by prescriptive and traditional grammarians. Although a Hindi sentence usually (but not invariably) begins with a subject and ends with a verb, if the sentence has an object, this is sandwiched between the subject and the verb. That is why Hindi is often called an SOV language (i.e. subject/object/verb language). However, Hindi speakers or writers enjoy considerable freedom in placing words to achieve stylistic effects. In dialogue 1 Sarita asks:

क्या	हाल	है?
kyā	**hāl**	**hɛ**?
what	condition	is

How are you?

Usually the question word क्या **kyā** 'what' does not appear in the sentence initial position. The ordinary form of the sentence is as follows:

हाल	क्या	है?
hāl	**kyā**	**hɛ**?
condition	what	is

How are you?

The question word क्या **kyā** 'what' is placed at the beginning of the sentence to give special emphasis to it. Also, you may have noticed the deletion of the implied element (i.e. the possessive pronoun 'your' modifying the subject noun 'condition') in the conversation. Such deletions also affect Hindi word order. For example, in the same dialogue, Mohan responds to Sarita's question in the following way:

ठीक	है।
T^hīk	**hɛ**
fine	is

I am fine.

Mohan's reply has no subject because the subject phrase is implied. The full version of the sentence is as follows:

मेरा	हाल	ठीक	है।
merā	**hāl**	**T^{h}īk**	**hɛ**
my	condition	fine	is

I am fine. (lit. 'My condition is fine.')

The implied subject (i.e. मेरा हाल **merā hāl**) is rarely spelled out in the reply.

Yes–no questions

Yes–no questions involve either an affirmative or a negative answer. In spoken Hindi, yes–no questions are much simpler than in English. They are usually formed by changing *intonation*, i.e. with a rising tone of voice at the end of the sentence. You do not need to place any form of the verb before the subject, as you do in English. In dialogue 2 above, Razia asks

सब	ख़ैरियत	है?
sab	**xɛriyat**	**hɛ**?
all	welfare	is

Is all well? *or* Is everything fine?

simply by 'yes–no question intonation', i.e. by raising the pitch of voice at the end of the sentence. The same sentence with a 'statement intonation' (pitch falling at the end), as in English, would mean 'All is well' = 'I am fine.'

Personal and demonstrative pronoun

The Hindi personal pronouns are

mɛ̃	मैं	I
tū	तू	you (singular)
<vo>	वह	she, he, it; that
<ye>	यह	this
ham	हम	we
tum	तुम	you (plural)
āp	आप	you (honorific)
ve	वे	they; those
ye	ये	these

There is no gender distinction in Hindi pronouns.

तू **tū** is considered to be either too intimate or too rude. We advise you not to use तू **tū** unless you are absolutely sure about your intimate relationship with the listener and your listener has already been using this pronoun in his/her exchanges with you. In short, you will not get much of a chance to hear and use तू **tū**. In the case of an emerging familiar relationship the only pronoun you will need is तुम **tum**.

तुम **tum** can be used with one or more than one addressee. However, like the English 'you', it never takes a singular verb form.

आप **āp** is used to show respect and politeness. You will use this pronoun most often in your exchange with friends and strangers. Indian society is changing quickly and you should avoid stereotyping. You may have heard about the distinction between lower and higher caste Indians. Our advice is use आप **āp** for everybody regardless of his/her caste and status. This approach is the safest form of address in the final analysis. आप **āp** always takes a plural verb (e.g. the Hindi equivalent of 'you are' and not 'you is') regardless of the number of addressees.

<vo> is written as **vah** वह, but is pronounced as वो **vo** most widely. वो **vo** 'that' and वे **ve** 'those' (called 'remote demonstrative' pronouns) are also used to refer to person(s) or object(s) far from the speaker.

<ye> 'this, these' (called 'proximate demonstrative' pronouns) can be used to refer to both singular and plural person(s) or object(s) close to the speaker. The only difference is the singular form **<ye>**, which is written differently. It is written as यह **yah**.

Number and gender (plural formation of unmarked nouns)

Hindi nouns (like nouns in Spanish, Italian and French) are marked for both number and gender. There are two numbers (singular and plural) and two genders (masculine and feminine). Adjectives and verbs agree with nouns in number and gender.

The following box will provide you with Magic Key 1 to open a treasure chest of different noun and verb forms. Just let your imagination capture the suffixes boxed, and then you can begin to make new forms of nouns, adjectives and verbs. The only limit is your imagination!

Magic Key 1

	Singular	*Plural*	
Masculine	**-ā**	**-e**	
Feminine	**-ī**	**-iā̃**	(nouns)
		-ī	(adjectives; verbs)

Here are some examples of nouns and adjectives. Examples of verbs will be given in the next unit. You will find slight changes in the feminine plural forms of verbs and these are discussed in Unit 5.

Masculine

Singular			*Plural*		
beTā	बेटा	son	**beTe**	बेटे	sons
baccā	बच्चा	child	**bacce**	बच्चे	children
burā	बुरा	bad	**bure**	बुरे	bad

Feminine

Singular			*Plural*		
beTī	बेटी	daughter	**beTiā̃**	बेटियाँ	daughters
baccī	बच्ची	child	**bacciā̃**	बच्चियाँ	children
burī	बुरी	bad	**burī**	बुरी	bad

Masculine nouns ending in **ā** and feminine nouns ending in **ī** are called *unmarked nouns* in Hindi grammars. Similarly, the adjectives that end in **ā** are called *unmarked* (or *majority*) *adjectives*.

Nouns have gender too. In fact, most of the boxed suffixes draw their cues from the gender and number markings of nouns. However, there are no absolutes, as is the case in the real world. The logical gender holds only in the case of animate nouns. Male human beings receive masculine gender, whereas females receive feminine gender. However, inanimate and abstract nouns can either be masculine or feminine. सेना **senā** 'army', which (in India) does not admit women, is feminine; in addition, दाढ़ी **dāR^{h}ī** 'beard' is also feminine. Some animate nouns (species of animals, birds, insects, etc.) are either masculine or feminine. For example, मच्छर **macc^{h}ar** 'mosquito', खटमल **k^{h}aTmal** 'bug', चीता **cītā** 'leopard' and उल्लू **ullū** 'owl', are masculine in gender, and nouns such as चिड़ी **ciRī** 'bird', मक्खी **makk^{h}ī** 'fly' and मच्छी **macc^{h}ī** 'fish' are feminine. However, do not worry about the absolute gender in the case of inanimate and abstract nouns. There follow some rules of thumb for you to navigate the unpredictable waters of gender.

Look at the following representative list of Hindi words and see if you can guess the gender rules.

Masculine			*Feminine*		
laRkā	लड़का	boy	**laRkī**	लड़की	girl
g^h^oRā	घोड़ा	horse	**g^h^oRī**	घोड़ी	mare
kamrā	कमरा	room	**kursī**	कुरसी	chair
darvāzā	दरवाज़ा	door	**k^h^iRkī**	खिड़की	window
landan	लन्दन	London	**dillī**	दिल्ली	Delhi
g^h^ar	घर	house	**kitāb**	किताब	book
hāt^h^	हाथ	hand	**nazar**	नज़र	vision
namak	नमक	salt	**mirc**	मिर्च	pepper
ādmī	आदमी	man	**aurat**	औरत	woman
c^h^ātā	छाता	umbrella	**mātā**	माता	mother

Most Hindi nouns ending in **ā** are masculine and those ending in **ī** are feminine. There are exceptions though: आदमी **ādmī** 'man' ends in **ī** and is masculine and माता **mātā** 'mother' ends in **ā** and is feminine. But you have probably guessed that the *logical gender* takes precedence over the word-final sound. After all, how could the word for 'mother' be other than feminine in gender and the word 'man' be other than masculine? These two criteria – logical gender and word-final sound – can solve the mystery of Hindi gender in nearly every case.

Agreement: adjectives and possessive adjectives

You have already come across one very productive adjective: अच्छा **acc^h^ā** 'good/fine' which ends in **ā**. It is a majority adjective. By substituting the suffixes given in the box, we can produce other forms. For example:

acc^h^ā	**laRkā**	अच्छा लड़का	**acc^h^e**	**laRke**	अच्छे लड़के
good	boy		good	boys	
acc^h^ī	**laRkī**	अच्छी लड़की	**acc^h^ī**	**laRkiyā̃**	अच्छी लड़कियाँ
good	girl		good	girls	

The question word कैसा **kɛsā** 'how' also behaves like an adjective ending in **ā**.

kɛsā laRkā	कैसा लड़का	**kɛse laRke**	कैसे लड़के
what kind of boy		what kind of boys	
kɛsī laRkī	कैसी लड़की	**kɛsī laRkiyā̃**	कैसी लड़कियाँ
what kind of girl		what kind of girls	

The Hindi equivalents of the English possessive pronouns ('my', 'our', etc.) are:

merā	मेरा	my
hamārā	हमारा	our
terā	तेरा	your (singular, most intimate/non-honorific)
tumhāra	तुम्हारा	your (plural, familiar)
āpkā	आपका	your (plural, honorific)
uskā	उसका	his/her (remote)
unkā	उनका	their (remote)
iskā	इसका	his/her (proximate)
inkā	इनका	their (proximate)

Hindi possessive pronouns listed above follow the pattern of adjectives which end in **ā**.

merā	**laRkā**	मेरा लड़का	**mere**	**laRke**	मेरे लड़के
my	boy		my	boys	
merī	**laRkī**	मेरी लड़की	**merī**	**laRkiyā̃**	मेरी लड़कियाँ
my	girl		my	girls	

From the above examples, it is clear that adjectives ending in **ā** agree with the nouns that follow them. Therefore, they behave like 'majority' adjectives.

In English, it is the gender of the *possessor* in third person singular pronouns (i.e. 'his girl', 'her girl') that is marked on possessive adjectives. Such a distinction is not made in Hindi. Notice, however, that because possessive adjectives agree with the nouns that follow them, the form of a possessive adjective can change in accordance with the gender and the number of the *possessed* noun. Thus, the following phrases are ambiguous in Hindi:

uskā	**laRkā**	उसका लड़का	**uske**	**laRke**	उसके लड़के
his/her	boy		his/her	boys	
uskī	**laRkī**	उसकी लड़की	**uskī**	**laRkīyā̃**	उसकी लड़कियाँ
his/her	girl		his/her	girls	

उसका लड़का **uskā laRkā** means both 'his boy' and 'her boy'. Since लड़का **laRkā** 'boy' is masculine, the possessive adjective उसका **uskā** 'his/her' takes the masculine form, regardless of whether the boy in question belongs to a man or a woman. Similarly, उसकी लड़की **uskī laRkī** can mean both 'his girl' or 'her girl'. It is the feminine gender of the word लड़की **laRkī** 'girl' that assigns gender to the possessive pronoun.

अभ्यास **ab^{h}yās Exercises**

Exercise 1

How would you reply to someone who said this to you?

1	namaste.	नमस्ते।
2	kyā haal hɛ?	क्या हाल है?
3	salām.	सलाम।
4	mizāj kɛse hɛ̃?	मिज़ाज कैसे हैं?
5	acc^{h}ā, namaste.	अच्छा, नमस्ते।
6	sat srī akāl jī.	सत् स्री अकाल जी।
7	sab xɛriyat hɛ?	सब ख़ैरियत है?
8	namaste jī.	नमस्ते जी।
9	hukam kījie.	हुकम कीजिये।

Exercise 2

Match the replies in column B with the greetings or questions in column A.

	A	B
1	नमस्ते। namaste	ठीक है। T^{h}īk hɛ
2	क्या हाल है? kyā hāl hɛ?	अल्लाह का शुक्र है। allāh kā shukra hɛ.
3	आपके मिज़ाज कैसे हैं? āp ke mizāj kɛse hɛ̃	नमस्ते। namaste.
4	खुदा हाफ़िज़ xudā hāfiz.	खुदा हाफ़िज़। xudā hāfiz.
5	सब ख़ैरियत है? sab xɛriyat hɛ?	सलाम। salām.
6	सलाम salām.	मेहरबानी है। meharbānī hɛ.

Exercise 3

Fill in the gaps in the two conversations given below:

Conversation 1

A: सलाम।
salām.
B: __________।
B: सब ख़ैरियत है?
sab xɛriyat hɛ?
A: _________है और आप के ____________ कैसे हैं?
_________hɛ, aur āp ke_________ kɛse hɛ̃?
B: अल्लाह का___________ ________।
allāh kā__________ _________ .

Conversation 2

A: _________________।
B: सत स्री अकाल जी।
sat srī akāl jī.
B: क्या________ है?
kyā________ hɛ?
A: ___________ है और __________?
_____________ hɛ, aur_______?
B: मैं भी ____________ _____________।
mɛ̃ bʰī__________ _____________.
A: अच्छा ______ _______ _______।
accʰā,______ ______ _______
B: सत स्री अकाल।
sat srī akāl.

Exercise 4

Answer the following questions:

1
Question: क्या हाल है?
kyā hāl hɛ?
Answer:
Question: और आप?
aur āp?
Answer:

2

Question: आप कैसे हैं?
āp kɛse hɛ̃?

Answer:

Exercise 5

Give short sentences corresponding to the long sentences in the left-hand column.

	Long sentences	*Short sentences*
1	और आप कैसे हैं?	____________________
	aur āp kɛse hɛ̃	____________________
2	मैं भी ठीक हूँ।	____________________
	mɛ̃ b^hi Thīk hū̃	____________________
3	आपकी मेहरबानी है।	____________________
	āpkī meharbānī hɛ.	____________________
4	आपके मिज़ाज कैसे हैं?	____________________
	āpke mizāj kɛse hɛ̃?	

Exercise 6 (CD 1; 15)

If you have the recording, listen to the dialogue and identify the religion of the speakers on the basis of their use of greetings and goodbyes.

A: Male voice B: Female voice

शब्दावली shabdāvalī Vocabulary

किताब	**kitāb** (f.)	book
के लिये	**ke liye**	for
कोई	**koī**	some
बात	**bāt** (f.)	matter

2 आप कहाँ के/की हैं?

Where are you from?

By the end of this unit you should be able to:

- introduce yourself and others
- say and ask what you and others do
- say and ask where you and others work
- learn self-disclosure techniques about you and your family
- ask someone's address
- refer to inseparable possessions
- use very frequent adjectives
- learn plural formation
- form the simple present tense

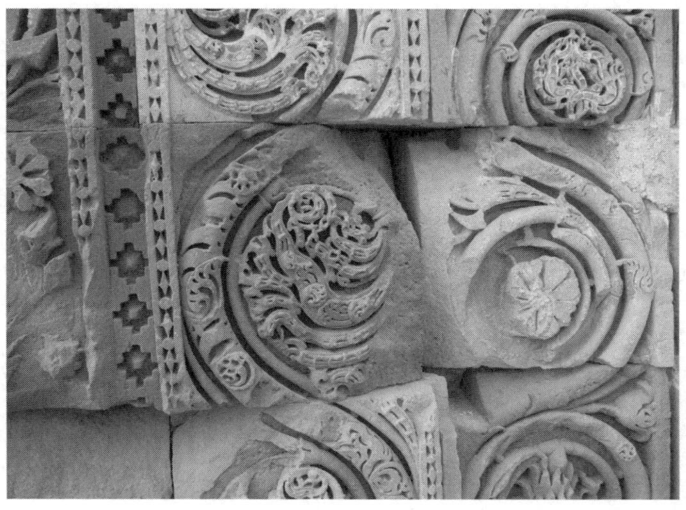

अंग्रेज़ी मना है?
English prohibition?

Hindi speakers are not snobbish in their linguistic attitude. They treat English as one of their languages. Therefore, many English words have been nativized into Hindi and they have their own Hindi pronunciation. The realization that English words are not alien to Hindi speakers will give you a thrill like running into a long-lost friend. Moreover, there are a number of modern contexts – such as jobs and titles – which cannot be adequately translated into Hindi because of their social meaning. Wait a minute! Do not be quick to value-judge Hindi or Indians. The lack of a word does not mean that the language is not rich enough. It simply means that Hindi responds to new contexts and needs by borrowing from English and other languages rather than inventing new words. In this way, Hindi is like English.

In the following dialogues, no attempt is made to artificially translate an English word/expression artificially into Hindi, if the English word has become a natural part of the Hindi language. The original English words in the text are italicized. Their native pronunciation is also given.

बातचीत **bātcīt** Dialogue 1 (CD 1; 17)

Small-talk

A young stock broker, Mukesh Bhargava, wants to meet a distinguished looking gentleman standing alone in a corner gazing at the wall. On learning from a friend that his name is Dr Anup Patel, Mr Bhargava approaches him. Having exchanged greetings, Mukesh Bhargava undertakes the task of introducing himself.

मुकेश: कहिए, आपका नाम डॉक्टर अनूप पटेल है न?
MUKESH: kahiye, āpkā nām DākTar Anūp Patel hɛ na?
अनूप: जी हाँ, मेरा नाम अनूप पटेल है।
ANUP: jī hā̃, merā nām Anūp Patel hɛ.
(*extending his hand to shake hands*)
मुकेश: मेरा नाम मुकेश है।
MUKESH: merā nām mukesh hɛ.
अनूप: मिल के बड़ी खुशी हुई। आप का पूरा नाम क्या है?
ANUP: mil ke baRī xushī huī. āp kā pūrā nām kyā hɛ?

मुकेश: मुकेश भार्गव है।
MUKESH: mukesh bʰārgav hɛ.
अनूप: आप क्या करते हैं?
ANUP: āp kyā karte hɛ̃?
मुकेश: मैं स्टाक ब्रोकर हूँ। आप मैडीकल डाक्टर हैं?
MUKESH: mɛ̃ sTāk brokar [*stockbroker*] hū̃. āp mɛDikal DākTar [*medical doctor*] hɛ̃?
अनूप: जी नहीं, मैं मैडीकल डॉक्टर नहीं हूँ। दूसरा डाक्टर हूँ।
ANUP?: jī nahī̃, mɛ̃ mɛDikal DākTar nahī̃ hū̃. dūsrā DākTar hū̃.

MUKESH: *Excuse me, you are Dr Anup Patel, aren't you?*
ANUP: *Yes, my name is Anup Patel.*
MUKESH: *My name is Mukesh.*
ANUP: *Pleased to meet (you). What is your full name?*
MUKESH: *My name is Mukesh Bhargava.*
ANUP: *What (work) do you do?*
MUKESH: *I am a stockbroker. Are you a medical doctor?*
ANUP: *No, I am not a medical doctor. (I) am the other (kind of) doctor.* (i.e. I am a PhD)

शब्दावली **shabdāvalī Vocabulary**

कहना	**kahnā** (+ne)	to say
कहिए/कहिये	**kahiye**	Excuse me!
नाम	**nām** (m.)	name
ना	**nā**	isn't it?
हाँ	**h**	yes
मिल के बड़ी ख़ुशी हई	**mil ke baRī xushī huī**	pleased to meet you
पूरा	**pūrā** (m. adj.)	full
करना	**karnā** (+ne)	to do
दूसरा	**dūsrā** (m. adj.)	second, other

Notes

Attention getters

The Hindi literal equivalent of the English expression '**Excuse me!**' is **māf kījiye**. However, the Hindi expression actually means 'I apologize' or 'I beg your pardon'. Therefore, it is not suited to those contexts observed in the above dialogue where the real aim of '**Excuse me**' is to get attention. Although some educated

English-speaking Indians tend to translate directly from English, this is not the natural tendency of native speakers. The expression 'Excuse me' is best paraphrased by the native Hindi speaker either as 'please say' कहिए **kahiye** or 'please listen' सुनिए **suniye**. In fact, this is true of many languages, for example Spanish.

*Do not use **māf kījiye** if you do not intend to apologize. Such an inappropriate choice could make a learner the easy target of unwanted jokes.*

Social linguistic rituals

Every language employs some expressions which are often fixed and invariable. For instance, in greeting someone, one might use the expression 'Hi there'; but if one examines this expression, it is rather a strange one as there is no subject, no verb and no chance of changing the expression even slightly, for example to 'Hi here'. In some respects, Hindi expressions such as 'Pleased to see you' belong to this category. For the time being, you should memorize them without going further into their composition. Also, learn their appropriate usage. They are used usually in introductions. However, if a waiter is introducing himself, you do not need to use this expression in response.

The mystery of what the correct subject of 'Pleased to see you' is will become clear later when the concept of **ko** subjects (called 'dative subjects' or 'experiential subjects') is introduced. For the time being, use the expression as if it were a subject-less sentence.

Word-for-word translation

The Hindi expression of 'I am pleased to meet you' is

मिल के	बड़ी	ख़ुशी	हुई।
mil ke	**baRī**	**xushī**	**huī**
met-having	big	happiness	happened

In the above expression, the object 'you' is implied. However, for emphasis, the object can be inserted into the above expression:

आपसे	मिल के	बड़ी	ख़ुशी	हुई।
āp se	**mil ke**	**baRī**	**xushī**	**huī**
you-with	met-having	big	happiness	happened

Notice the Hindi equivalent of the English 'I am pleased to meet you' is 'Having met you, I am pleased.'

Word order of the question word 'what'

Observe the place of the question word क्या **kyā** 'what' in the following sentences:

आपका	पूरा	नाम	क्या	है?
āp kā	**pūrā**	**nām**	**kyā**	**hɛ**?
your	full	name	what	is

What is your full name?

आप	क्या	काम	करते	हैं?
āp	**kyā**	**kām**	**karte**	**hɛ̃**?
you	what	work	do	are

What do you do? = What is your job?

When one compares these sentences with the socially ritualistic expression क्या हाल है **kyā hāl hɛ**, one might be tempted to conclude that 'anything goes' regarding the placement of क्या **kyā** in a sentence. These examples strengthen this belief further because one can say the above two sentences in the following way:

आपका	क्या	पूरा	नाम	है?
āpkā	**kyā**	**pūrā**	**nām**	**hɛ**?
your	what	full	name	is

What is your full name?

आप	काम	क्या	करते	हैं?
āp	**kām**	**kyā**	**karte**	**hɛ̃**?
you	work	what	do	are

What do you do? = What is your job?

The placement of क्या **kyā** at the beginning or at the end of the sentence, or between the two verbal elements, causes some problems. It changes the meaning of the sentences and may even sound abrupt and impolite. Therefore, the rule of thumb is to keep the question word closer to the word that is the subject of the inquiry. क्या **kyā** is usually placed before the noun or the verb it modifies. If the noun phrase is modified, as the noun नाम **nām** is modified in the following sentence by two modifiers ('your' and 'full'), rather than breaking the bond between the noun and the modifier as in

आपका	क्या	पूरा	नाम	है?
āpkā	**kyā**	**pūrā**	**nām**	**hɛ?**

the question word is placed after the noun.

आपका	पूरा	नाम	क्या	है?
āpkā	**pūrā**	**nām**	**kyā**	**hɛ?**

In the following sentence, the noun काम **kām** is, however, not modified further; thus, it is better to say

आप	क्या	काम	करते	हैं?
āp	**kyā**	**kām**	**karte**	**hɛ̃?**

i.e. lit. 'What work do you do?' instead of the following sentence, which has some negative connotations as in the English sentence 'Tell me, what do you do anyway?'

आप	काम	क्या	करते	हैं?
āp	**kām**	**kyā**	**karte**	**hɛ̃?**

बातचीत **bātcīt** **Dialogue 2** (CD 1; 19)

Where are you from?

Indian train travel can be nostalgic. Two female college students on their way to Banaras from Delhi engage in a dialogue which is typical of Indian travellers whether from urban or rural areas. After asking each other their names, Kanika Bhatia and Sunita Divan start inquiring about each other's family background.

कनिका: आप कहाँ की हैं?
KANIKA: āp kahā̃ kī hɛ̃?
सुनीता: मैं दिल्ली की हूँ और आप?
SUNITA: mɛ̃ dillī kī hū̃. aur āp?
कनिका: मैं बनारस में रहती हूँ।
KANIKA: mɛ̃ banāras mẽ rɛhtī hū̃.

सुनीता: आपके कितने भाई बहनें हैं?
SUNITA: āpke kitne b^{h}āī-bɛhɛnẽ hɛ̃?
कनिका: हम चार भाई और दो बहनें हैं।
KANIKA: ham cār b^{h}āī aur do bɛhɛnẽ hɛ̃.
सुनीता: मेरा एक भाई और एक बहन है।
SUNITA: merā ek b^{h}āī aur ek bɛhɛn hɛ.

KANIKA: *Where are you from?*
SUNITA: *I am from Delhi. And you?*
KANIKA: *I live in Banaras.*
SUNITA: *How many brothers and sisters do you have?*
KANIKA: *We are four brothers and two sisters.*
SUNITA: *I have one brother and a sister.*

शब्दावली **shabdāvalī Vocabulary**

कहाँ	**kahā̃**	where
में	**mẽ**	in
दिल्ली	**dillī** (f.)	Delhi (the capital city)
की	**kī** (f.)	of
बनारस	**banāras**	Banaras (one of the oldest cities of India)
रहना	**<rɛhnā>**	live
कितना	**kitnā** (m.)	how many?
कितने	**kitne**	how many?
भाई	**b^{h}āī** (m.)	brother/brothers
बहन	**<bɛhɛn>** (f.)	sister
चार	**cār**	four
दो	**do**	two
एक	**ek**	one

Pronunciation

The word for sister is written as बहन **bahan** but is pronounced as **bɛhɛn**. You must have noticed by now that the sound **h** in the middle of a word (when sandwiched between the vowels **a** and the final position) alters the pronunciation of the preceding vowel. Go back to Unit 1 and check the pronunciation of third person singular pronouns. Similarly, the verb 'live' is written as रह **rah** but is pronounced as **rɛh**.

Notes

Word-for-word translation: 'Where are you from?'

The Hindi equivalent of the English 'Where are you from?' is

आप	कहाँ	की	हैं?
āp	**kahā̃**	**kī**	**hɛ̃**?
you	where	of	are

The response to the English question in Hindi is

मैं	दिल्ली	की	हूँ।
mɛ̃	**dillī**	**kī**	**hū̃**.
I	Delhi	of	am

As we saw in the last chapter, like other possessive pronouns, की **kī** agrees with the number and the gender of its possessor. In the above two sentences the subject pronoun is the possessor. Since the subjects are feminine, the feminine form की **kī** is selected. It is not difficult to guess what would happen if the subjects were masculine. If these sentences are uttered by males, they are

आप	कहाँ	के	हैं?
āp	**kahā̃**	**ke**	**hɛ̃**?
you	where	of	are

मैं	दिल्ली	का	हूँ।
mɛ̃	**dillī**	**kā**	**hū̃**.
I	Delhi	of	am

Remember the honorific pronoun आप **āp** always takes the plural form.

Don't be surprised if you hear someone using से **se** 'from' instead of का **kā**, का **ke** or की **kī**.

आप	कहाँ	से	हैं?
āp	**kahā̃**	**se**	**hɛ̃**?
you	where	from	are

मैं	दिल्ली	से	हूँ।
mɛ̃	**dillī**	**se**	**hū̃**.
I	Delhi	from	am

Usually, an educated Hindi–English bilingual would construct such a sentence. The important thing is to know that से **se** is invariable whereas का **kā** is variable. You will learn about the invariable elements such as से **se** later in the section on invariable postposition.

Notice also the placement of the English 'from' in the Hindi sentence.

Postpositions

The Hindi equivalents of English 'in Banaras' and 'from Delhi' are

बनारस	में	दिल्ली	से
banāras	**mẽ**	**dillī**	**se**
Banaras	in	Delhi	from

Notice the English prepositions placed after the noun of the prepositional phrase. In other words, the word order of the prepositional phrase is reversed in Hindi. Since the prepositional elements always follow the noun they modify, they are called *post*positions in Hindi grammar.

Question words: 'where' and 'how many/much'

From the Hindi sentence 'Where are you from?' it should be obvious that the Hindi word for where is कहाँ **kahā̃**. Like the English question word, Hindi कहाँ **kahā̃** does not change its shape. It is also not placed at the beginning of the sentence. Its usual place is before the verb. However, this word is can be quite mobile within a sentence.

The Hindi equivalent of 'how many/much' is कितना **kitnā**. This question word agrees with its following noun in number and gender.

कितना	काम	
kitnā	**kām**	how much work
कितने	भाई	
kitne	**b^hai̅**	how many brothers
कितनी	बहनें	
kitnī	**bɛhɛnẽ**	how many sisters

This question word is like a (an inflecting) possessive adjective.

बातचीत **bātcīt** **Dialogue 3** (CD 1; 21)

Where are you from?

During the train journey, Kanika and Sunita become friends; they are ready to exchange their addresses.

सुनीता: यह मेरा पता है।
SUNITA: ye merā patā hɛ.
कनिका: यह पता बड़ा है।
KANIKA: ye patā bahut baRā hɛ.
सुनीता: हाँ, बड़ा शहर, बड़ा पता।
SUNITA: hā̃ baRā shɛhɛr, baRā patā.
कनिका: लेकिन छोटा शहर, छोटा पता।
KANIKA: lekin, c^{h}oTā shɛhɛr, choTā patā.
(both laugh)
सुनीता: अच्छा, फिर मिलेंगे।
SUNITA: acc^{h}ā, p^{h}ir milẽge.
कनिका: मिलेंगे।
KANIKA: milẽge.

SUNITA: *This is my address.*
KANIKA: *This address is very big.* (i.e. long)
SUNITA: *Yes, big city, big address.*
KANIKA: *But small city, small address!*
(both laugh)
SUNITA: *Okay, (we) will meet again.*
KANIKA: *Okay, (we) will meet.*

शब्दावली **shabdāvalī** **Vocabulary**

पता	**patā** (m.)	address
बहुत	**bahut**	very
बड़ा	**baRā** (m. adj.)	big
शहर	**<shɛhɛr>** (m.)	city
लेकिन	**lekin**	but
छोटा	**c^{h}oTā** (m. adj.)	small
फिर	**p^{h}ir**	again, then
अच्छा	**acc^{h}ā** (m. adj.)	good, okay
मिलना	**milnā** (–ne)	to meet
मिलेंगे	**milẽge**	will meet

Pronunciation

Like the word बहन **bahan**, the word for 'city' is written as शहर **shahar** but it is pronounced **shɛhɛr**. However, the pronunciation of बहुत **bahut** does not change because **h** is not surrounded by the vowel **a** on both sides.

Notes

Word-for-word translation

यह	पता	बहुत	बड़ा	है।
ye	**patā**	**bahut**	**baRā**	**hɛ**.
this	address	very	big	is

Notice the sentence ends with a verb and not with an adjective as is the case with 'This address is very long.'

Subject omission

The Hindi expression of 'we will meet again' is

फिर	मिलेंगे।
p^{h}ir	**milẽge**.
again	will meet

The subject 'we' is implied. It is rarely spelled out. Normally such subjectless expressions are considered ungrammatical in many languages including English; however, they are quite normal in Hindi. Many languages, such as Chinese, follow the tendency to drop subjects. Subject/pronoun dropping languages are called 'pro-drop' languages.

व्याकरण **vyākaraNa** Grammar

Tag question

A tag question is usually tagged to a statement. The Hindi equivalent of 'You are Dr Anup Patel, aren't you?' is very simple – just add न **na** at the end of the statement. It will take care of both the positive tags (e.g. 'is it?', 'will you?', 'do you?', etc.) and the negative tags (e.g. 'isn't it?', 'won't you?', 'don't you?', etc.) attached to a statement in English. The only difference is that whereas English speakers will pause at the point where a comma is placed in the English sentence Hindi speakers will not do so. Therefore, no comma is placed between the statement and the tag. However, in both English and Hindi a tag question has a rising intonation.

Verb 'to be'

This section will guarantee plain sailing into the sea of different tenses. Once you have mastered the forms given below, your adventure into different tenses becomes more rewarding and worthwhile.

There is a striking resemblance between the English and Hindi verb 'to be'. In Hindi just as in English one cannot say 'you am', 'I is', 'he am' or 'they is'. Different forms are used depending upon the person and number of the subject. The Hindi counterparts of the English verb 'to be' are given below in Magic Key 2.

Magic Key 2

	Singular	*Plural*	*Honorific*
First person	हूँ **hū̃** (I) am	हैं **hɛ̃** (we) are	–
Second person	है **hɛ** (you sg.) are	हो **ho** (you pl.) are	हैं **hɛ̃** (you honorific) are
Third person	है **hɛ** (he/she/it) is	हैं **hɛ̃** (they) are	–

Certainly there are some differences between Hindi and English. In Hindi it is possible to say 'you is', provided the Hindi singular 'you' तू **tū** is selected. Of course, the second person honorific pronoun आप **āp** always takes a plural form. As we mentioned in the first unit, be careful when using Hindi second person pronouns. Chances are you will rarely get to use the pronoun तू **tū** and, thus, the singular second person form of 'to be'.

Present habitual actions = simple present tense

The Hindi sentences

आप	क्या	करते	हैं?
āp	**kyā**	**karte**	**hɛ̃**?
you	what	do	are

मैं	बनारस	में	रहती	हूँ।
mɛ̃	**banaras**	**mẽ**	**rɛhtī**	**hū̃**
I	Banaras	in	live	am

are equivalent to the English 'What do you do?' and 'I live in Banaras,' which refer to habitual or regularly repeated acts. Look at the verb form/phrase, and you will see that there are two main parts of the Hindi verb form. The first, usually called the 'main verb', is composed of three elements:

कर	+ त	+ े
kar	+ **t**	+ **e**
stem 'to do'	+ aspect marker	+ gender-number marker (m. pl.)

रह	+ त	+ ी
rɛh	+ **t**	+ **ī**
stem 'to live'	+ aspect marker	+ gender-number marker (f. sg.)

The first element of the first part is the verb stem. The second element is the aspect marker. The aspect marker simply shows whether the act is completed or ongoing. At this point it is important to understand the difference between tense and aspect. As mentioned just now, aspect is concerned about the ongoing, repeated or completed state of the action whereas tense (present, past or future) renders time information, i.e. as to what point in time the action took place. The third element of the main verb is the same masculine plural ending from Magic Key 1 discussed in the previous chapter.

The second part of the verb is called the 'auxiliary verb'. In our two sentences, the auxiliary verb is the same 'to be' verb form discussed above in Magic Key 2.

This verb form has various technical names. The most widely used forms are the following three: present imperfect tense, present habitual tense and simple present tense. Here we will call it the *simple present tense*. The full paradigm is given in the Grammatical Summary.

Verb 'to have'

The Hindi expression for 'How many brothers and sisters do you have?' is

आपके	कितने	भाई	बहनें	हैं?
āpke	**kitne**	**b^{h}āī**	**bɛhɛnẽ**	**hɛ̃**?
your	how many	brothers-sisters		are

Notice that the Hindi sentence contains neither an equivalent to the English verb 'to have' nor the subject 'you'. In Hindi, the subject takes a possessive form and the verb 'to have' becomes the verb 'to be'. As we proceed further, it will become clear that many languages do not have the exact equivalent of English 'have'. This Hindi construction is used to express inseparable or non-transferable possessions (such as body parts, relationships or dearly held possessions such as a job, house or shop). Transferable possessions will be dealt with later on.

Number and gender (plural formation of marked 'nerd' nouns)

Now do some detective work and discover Magic Key 3 for the following nouns:

Masculine					
Singular			*Plural*		
भाई	**b^{h}āī**	brother	भाई	**b^{h}āī**	brothers
घर	**g^{h}ar**	house	घर	**g^{h}ar**	houses
हाथ	**hāt^h**	hand	हाथ	**hāt^h**	hands
मर्द	**mard**	man	मर्द	**mard**	men
आदमी	**ādmī**	man	आदमी	**ādmī**	men
Feminine					
Singular			*Plural*		
बहन	**bɛhɛn**	sister	बहनें	**bɛhɛnẽ**	sisters
किताब	**kitāb**	book	किताबें	**kitābẽ**	books
औरत	**aurat**	woman	औरतें	**auratẽ**	women
माता	**mātā**	mother	माताएँ	**mātāẽ**	mothers

If you think that the masculine nouns that do not end in **ā** remain unchanged and the feminine nouns which do not end in **ī** take **ẽ** to form plurals, you are right. The masculine nouns which depart from the normal trend, i.e. those that do *not* end in **ā** and the feminine nouns that do *not* end in **ī**, are called 'marked' nouns. We affectionately call them 'nerd' nouns as an aid to memory.

Magic Key 3

	Singular	*Plural*
Masculine	non-**ā**	0 (zero = unchanged)
Feminine	non-**ī**	**ẽ**

अभ्यास **ab^{h}yās Exercises**

Exercise 1

Pac-man has swallowed either some parts of the words or whole words. Supply the missing part where you see the * sign:

मैं दिल्ली * हूँ। मे* चार भाई *। मेरा छोट* भाई शिकागो में काम कर* है। मे* दो बड़* भाई इंग्लैड़ में रहत* *। मेरा नाम अमर *। मैं स्कूल जा* हूँ। मेर* दो बहन* भी * ।मेर* पिता जी भी काम करत* हैं। आप * रहते है? आप* कित* भाई–बहनें हैं। आप* माता जी क्या * कर* हैं?

mɛ̃ dillī * hũ. me* cār b^{h}āi *. merā c^{h}oT* b^{h}āī *Chicago* mẽ kām kar* hɛ. mer* do baR* b^{h}āī *England* mẽ rɛht* *. merā nām amar *. mɛ̃ *school* jā* hũ. mer* do bɛhɛn* b^{h}ī *. mer* pitā jī b^{h}ī kām kart* hɛ̃. āp * rɛhte hɛ̃? āp kit* b^h āī-bɛhɛnẽ. āp* mātā jī kyā * kar* hɛ̃?.

Exercise 2

Pair the words on the right with those on the left:

अच्छा
acc^{h}ā | छोटा
c^{h}oTā

बड़ा
baRā | लड़की
laRkī

बहन bɛhɛn	औरत aurat
लड़का laRkā	बुरा burā
आदमी ādmī	नहीं nahī̃
हाँ hā̃	भाई b^{h}āī

Exercise 3

The software system of our computer has imposed some weird system on the following Hindi phrases. It's your job to correct them.

से se	बनारस banāras
में mẽ	शहर shɛhɛr
दस das	बहन bɛhɛn
चार cār	भाईयाँ b^{h}āīyā̃
दो do	आदमीयाँ ādmīyā̃
कितना kitnā	भाईयाँ b^{h}āīyā̃
पीला pīlā	साड़ी sāRī

Exercise 4

Unscramble the following words/phrases and fill in the unscrambled expression in the blank spaces on the right:

hiyeka	________		
shīxu	________		
bīRa xuīsh hīu	________	________	________
rūpā mnā	________	________	
dūrās	________		
kinte b^{h}āī	________	________	
mẽlieg	________		

Exercise 5

In this puzzle there are four Hindi words from our dialogues. Find the words and circle them. They can be found horizontally and vertically.

a d g a b a d z x s u n i y e z y x u f g
l l k j a z x c v b n m a s p q w e r t y
z x c v R a d g a r t y f g h a s g h j o
r t y f i b g t x u s h i i z q t s k x p
c v b n i w s x e d v r a t g h t a h z c
q a z w c w s v f r y h n m h u i k a u c

Exercise 6 (CD 1; 23)

If you have the recording, listen to it, and then play the role of Meenu Bharati. You can record your response.

Setting: a crowded store

अभिलाषा: (*bumps into Meenu*) माफ़ कीजिये।
मीनू: ________________। बहुत भीड़ है।
अभिलाषा: सच।
मीनू: ________________________।
अभिलाषा: और मेरा नाम अभिलाषा पाँडे है।
मीनू: ______________________।
अभिलाषा: आप दिल्ली की हैं, न?
मीनू: ______________________।

ABHILASHA: (*bumps into Meenu*) māf kījiye.
MEENU: ________________. bahut b^{h}īR hɛ.
ABHILASHA: sac.
MEENU: ________________.
ABHILASHA: aur merā nām Abhilasha Pande hɛ.
MEENU: ________________.
ABHILASHA: āp dillī kī hɛ̃ na?
MEENU: ________________.

शब्दावली shabdāvalī Vocabulary

माफ़ी	**māfī** (f.)	apology
भीड़	**bhīR** (f.)	crowd

3 आपको क्या चाहिए? āpko kyā cāhiye?

What would you like?

By the end of this unit you should be able to:

- tell someone what you wish to get
- describe locations
- use some negotiation skills
- make reservations
- describe possessions (transferable)
- understand verb agreement with subjects and objects
- express physical states (e.g. fever, headache)

बातचीत **bātcīt Dialogue 1** (CD 1; 24)

साड़ी ख़रीदना ***sāRī xarīdnā Buying a saree***

Meghan Ashley and Anita Sharma go to a saree shop in Jaipur. Anita visits the shop quite regularly. After they have greeted each other, Anita tells the shopkeeper that Meghan is visiting from London and wants a saree.

अनिता:	ज़रा नये फैशन की साड़ी दिखाइए।
ANITA:	zarā naye *fashion* kī sāRī dikʰāīye.
राजेन्द्र:	कौन–सी साड़ी चाहिए? रेशमी या सूती?
RAJINDER:	kaun sī sāRī cāhiye? reshmī yā sūtī?
अनिता:	रेशमी।
ANITA:	reshmī.
राजेन्द्र:	ये देखिये, आज कल इसका बहुत रिवाज है। देखिये, सिल्क कितना अच्छा है।
RAJINDER:	ye dekʰiye. āj-kal iskā bahut rivāj hai. dekʰiye, silk kitnā accʰā hɛ!

(Rajinder shows a number of sarees. Anita asks Meghan about her choice.)

अनिता:	मेगन, आपको कौन सी साड़ी पसन्द है?
ANITA:	Meghan, āpko kaun sī sāRī pasand hɛ?
मेगन:	ये पीली।
MEGHAN:	ye pīlī.

(turning to Rajinder to ask the price)

अनिता:	इसका दाम क्या है?
ANITA:	iskā dām kyā hɛ?
राजेन्द्र:	बारह सौ रुपये।
RAJINDER:	bārā sau rupaye.
अनिता:	ठीक बताइये, ये बाहर से आयी हैं।
ANITA:	Tʰīk batāiye, ye bāhar se āyī hɛ̃.
राजेन्द्र:	आज–कल इतना दाम है . . . अच्छा, ग्यारह सौ।
RAJINDER:	āj-kal itnā dām hɛ . . . accʰā, gyāra sau.
अनिता:	अच्छा, ठीक है।
ANITA:	accʰā Thīk hɛ.

ANITA:	*Please show me a saree that is in fashion.*
RAJINDER:	*What kind of saree (do you) desire/want? Silk(en) or cotton?*
ANITA:	*Silk(en).*
RAJINDER:	*Look at this. Nowadays it is very much in fashion. See how good the silk is!*

(Rajinder shows a number of sarees. Anita asks Meghan about her choice.)

ANITA: *Meghan, which saree do you want?*

MEGHAN: *(I want) this yellow (one).*

(Turning to Rajinder to ask the price)

ANITA: *What is its price?*

RAJINDER: *Twelve hundred rupees.*

ANITA: *Please tell (me) the right (price); she is the visitor.* (lit. she has come from abroad)

RAJINDER: *This is the price nowadays . . . okay, eleven hundred (rupees).*

ANITA: *Okay, (that) is fine.*

शब्दावली **shabdāvalī Vocabulary**

ज़रा	**zarā**	little, somewhat
नया	**nayā** (m. adj.)	new
नये	**naye**	new
साड़ी	**sāRī**	saree
दिखाना	**dik^{h}ānā** [+ne]	to show
दिखाइये	**dik^{h}āiye**	please show
कौन सा	**kaun sā** (m. adj.)	which one
कौन सी	**kaun sī**	which one
चाहिये/चाहिए	**cāhiye**	desire, want
रेशम	**resham** (m.)	silk
रेशमी	**reshmī**	silken
या	**yā**	or
सूत	**sūt** (m.)	cotton
सूती	**sūtī**	cotton (adj.)
देखना	**dek^{h}nā** (+ne)	to see
देखिये/देखिए	**dek^{h}iye**	please see
आजकल	**āj-kal**	nowadays
रिवाज	**rivāj** (m.)	custom
आपको	**āp-ko**	to you
पसन्द	**pasand** (f.)	choice, liking
पीला	**pīlā** (m. adj.)	yellow
पीली	**pīlī** (f. adj.)	yellow
दाम	**dām** (m.)	price
बारह	**<bārā>**	twelve
सौ	**sau**	hundred
रुपये	**rupaye** (m.)	Rupees (Indian currency)
बताइये/बताइए	**batāiye**	please tell

बाहर	**bāhar**	outside
आयी/आई	**āyī**	came
इतना	**itnā** (m. adj.)	this much
ग्यारह	**<gyārā>**	eleven

Pronunciation

The numerals eleven and twelve are written ग्यारह **gyārah** and बारह **bārah**, but are pronounced ग्यारा **gyārā** and बारा **bārā** in Standard Hindi. In the other varieties of Hindi, they are pronounced **gyārɛ** and **bārɛ**, respectively.

The Hindi word for 'silken' is written as रेशमी **reshamī** but the vowel अ **a** is dropped. Therefore, it is pronounced रेश्मी **reshmī**. For the time being, satisfy yourself with this observation. The rule for dropping अ **a** is given in Script Unit 4.

Notes

Rules of negotiation: direct and indirect strategies

The rules of bargaining or negotiating can be very complex indeed, and are beyond the scope of this book. However, one strategy deserves special mention. Towards the end of the conversation, the subject of visitors is brought up. Since Indian culture shows a great deal of sensitivity towards foreign visitors, this is a signal to request a discount. In this case, the shopkeeper appropriately obliges.

It is also quite common to ask the price indirectly by saying:

Asking the price (directly)				*Asking how much the total comes to (indirectly)*		
इसका	दाम	क्या	है?	कितने	[पैसे]	हुए?
iskā	**dām**	**kyā**	**hɛ?**	**kitne**	**paise**	**hue?**
Its	price	what	is	how much	money	happened
ये	कितने	का	है?	कितना	हुआ/होगा?	
ye	**kitne**	**kā**	**hɛ?**	**kitnā**	**huā/hogā?**	
this	how much	of	is	how much	happened/will happen	
इसकी	कीमत	क्या	है?			
iskī	**kīmat**	**kyā**	**hɛ?**			
its	price	what	is			

Politeness bug

As we saw in the last unit, Hindi is a very rich language from the point of view of politeness.

When ज़रा **zarā** 'little', 'somewhat' is used at the beginning of a request, its main function is politeness. It is a little like the English 'I do not want to impose on you but . . .'. By adding ज़रा **zarā**, Hindi speakers convey the meaning 'I want to put as little burden as possible on you by my request'. ज़रा **zarā** remains invariable.

चाहना cāhnā 'want' vs चाहिए cāhiye 'desire/want'

Just as the English expression 'What do you want?' would be considered less polite than 'What would you like to have?', similarly in Hindi

आप	कौन	सी	साड़ी	चाहती	हैं?
āp	**kaun**	**sī**	**sāRī**	**cāhtī**	**hɛ̃**
you	what kind of		saree	want	are

would be considered less polite than

आपको	कौन सी	साड़ी	चाहिए?
āpko	**kaun sī**	**sāRī**	**cāhiye?**
you-to	what kind of	saree	desire

(lit. What kind of saree is desirable to you?)

In the first sentence the subject आप **āp** indicates a *deliberate* subject whereas in the second sentence the subject आपको **āpko** is an *experiencer* one. Sometimes politeness is achieved in Hindi by means of experiencer subjects. In other words, the verb चाहिए **cāhiye** is the relatively polite counterpart of English 'to want' (and Hindi चाहना **cāhnā** 'to want') because it always selects an experiencer subject. Experiencer subjects render polite reading in some contexts. Hereafter the Hindi verb चाहिए **cāhiye** will be glossed as 'want' because 'desire' is not its best translation.

For more information, see the discussion of the experiencer subject in the next unit.

Word-for-word translation

The Hindi equivalent of English 'It is very much in fashion' is

इसका	बहुत	रिवाज	है।
iskā	**bahut**	**rivāj**	**hɛ.**
its	very	custom	is

Similarly, the English expression 'This (she) is a visitor' is realized in Hindi as

ये	बाहर	से	आई	हैं।
ye	**bāhar**	**se**	**āyī**	**hɛ̃.**
this (hon.)	outside	from	came	are

In other words, the Hindi expression is literally 'She has come from outside.' The past tense will be dealt with later on; for the time being memorize this sentence and learn to make number and gender changes in आई **āyī** (आया **āyā** for masculine singular subjects, आए/आये **āye** for masculine plural and आईं/आयीं **āyī̃** for feminine plural) and person and number changes in the 'to be' form.

Polite commands

The Hindi equivalent of English 'please show' and 'please see' are

दिखाइए	देखिए
dik^{h}ā-iye	**dek^h-iye**
show-imperative (polite)	see-imperative (polite)

The other examples of polite commands you have encountered earlier are:

कहिए	सुनिए
kah-iye	**sun-iye**
say-imperative (polite)	listen-imperative (polite)

In short, **iye** is added to a verbal stem to form polite commands. It is called the 'polite imperative' in grammatical literature.

No word for 'please'

There is really no *exact* equivalent of the English word 'please'. The most important way of expressing polite requests is by means of the polite verb form, i.e. by adding **-iye** to a verb stem. If one looks for word-for-word Hindi equivalents of 'please', there are two: कृपया **kripyā** or मेहरबानी करके **meharbānī karke**; even then the verbal form with **-iye** must be retained. कृपया **kripyā** and मेहरबानी करके **meharbānī karke** mean 'kindly' in Hindi.

Context

Note the use of the change in meaning of Hindi कौन सा **kaun sā** 'which one' in the following two contexts: when a saree has yet to be shown by the shopkeeper

कौन सी	साड़ी	चाहिए?
kaun sī	**sāRī**	**cāhiye?**
what kind of	saree	want

What kind of saree do (you) want?

and in the context of choosing a saree from a set of sarees which are being shown to the customer

आपको	कौन	सी	साड़ी	पसंद	है?
āpko	**kaun**	**sī**	**sāRī**	**pasand**	**hɛ?**
you-to	which	one	saree	choice/liking	is

Which saree do (you) like?

Subject omission

कौन	सी	साड़ी	चाहिए?
kaun	**sī**	**sāRī**	**cāhiye?**
what	kind of	saree	want

What kind of saree do (you) want?

बातचीत **bātcīt Dialogue 2** (CD 1; 26)

Booking a flight

John Smith goes to the airline booking office to make an airline reservation for Jaipur (the Pink City). He talks with the agent.

जान: जयपुर की एक टिकट चाहिए।
JOHN: jaipur kī ek TikaT (*ticket*) cāhiye.
एजेंट: कौन से दिन के लिये?
AGENT: kaun se din ke liye?
जान: कल के लिए।
JOHN kal ke liye.

एजेंट: कम्प्यूटर पर देखता हूँ, है या नहीं।
AGENT: kampuTar (*computer*) par dek^{h}tā hũ, hɛ yā nahī̃.
जान: सुबह की फ़्लाइट चाहिये।
JOHN: subā kī flāiT (*flight*) cāhiye.
एजेंट टिकट है।
AGENT: Ticket (*ticket*) hɛ.
जान: तो दीजिए। फ़्लाइट कब चलती है?
JOHN to dījiye. *flight* (*flight*) kab caltī hɛ?
एजेंट: सुबह दस बजे ।
AGENT: subā das baje.
जान: मेरे पास कैश नहीं है।
JOHN: mere pās *cash* nahī̃ hɛ.
एजेंट: तो कैडिट कार्ड दीजिए।
AGENT: to krɛDiT kārDa (*credit card*) dījiye.

JOHN: *(I) want one ticket for Jaipur*
AGENT: *For which day?*
JOHN: *For tomorrow.*
AGENT: *(I) must look at the computer (to see), whether or not (I have it).* (lit. [it] is or not).
JOHN: *(I) need a morning flight.*
AGENT: *(I) have a ticket.*
JOHN: *Then (please) give (it to me). When does the flight leave?*
AGENT: *10 o'clock (in the) morning.*
JOHN: *I do not have cash.*
AGENT: *Then use a credit card. (lit. give a credit card)*

शब्दावली **shabdāvalī Vocabulary**

दिन	**din** (m.)	day
के लिये	**ke liye**	for
कल	**kal**	yesterday, tomorrow
पर	**par**	on, at
देखना	**dek^{h}nā** (+**ne**)	to see
सुबह	**<subā>**	morning
तो	**to**	then
देना	**denā** (+**ne**)	to give
दीजिए	**dījiye**	please give
कब	**kab**	when (question word)
चलना	**calnā** (–**ne**)	to leave, to walk
दस	**das**	ten
बजे	**baje**	o'clock
पास	**pās**	near, possession (have)

Pronunciation

The word for morning is written as सुबह **subah**, but is pronounced **subā** सुबा.

In the borrowed words from English such as *computer* and *ticket*, the English *t* is pronounced with the retroflex ट **T** (see chapter on Hindi writing system and pronunciation for the pronunciation of Hindi retroflex sounds).

Notes

Word-for-word translation

जयपुर	की	टिकट
jaipur	**kī**	**TikaT**
Jaipur	of (f.)	ticket (f.)

A ticket for Jaipur. (lit. Jaipur's ticket)

The borrowed English words 'ticket' and 'computer' have been assimilated into Hindi and assigned feminine and masculine gender, respectively.

The equivalent Hindi expression for 'morning flight' is

सुबह	की	फ़्लाइट
subā	**kī (f.)**	**flāiT**
morning	of	flight

Guess the gender of 'flight' in Hindi. Of course, it is feminine (clue: the feminine form **kī**).

Short form of तब tab 'then'

The short form of तब **tab** 'then' is तो **to**, as in

तो	दीजिए
to	**dījiye**
then	please give

Compound and oblique (peer pressure) postpositions

Observe the structure of the English preposition in Hindi:

(noun)	*postposition*	*postposition*
कल	के	लिए
kal	**ke**	**liye**
tomorrow	of	for

As we proceed further we will introduce the concept of the 'oblique' case in Hindi, which I affectionately call the 'peer pressure' case. Languages do show the effects of peer pressure! You will notice, as we go on, that the compound postpositions will either begin with के **ke** or की **kī**, but never with का **kā**. The reason is that का **kā** and की **kī** have to be followed by another postposition in the compound postposition, and the succeeding postposition influences the preceding one. In the above expression लिए **liye** changes का **kā** to के **ke**. That is, the postposition ending **ā** becomes **e**.

The oblique effect does not last to the preceding postposition but to the phrase as a whole.

कौन	सा	दिन
kaun	**sā**	**din**
which		day (m.)

Notice that the सा **sā** part of the question word 'which' agrees in number and gender with the following noun, i.e. दिन **din** 'day', which is masculine singular. Now let us expand this phrase by adding the Hindi compound postposition के लिए **ke liye**

कौन	से	दिन	के	लिए
kaun	**se**	**din**	**ke**	**liye**
which		day (m.)	of	for

Now the peer pressure of लिए **liye** not only extends to के **ke** but all the way to से **se**. The way का **kā** gives in to the peer pressure of लिए **liye** is similar to the way सा **sā** gives in to से **se**. As a matter of fact, even the noun दिन **din** is affected too. The only exceptions are the marked nouns (or nerd nouns: remember this distinction from the last chapter), where the effect does not surface. However, if we replace the marked noun with an unmarked noun, लड़का **laRkā** 'boy', you can see a clear change.

कौन	से	लड़के	के	लिए
kaun	**se**	**laRke**	**ke**	**liye**
which		boy (m.)	of	for

For which boy

Although लड़का **laRkā** 'boy' changes to लड़के **laRke** under peer pressure, its meaning does not change. It still keeps its singular identity. Remember, people usually give in to peer pressure only superficially!

Separable or transferable possessions

In the last unit we dealt with non-transferable and inseparable possessions, i.e. expressions such as 'I have four brothers.' Let us turn our attention to separable possessions, as in

मेरे	पास	कैश	नहीं	है।
mere	**pās**	***cash***	**nahī̃**	**hɛ**
my	near	cash	not	is

I do not have cash.

Similarly, in Hindi the expression 'You have a ticket' is

आपके	पास	टिकट	है।
āpke	**pās**	**TikaT**	**hɛ.**
your	near	ticket	is

You have a ticket.

In other words, in the case of separable possession the subject receives के पास **ke pās** compound postposition and, subsequently, the following changes take place. Notice के **ke** makes the subject oblique masculine possessive.

मैं		के पास		मेरे पास	
mɛ̃	+	**ke pās**	⇒	**mere pās**	I have
आप		के पास		आपके पास	
āp	+	**ke pās**	⇒	**āp ke pās**	You have

बातचीत **bātcīt** Dialogue 3 (CD 1; 28)

डॉक्टर के पास जाना ***DākTar ke pās jānā***
A visit to the doctor

Kushwant Singh is under the spell of cold weather. He has a fever and headache. He goes to his doctor, Charan Chaturvedi. After exchanging greetings, Kushwant tells Charan the purpose of his visit.

कुशवंत: डॉक्टर साहिब, मुझको कुछ बुख़ार है।
KUSHWANT: DākTar sāhib, muj^{h}ko kuc^{h} buxār hɛ.
चरन: कब से है?
CHARAN: kab se hɛ?
कुशवंत: कल रात से।
KUSHWANT: kal rāt se.
चरन: सिर–दर्द भी है।
CHARAN: sir-dard b^{h}ī hɛ?
कुशवंत: जी हाँ।
KUSHWANT: jī hā̃.
(putting the thermometer in Kushwant's mouth)
चरन: थरमामीटर लगाइए।
CHARAN: thermometer lagāiye.
(after taking the thermometer from Kushwant's mouth)
चरन: थोड़ा बुख़ार है . . . यह दवाई दिन में दो बार लीजिये . . . जल्दी ठीक हो जायेंगे।
CHARAN: t^{h}oRā buxār hɛ . . . ye davāī din mẽ do bār lījiye . . . jaldī Thīk ho jāẽge.

KUSHWANT: *Doctor sir, I have some fever.*
CHARAN: *Since when (i.e. is it)?*
KUSHWANT: *Since last night.*
CHARAN: *(Do you have) a headache too?*
KUSHWANT: *Yes.*
CHARAN: *Put the thermometer (into your mouth)*
(putting the thermometer into Kushwant's mouth)
CHARAN: *(You have) a little fever . . . please take this medicine twice a day. (You) will be fine.*

शब्दावली **shabdāvalī Vocabulary**

डॉक्टर	**DākTar**	Doctor
साहिब	**<sāhib>**	sir
मुझको	**muj^{h} ko**	to me
कुछ	**kuc^{h}**	some
बुख़ार	**buxār** (m.)	fever
कब	**kab**	when
कल	**kal**	yesterday/tomorrow
रात	**rāt** (f.)	night
सिर	**sir** (m.)	head
दर्द	**dard** (m.)	pain
लगाना	**lagānā (+ne)**	to fix, to put into, to stick

लगाइए/लगाइये	**lagāiye**	please fix, put into, stick
थोड़ा	**thoRā** (m. adj.)	little
दवाई	**davāī** (f.)	medicine
दो	**do**	two
बार	**bār** (f.)	time, turn
लेना	**lenā** (+ne)	to take
लीजिए/लीजिये	**lījiye**	please take
जल्दी	**jaldī**	soon, quickly
हो जाएँगे/जायेंगे	**ho jāẽge**	will become

Pronunciation

The word साहिब **sāhib** also has other variants: **sāhab** साहब and more colloquial साब **sāb**.

Notes

साहिब sāhib

The original meaning of Hindi साहिब **sāhib** is 'master' or 'lord'. This word is more formal than the English 'sir'. In highly formal addresses, साहिब **sāhib** can be substituted for the Hindi जी **jī**. Usually it is used with last names and titles (e.g. जज **jaj** 'judge'; **sāhib**). The other two variants are: **sāhab** साहब and **sāb** साब.

'Since'

The Hindi equivalent of 'since' is the postposition से **se** 'from', e.g.

कब	से	कल	रात	से
kab	**se**	**kal**	**rāt**	**se**
when	from	yesterday	night	from
Since when		Since last night		

'Tell me why' column

सवाल:	हिन्दुस्तानी औरतें बिन्दी क्यों लगाती हैं?
savāl:	**hindustānī auratẽ bindī kyõ lagātī hẽ?**
Question:	Why do Indian women put a dot (on their foreheads)?

Circle the correct response:

1 **singār** सिंगार (for) make up
2 **shādī-shudā hɛ** शादी-शुदा है (to show she) is married
3 **donõ** दोनों (for) both (reasons)

दोनों

javāb: 3 **donõ** दोनों
Answer: 3 both

शब्दावली **shabdāvalī** **Vocabulary**

भारत	**b^hārat** (m.)	India
हिन्दुस्तान	**hindustān** (m.)	India
भारतीय	**b^hāratīya**	Indian
हिन्दुस्तानी	**hindustānī**	Indian
सवाल	**savāl** (m.)	question
बिन्दी	**bindī** (f.)	dot
क्यों	**kyõ**	why
लगाना	**lagānā (+ne)**	to attach, to fix
जवाब	**javāb** (m.)	answer
सिंगार	**singār** (m.)	make up
शादीशुदा	**shādī-shudā**	married
दोनों	**donõ**	both

बातचीत **bātcīt** **Dialogue 4** (CD 1; 30)

मज़ाक ***mazāk*** ***Humour column***

Two thieves are being interrogated in a Delhi Police Station. The inspector is interrogating the thieves and his assistant is taking notes.

इंस्पैक्टर: तुम्हारा नाम?
INSPECTOR: tumhāra nām?
चोर: बैनरजी।
THIEF: Banerjī.
(inspector now turns to the other)
इंस्पैक्टर : तुम्हारा नाम?
INSPECTOR: tumhāra nām?
चोर: चैटरजी।
THIEF: Chatterjī.
(inspector talks to both thieves)

इंस्पैक्टर: चोरी करते हो और नाम के साथ 'जी' लगाते हो।
INSPECTOR: corī karte ho aur nām ke sāt^h 'jī' lagāte ho.
(turning to his assistant)
इंस्पैक्टर: इनका नाम लिखिये, बैनर और चैटर।
INSPECTOR: inkā nām lik^hiye, Baner aur Chatter.

INSPECTOR: *Your name?*
THIEF: *Banerjī.*
(inspector now turns to the other)
INSPECTOR: *Your name?*
THIEF: *Chatterjī.*
(inspector talks to both thieves)
INSPECTOR: *(You) steal and use '**jī**' with your name.*
(turning to his assistant)
INSPECTOR: *Write their names, Baner and Chatter.*

शब्दावली **shabdāvalī Vocabulary**

चोरी करना	corī karnā (+**ne**)	to steal
लिखना	lik^hnā (+**ne**)	to write
के साथ	ke sāth	with
लगाना	lagānā (+**ne**)	to attach, to fix
लिखिये/लिखिए	lik^hiye	please write

Note (cultural)

Some common last names in the state of Bengal end in जी **–jī**. However, this जी **jī** is not an honorific as in Hindi.

व्याकरण **vyākaraNa Grammar**

चाहिए *cāhiye and verb agreement*

The verb चाहिए **cāhiye** is a frozen verb. It agrees neither with a subject nor with an object in Standard Hindi.

Simple present tense: subject–verb agreement

As pointed out earlier, the verb agrees with the subject in person, number and gender. The first part of the verb (called the 'main verb') agrees in number and gender, and the second part of the verb (called the 'auxiliary verb') agrees in person and number with the subject.

फ्लाइट कब चलती है?
flight kab caltī hɛ?
flight (f.) when move/walk is
When does the flight leave?
(lit. when does the flight walk/move?)

Object–verb agreement (postposition syndrome)

आपको साड़ी पसन्द है?
āpko sāRī pasand hɛ?
you-to saree (f.) choice/liking is
Do you like the saree?

Note that, unlike in English, the Hindi verb does not agree with the subject. Instead, it agrees with the object. The rule of thumb is that whenever the subject is followed by any postposition, the verb does not agree with it. Recall the 'have' construction:

मेरे चार भाई हैं।
mere cār b^{h}āī hɛ̃
my four brothers (m. pl.) are
I have four brothers.

In the above sentence, the verb form is not हूँ **hũ**, indicating that the verb does not agree with the subject. The verb agrees with भाई **b^{h}āī** 'brothers' and takes the plural ending.

मेरे पास साड़ियाँ हैं।
mere pās sāRiãyã hɛ̃
my near sarees are
I have sarees.

Similarly, the verb agrees with साड़ियाँ **sāRiã**, which is plural.
How about the expression 'I have some fever'?

मुझको कुछ बुखार है।
muj^{h}ko kuc^{h} buxār hɛ
me-to some fever is
I have some fever.

Once again the verb does not agree with the subject because it is followed by the postposition को **ko**. Instead, it agrees with 'fever'.

In fact, if both the subject and the verb are followed by a postposition, the verb never agrees with either. In this case, it stays masculine singular (called 'default agreement').

When does the subject take a postposition?

Hindi verbs such as पसंद होना **pasand honā** 'to like' and चाहिए **cāhiye** 'to want' select the को **ko** postposition with their subject. You will need to remember which verb takes which postposition with the subject. For example, you will need to know that the English verb 'to have' takes three different postpositions in the Hindi subject:

Subject postposition		*Possession*
के पास	**ke pās**	separable, transferable
का, के, की	**kā, ke, kī**	inseparable
को	**ko**	physical states (such as fever, headache)

अभ्यास **ab^hyās Exercises**

Exercise 1

Translate the following sentences into Hindi according to the model example. (Remember that Hindi does not have articles so the articles 'a', 'an' and 'the' cannot be translated into Hindi.)

Model

आपको किताब चाहिए
āpko kitāb cāhiye. You want a book.

मुझको किताब चाहिए
muj^hko kitāb cāhiye. I want a book.

1 I want a ticket for Jaipur.
2 Do you want medicine?
3 I want two houses.
4 I want a car in my garage. (garage: use the English word)
5 You want this beautiful saree. (beautiful: सुन्दर **sundar**)

Exercise 2

Fill in the blanks by making an appropriate choice from the following Hindi subjects.

मेरा	मेरे	मेरी	मेरे पास	मुझको
merā	mere	merī	mere pās	mujʰko

1 __________ एक बहन है।
__________ek bɛhɛn hɛ.
2 ___________दो भाई हैं।
___________do bʰāī hɛ̃.
3 __________ एक कम्प्यूटर है।
__________ ek *computer* hɛ.
4 ___________हाल ठीक है।
___________hāl Tʰīk hɛ.
5 __________ सिर–दर्द है।
__________ sir-dard hɛ.
6 ___________ काम चाहिए।
___________kām cāhiye.
7 ___________ लड़का घर लेता है।
___________laRkā gʰar letā hɛ.

Exercise 3

Match the parts of the sentences given on the right with those on the left to make a complete sentence.

मुझको mujʰko	घर में कितने आदमी हैं? gʰar mẽ kinte ādmī hɛ̃?
मेरे पास mere pās	क्या है? kyā hɛ?
आपके āpke	बुखार है। buxār hɛ.
मेरा शहर merā shɛhɛr	आपके लिये है। āpke liye hɛ.
ये फ़्लाइट ye *flight*	बहुत सुंदर है। bahut sundar hɛ.

इसका दाम रुपये हैं।
iskā dām rupiye hɛ̃.

Exercise 4 (CD 1; 31)

Listen to what the waiter is saying in the recording and answer each question in Hindi. Your part of the answer is given below in English. After the beep there is a pause for you to reply. After your reply, listen to the correct recorded version. To distinguish you from the waiter, your voice is represented by a female voice.

Use the glossary to familiarize yourself with food items.

WAITER:
YOU: (appropriate greeting)
WAITER:
YOU: *I am fine.*
WAITER:
YOU: *No, what is the special for lunch?*
WAITER:
YOU: *The vegetarian special is fine. What is it?*
WAITER:
YOU: *I need my daal a little spicy.* (No need to translate 'my' here.)
WAITER: ठीक है Tʰīk hɛ.

4 आपके शौक क्या हैं? āpke shauk kyā hε̃?

What are your hobbies?

By the end of this unit you should be able to:

- talk about your and others' hobbies and interests
- talk about your and others' likes and dislikes
- manage some more expressions of health and ailments
- learn expressions with 'generally'
- form derived adjectives
- note asymmetry between English and Hindi expressions

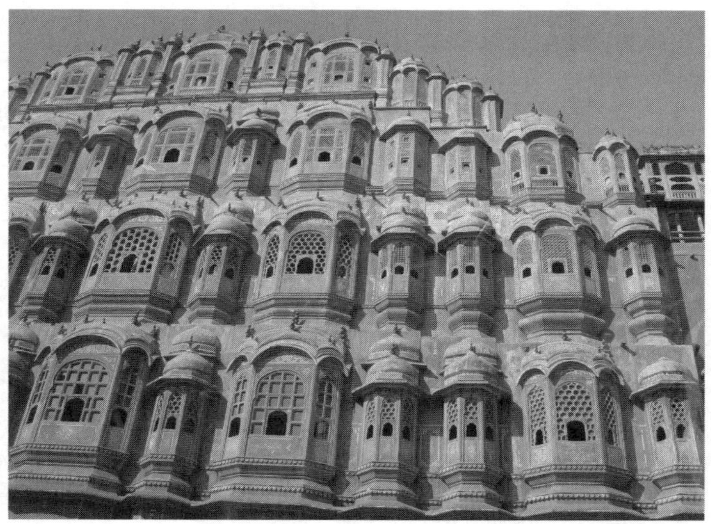

बातचीत **bātcīt Dialogue 1** (CD 1; 32)

आपके शौक क्या हैं? āpke shauk kyā hɛ̃?
What are your hobbies?

Professor James Jones, an internationally acclaimed expert on international adverstising, is being profiled in an ethnic Indian newspaper from California. After talking about his research, the interviewer, Y. Malik, wants to report Professor Jones' interests to his readers

मलिक: क्या आप भारत जाते हैं?
MALIK: kyā āp b^hārat jāte hɛ̃?
जोन्ज़: जी हाँ, कई बार।
JONES: jī hā̃ kaī bār.
मलिक: आपको हिन्दुस्तानी खाना पसन्द है?
MALIK: āpko hindustānī k^hānā pasand hɛ?
जोन्ज़: जी हाँ, तन्दूरी चिकन, डोसा . . . वैसे समोसा भी पसन्द है।
JONES: jī hā̃, tandūrī cikan (*tandoori chicken*), Dosā (*dosa*) . . . vɛse samosā b^hī bahut pasand hɛ.
मलिक: आपके शौक क्या-क्या हैं?
MALIK: āpke shauk kyā-kyā hɛ̃?
जोन्ज़: मुझको तैरने का शौक है, इसके अलावा भारतीय संगीत का भी शौक है।
JONES: muj^h ko tɛrne kā shauk hɛ, iske alāvā b^hāratīya saŋgīt kā b^hī shauk hɛ.
मलिक: गाने का भी?
MALIK: gāne kā b^h ī?
जोन्ज़: ज़रूर, मेरे गाने पर मेरे बच्चे हैड फ़ोन लगाते हैं।
JONES: zarūr, mere gāne se mere bacce hɛD fon (*head phone*) lagāte hɛ̃.
मलिक: वाह वाह।
MALIK: vāh, vāh.

MALIK: *Do you visit India (quite frequently)?*
JONES: *Yes, quite often.* (lit. several times)
MALIK: *Do you like Indian food?*
JONES: *Yes, tandoori chicken, dosa . . . in addition (I) like samosas very much.*
MALIK: *What are your hobbies?*
JONES: *I am fond of swimming; besides this, (I) am fond of Indian music.*
MALIK: *(Fond) of singing too?*

JONES: *Of course, my children put on headphones (because of) my singing.*
(lit. (my) children put on head phones from my singing)

MALIK: *Excellent!* (i.e. what an excellent sense of humour!)

शब्दावली **shabdāvalī** **Vocabulary**

जाना	**jānā** (–**ne**)	to go
कई	**kaī**	several
खाना	**k^{h}ānā** (m.), **v** (+**ne**)	food (n.), to eat (v.)
वैसे	**vɛse**	otherwise, in addition
शौक	**shauk** (m.)	hobby, fondness, interest
तैरना	**tɛrnā** (–**ne**)	to swim
संगीत	**saŋgīt** (m.)	music
के अलावा	**ke <alāvā>**	beside, in addition to
गाना	**gānā** (m.); v. (+**ne**)	song (n.); to sing (v.)
ज़रूर	**zarūr**	of course, certainly
पर	**par**	on, at
वाह	**vāh**	ah!, excellent!, bravo!

Pronunciation

अलावा **alāvā** is also pronounced as इलावा **ilāvā**.

Notes

The experiential (dative) subject: (को ko-subjects)

The Hindi equivalent of the English 'I am fond of swimming' is

मुझको	तैरने	का	शौक	है।
muj^{h}ko	**tɛrne**	**kā**	**shauk**	**hɛ**
me-to	swimming	of	fondness	is

In English 'I' is the subject of the sentence. However, in Hindi the equivalent of the English 'I' is मुझको **muj^{h}ko** 'to me'. Such a distinction is very important in South Asian languages. The nominative subjects (e.g. 'I') denote volitional/deliberate subjects, as in the English 'I met him.' The experiential (**ko** को) subjects are non-volitional/non-deliberate, as in the English 'I ran into him.' को **ko** subjects emphasize something happening without any deliberate effort being made. In other words, expressions such as the following are expressed in a slightly different fashion:

English	*Hindi*
I am fond of swimming	The fondness of swimming is to me.
You want a ticket	The desire of a ticket is to you.
I have some fever.	Some fever is to me.
She likes this book.	The choice of this book is (i.e. experienced by) to her.

The experiencer subjects receive the को **ko** postposition in Hindi. Recall the postposition syndrome of Hindi verbs which refuse to agree with any element that contains a postposition. As a result, the verb 'to be' in Hindi does not agree with the को **ko** subject. Instead, शौक **shauk** 'fondness' becomes the element of agreement.

There are two other terms for experiential subjects – dative subjects and को **ko** subjects. We will call them experiential subjects in this book.

Verbal nouns (infinitive verbs)

Now note the status of the word 'swimming' in the English sentence: 'I am fond of swimming.' The word 'swimming' functions like a noun in the sentence. As a matter of fact, one could replace it with a noun, e.g. 'I am fond of chocolate.' The only difference is that 'chocolate' is a noun to begin with and 'swimming' is derived from the verb 'swim' by adding '-ing' to it. Such derived nouns are called verbal nouns or gerunds. We will call them verbal nouns throughout this book.

Hindi does not distinguish verbal nouns and infinitive forms, e.g. 'to swim'. You get two for one. Examples of Hindi verbal nouns or infinitive forms are given below:

Verb stems			*Verbal nouns/infinitive verbs*		
कर	**kar**	do	करना	**karnā**	to do/doing
आ	**ā**	come	आना	**ānā**	to come/coming
जा	**jā**	go	जाना	**jānā**	to go/going
देख	**dek^h**	see	देखना	**dek^{h}nā**	to see/seeing
बता	**batā**	tell	बताना	**batānā**	to tell/telling
तैर	**tɛr**	swim	तैरना	**tɛrnā**	to swim/swimming
खा	**k^{h}ā**	eat	खाना	**k^{h}ānā**	to eat/eating
गा	**gā**	sing	गाना	**gānā**	to sing/singing
लिख	**lik^h**	write	लिखना	**lik^{h}nā**	to write/writing

You must have discovered by now that the only counterpart of the English infinitive 'to' (as in 'to leave') and the verbal noun marker '-ing' (as in 'leaving') in Hindi is ना **nā**. It is like English '-ing' in the sense that it follows a verbal stem rather than the English infinitive marker 'to', which precedes a verbal stem rather than following it.

Oblique verbal nouns

Remember the peer-pressure influence of postposition on the words in a phrase? See the section on 'compound and oblique postposition' in case you have forgotten it.

Now consider the Hindi counterpart of the English 'of swimming', as in 'I am fond of swimming':

तैरने	का
tɛrne	**kā**
swimming	of

Under peer pressure from the postposition का **kā**, the Hindi verbal noun तैरना **tɛrnā** 'swimming' undergoes a change exactly like the noun लड़का **laRkā**: it becomes तैरने **tɛrne**. Study the following sentences carefully. Do you see the same change?

मुझको	गाने	का	शौक	है।
muj^{h}ko	**gāne**	**kā**	**shauk**	**hɛ.**
me-to	singing	of	fondness	is

I am fond of singing.

मुझको	खाने	का	शौक	है।
muj^{h}ko	**k^{h}āne**	**kā**	**shauk**	**hɛ.**
me-to	eating	of	fondness	is

I am fond of eating.

आपको	मूवी	देखने	का	शौक	है।
āpko	**movie**	**dek^{h}ne**	**kā**	**shauk**	**hɛ.**
you-to	movie	seeing	of	fondness	is

You are fond of watching movies.

आपको	खाने	का	शौक	है।
āpko	**k^{h}āne**	**kā**	**shauk**	**hɛ.**
you-to	eating	of	fondness	is

You are fond of eating.

Yes–no questions with क्या kyā

In Unit 1, we showed you how to change a statement into a yes–no question with a mere change of intonation. One can also place क्या **kyā** in front of a statement and form a yes–no question from it. (Yes, this is the same word क्या **kyā** that means 'what'!) Even if क्या **kyā** is placed at the beginning of a sentence, the rising question intonation is imperative. Since it is difficult to show intonation in writing, क्या **kyā** is more prevalent in written Hindi, and its omission is common in speech.

The statement

आप	भारत	जाते	हैं।
āp	**b^hārat**	**jāte**	**hɛ̃.**
you	India	go	are

You go to India.

becomes a yes–no question with the addition of क्या **kyā** to its front:

क्या	आप	भारत	जाते	हैं?
kyā	**āp**	**b^hārat**	**jāte**	**hɛ̃?**
(Q)	you	India	go	are

Do you go to India [often/regularly]?

You do not need any verb forms at the beginning of a yes–no question in Hindi.

Reduplication of question words

The repetition of a question word is quite common in Hindi. In many languages of South East Asia repetition indicates plurality. Much the same is true of Hindi.

आपके	शौक	क्या	क्या	हैं?
āpke	**shauk**	**kyā**	**kyā**	**hɛ̃?**
your	interests/hobbies	what	what	are

What are your interests/hobbies?

In English you cannot repeat the question word 'what' even if you know that the person in question has many interests. However, the repetition of क्या **kyā** has a 'listing' function, and thus asks the person to give a list of more than one interest from the viewpoint of the speaker.

Similarly, if someone asks in Hindi

आप	कहाँ	कहाँ	जाते	हैं?
āp	**kahā̃**	**kahā̃**	**jāte**	**hɛ̃?**
you	where	where	go	are

What places do you go to?

the speaker has reason to believe that the listener goes (often/ regularly) to more than one place.

बातचीत **bātcīt** Dialogue 2 (CD 1; 34)

भारतीय फिल्में ***b^{h}ārtīya* filmẽ** ***Indian films***

India is the largest producer of films in the world. More movies are produced by the Bombay film industry (Bollywood) than by Hollywood. It is no wonder, therefore, that Hindi films dictate social conversation and are an excellent mode of expressing agreement–disagreement, likes–dislikes, and social and political thoughts. In this dialogue, the topic of discussion is Hindi films. The participants are Akbar Ali and Suhas Ranjan. Suhas saw the movie Black *and he is ready to express his delight over it.*

सुहास: ‘ब्लैक’ मेरी मन-पसन्द फिल्म है।
SUHAS: *Black* merī man-pasand film hɛ.
अकबर: वह कैसे?
AKBAR: vo kɛse?
सुहास: गाने बहुत अच्छे है, कहानी और ऐकटिंग भी शानदार है।
SUHAS: gāne bahut acc^{h}e hɛ̃, kahānī aur *acting* b^{h}ī shāndār hɛ.
अकबर: हिन्दी फिल्में तो मुझको बिल्कुल पसन्द नहीं। सिर्फ फ़ार्मूला।
AKBAR: Hindi *filmẽ* to muj^{h}ko bilkul pasand nahī̃. sirf formula.
शुहास: लेकिन यह फ़ार्मूला फिल्म नहीं, इसका अन्दाज़ और है।
SUHAS: lekin ye *formula film* nahī̃, iskā andāz aur hɛ.
अकबर: सब हिन्दी फिल्में एक-सी होती हैं, लड़का लड़की से मिलता है, दोनों में प्यार होता है, फिर खलनायक आता है।
AKBAR: sab Hindi *filmẽ* ek-sī hotī hɛ̃, laRkā laRkī se miltā hɛ, donõ mẽ pyār hotā hɛ, p^{h}ir k^{h}alnāyak ātā hɛ.

(Suhas interrupts)

सुहास: और दोनों की शादी होती है। जी नहीं, यह ऐसी फिल्म नहीं।
SUHAS: aur donõ kī shādī hotī hɛ. jī nahī̃, ye ɛsī *film* nahī̃.
अकबर: तो पश्चिम की नकल होगी।
AKBAR: to pashcim kī nakal hogī.
सुहास : तो आप के ख़्याल से सिर्फ़ पश्चिमी फिल्में अच्छी होती हैं?
SUHAS: to āp ke xayāl se sirf pashcimī *filmẽ* acchī hotī hɛ̃?
अकबर: मैं यह नहीं कहता, पुरानी हिन्दी फिल्में अच्छी होती हैं।
AKBAR: mɛ̃ ye nahī̃ kɛhtā, purānī hindī filmẽ acc^{h}ī hotī hɛ̃.
(Ajit Singh patiently listens to this discussion and intervenes:)
अजीत: फिल्म की बात पर महाभारत क्यों?
AJIT: film kī bāt par mahāb^{h}ārat kyõ?

SUHAS: *'Black' is my favourite movie.*
AKBAR: *How come?*
SUHAS: *(The) songs are very good; (the) plot and acting are great too.*
AKBAR: *I dislike Hindi films – (they are) only formula (films).*
SUHAS: *But this (one is) not a formula film. Its style is different.*
AKBAR: *All Hindi films are alike – a boy meets a girl, both fall in love, then a villain comes . . .*
(Suhas interrupts)
SUHAS: *And both get married. No, this is not such a film.*
AKBAR: *Then it must be an imitation of the West.*
SUHAS: *(Do) you think only Western films are (generally) good?* (lit. in your opinion only Western films are (generally) good)
AKBAR: *I do not say this: the old Hindi films are good.*
(Ajit Singh listens patiently to this discussion and intervenes:)
AJIT: *Why* (*wage a*) *fierce battle over the topic of films?* (implying that the topic of films is not worthy of such a serious discussion)

शब्दावली **shabdāvalī Vocabulary**

'ब्लैक'	***Black***	*black*
मन-पसन्द	**man-pasand**	favourite
वह कैसे	**vo kɛse**	how come?
कहानी	**kahānī** (f.)	story
शानदार	**shāndār**	splendid, great
बिल्कुल	**bilkul**	absolutely
नापसन्द	**pasand** (f.)	like
और	**aur**	and, more, other, else
अन्दाज़	**andāz** (m.)	style

एक-सा	**ek-sā**	alike
नायक	**nāyak**	hero
खलनायक	**k^{h}alnāyak**	villain
नायिका	**nāyikā**	heroine
प्यार	**pyār** (m.)	love
शादी	**shādī** (f.)	marriage
होना	**honā** (–**ne**)	to be/happen
होती हैं	**hotī hɛ̃**	generally happen, generally take place (pl.)
होती है	**hotī hɛ**	generally happens, generally takes place (sg.)
होगी	**hogī**	will be
ऐसा	**ɛsā**	such
पश्चिम	**pashcim** (m.)	West
पश्चिमी	**pashcimī**	Western
नकल	**nakal** (f.)	copy, fake, imitation
ख़्याल	**<xayāl>** (m.)	opinion, view
सिर्फ़	**sirf**	only
कहना	**<kɛhnā>** (+**ne**)	to say
पुराना	**purānā** (adj. m.)	old (inanimate)
बात	**bāt** (f.)	matter, conversation, topic
महा	**mahā**	great
महाभारत	**mahāb^{h}ārat**	one of the two greatest epics from Sanskrit; fierce battle (non-literal context)
क्यों	**kyõ**	why

Pronunciation

The Hindi word for 'opinion' can be pronounced and written in two ways: ख़याल **xayāl** and ख़्याल **xyāl**. The latter form is more frequent among the educated; we will use this form here.

The verb 'to say' is pronounced **kɛh** but is written कह **kah**.

Notes

फ़िल्में *filmẽ*

The English word 'film' has been assimilated into Hindi. It is no longer treated as a foreign word in the language; therefore, it has gender. From the plural ending एँ **ẽ**, you can predict its gender. It is, of course, feminine. (It is treated as a feminine of the nerd category, i.e. marked.)

Negative markers: नहीं nahī̃, न na

The short version of नहीं **nahī̃** 'not' is न **na**. It is written न **na** but in pronunciation the vowel **a** often becomes long, i.e. **ā**.

In polite orders न **na** is used instead of नहीं **nahī̃**. It is also used with subjunctives. Do not worry about subjunctives for now. However, observe the use of न **na** in polite orders ('polite imperatives').

न	दीजिए
na	**dījiye**
not	please give

Please do not give.

It is also used with the word नापसन्द **nāpasand** 'dislike'. However, with nouns it is not as productive as with polite commands. For example, you cannot make the word 'dissatisfaction' using न **nā** with the Hindi equivalent of 'satisfaction'.

और aur as an adjective or adverb

इसका	अन्दाज़	और	है।
iskā	**andāz**	**aur**	**hɛ.**
its	style	different	is

The conjunction 'and' in Hindi expresses a range of meanings when used either as a predicate, as in the above sentence, or as an adjective, as below:

और	चाय	दीजिए।
aur	**cāy**	**dījiye.**
more	tea	please give

Please give me (some) more tea.

और	साड़ी	दिखाइए।
aur	**sāRī**	**dik^{h}āiye.**
other	saree	please show

Please show (me some) other saree.

और **aur** is equivalent to the English 'different', 'more', 'else.' Observe another frequent expression with और **aur**.

और	कुछ	चाहिए?
aur	**kuc^h**	**cāhiye?**
else	some	want

Do you want something else?

Note the difference in word order.

एक-सा ek-sā: 'same', 'alike'

सब	हिन्दी	फिल्में	एक	सी	होती	हैं।
sab	**Hindi**	**filmẽ**	**ek**	**sī**	**hotī**	**hɛ̃**
all	Hindi	films	one	-ish	generic Be	are

Generally all Hindi films are alike.

The सा **-sā** is like the English '-ish' (e.g. 'boyish'). So the Hindi sentence in English is literally 'Generally all Hindi films are one-ish.'

Generic होता होना 'be'

The sentence above gives the generic meaning. There is no separate word exactly equivalent to the English 'generally' in the sentence. It is the verb होती **hotī** that contributes to this meaning. Compare this sentence with the following:

सब	हिन्दी	फिल्में	एक	सी	हैं।
sab	**Hindi**	**filmẽ**	**ek**	**sī**	**hɛ̃**
all	Hindi	films	one	-ish	are

All Hindi films are alike.

which expresses the universal truth, i.e. without exception, Hindi films are alike.

Note the slight difference in the *two conjugations* of होना **honā** 'to be':

Generic			*Non-generic*
ho + t	**+ ī**	**hɛ̃**	**hɛ̃**
be + aspect	+ number, gender	are	

It is the generic conjugation which contains the English word 'generally' in Hindi. The verb agrees with the subject. Now observe the two other examples of the generic Be in Hindi:

दोनों	में	प्यार	होता	है।
donõ	**mẽ**	**pyār**	**hotā**	**hɛ.**
both	in	love (m.)	generic Be	is

Generally, love blossoms (lit. happens) between the two.

दोनों	की	शादी	होती	है।
donõ	**kī**	**shādī**	**hotī**	**hɛ**
both	of	marriage (f.)	generic Be	is

Generally, their marriage (lit. the marriage of both) takes place.

होता **hotā** agrees with प्यार **pyār** 'love', which is masculine singular in Hindi, whereas होती **hotī** agrees with शादी **shādī** 'marriage.' Similarly, है **hɛ** agrees with its respective subjects.

Direct object: को ko or से se

In Hindi the English expression 'boy meets girl' is

लड़का	लड़की	से	मिलता	है।
laRkā	**laRkī**	**se**	**miltā**	**hɛ**
boy	girl	with	meet	is

The boy meets the girl.

लड़का	लड़की	को	देखता	है।
laRkā	**laRkī**	**ko**	**dekhtā**	**hɛ**
boy	girl	object	see	is

The boy sees the girl.

Notice that the English animate object 'girl' is followed by a postposition, either से **se** or को **ko**. Usually, the most frequent object postposition is को **ko**. Only some verbs, such as 'meet' and the verbs of communication (e.g. ask, say, speak, even love), are exceptions – they take से **se** instead of को **ko**.

Remember that only animate objects take को **ko**. *Inanimate objects do not take any object marker.*

लड़का	घर	देखता	है।
laRkā	**g^{h}ar**	**dek^{h}tā**	**hɛ**
boy	house	see	is

The boy sees a house.

The object घर **g^{h}ar** 'house' is not marked with को **ko** because it is an inanimate noun. More details are given in the discussion of articles in the Reference grammar section.

Word-for-word translation

पश्चिम	की	नकल	होगी।
pashcim	**kī**	**nakal**	**hogī**
West	of	copy	be-will

(The film) will be an imitation of the West.

The verb formation is as follows:

ho	+	**g**	+	**ī**
be	+	future tense	+	number gender

'Tell me why' column

१	सवाल:	क्या हिन्दुस्तानी लोग कहते हैं: *'I love you'*?
1	**savāl:**	**kyā hindustānī log kɛhte hɛ̃: *'I love you'*?**
	Question:	Do Indians say: 'I love you'?

• जवाब: (a) आँखों से, लेकिन शब्दों से नहीं ।
(b) सिर्फ़ शब्दों से।
javāb: (a) **ā̃khõ se, lekin shabdõ se nahī̃.**
(b) **sirf shabdõ se.**
Answer: (a) By eyes, but not in words.
(b) Only by words.

Circle the correct answer.

ठीक जवाब:	(a)
Tʰīk javāb:	(a)
Correct answer:	(a) आँखों से, लेकिन शब्दों से नहीं ।
	(a) ā̃khõ se, lekin shabdõ se nahī̃

२	सवाल:	हिन्दुस्तानी शब्दों से कभी कहते हैं: 'I love you'?
2	**savāl:**	**hindustānī shabdõ se kabhī kɛhte hɛ̃: 'I love you'?**
	Question:	Do Indians ever say: 'I love you'?

• जवाब: (a) कभी नहीं
(b) कभी कभी।
javāb: (a) **kabʰī nahī̃**
(b) **kabʰī kabʰī**
Answer: (a) Never
(b) Sometimes

Circle the correct answer.

ठीक जवाब:	(b)
Tʰīk javāb:	(b)
Correct answer:	(b) कभी कभी। kabʰī kabʰī.

३ सवाल: हिन्दुस्तानी शब्दों से कैसे कहते हैं 'I love you.'?
3 **savāl:** **hindustānī shabdõ se kɛse kɛhte hɛ̃ 'I love you.'**
Question: How do Indians say in words: 'I love you'?

- जवाब: (a) मैं तुम से प्यार करता हूँ।
  (b) मुझ को तुम से प्यार है।

  javāb: (a) **mɛ̃ tum se pyār kartā hũ.**
  (b) **mujʰko tum se pyār hɛ.**

  Answer: (a) I love you.
  (b) Love with you is to me.

Circle the correct answer.

ठीक जवाब:	(b)
Tʰīk javāb:	(b)
Correct answer:	(b) मुझ को तुम से प्यार है। mujʰko tum se pyār hɛ

शब्दावली **shabdāvalī** **Vocabulary**

लोग	**log** (m.)	people
आँख	**ãkʰ** (f.)	eye
आँखों	**ãkʰõ** (f. oblique)	eyes
से	**se**	from, with, by
शब्द	**shabda** (m.)	word
शब्दों	**shabdõ** (m. oblique)	words
सिर्फ़	**sirf**	only
कभी	**kabʰī**	ever
कभी नहीं	**kabʰī nahī̃**	never
कभी-कभी	**kabʰī kabʰī**	sometimes

Note

'I love you' prohibition

The name for 'Cupid' is काम देव **kāma Dev** ('the God Kāma'). काम देव **kāma Dev** carried bows and arrows exactly the same way as 'Cupid'

in the West. Did you notice the similarity between the two words – 'Cupid' and काम **kāma**? Although काम **kāma** has delighted Indians since approximately 3000 BC, Indians do not like to express 'I love you' in exactly the same way as in English. Some expressions are better made non-verbally than verbally. Such is the preference of Indians. If one has to say 'I love you' in words, it is better to express it by means of *experiential subject* construction rather than using the *non-experiential deliberate subject*. The following expression is almost vulgar. (Although such expressions are now common in Bollywood films. The language is changing!)

मैं	तुमसे	प्यार	करता	हूँ।
mɛ̃	**tumse**	**pyār**	**kartā**	**hū̃**
I	you-with	love	do	am

Therefore, the expression 'I love you' is best expressed in the following words:

मुझको	तुमसे	प्यार	है।
muj^{h}ko	**tum-se**	**pyār**	**hɛ.**
me-to	you with	love	is

However, nowadays among the educated and the younger generation the English expression 'I love you' is becoming quite popular.

Reduplication and pluralization

The reduplication of the adverb कभी **kab^{h}ī** 'ever' gives the plural meaning 'sometimes'.

Oblique plural nouns

Remember peer pressure. Notice the influence of a postposition on plural nouns.

	Masculine			*Feminine*		
Singular	**shabda**	शब्द	word	**ā̃kh**	आँख	eye
Plural	**shabda**	शब्द	words	**ā̃k^{h}ẽ**	आँखें	eyes

Plural nouns yield to the pressure of postposition and take the ending **õ**.

shabdõ	**se**	शब्दों से	by words
ā̃khõ	**se**	आँखों से	by eyes

बातचीत **bātcīt Dialogue 3** (CD 1; 36)

नाश्ते में आप क्या खाते हैं? ***nāshte mẽ āp kyā kʰāte hɛ̃? What do you eat for breakfast?***

Rakesh Seth visits his doctor and complains about his stomach problems. Apparently, he suffers from gas. The doctor begins by inquiring about his eating habits.

डॉक्टर:	राकेश जी, नाश्ते में आप क्या खाते हैं?
DOCTOR:	Rakesh jī, nāshte mẽ āp kyā kʰāte hɛ̃?
राकेश:	दस समोसे।
RAKESH:	das samose.
डाक्टर:	और क्या पीते हैं?
DOCTOR:	aur, kyā pīte hɛ̃?
राकेश:	मुझे चाय बहुत अच्छी लगती है। सवेरे बहुत चाय पीता हूँ।
RAKESH:	mujʰe cāy bahut acchī lagtī hɛ. savere bahut cāy pītā hū̃.
डाक्टर:	आपको शरीर की बिमारी नहीं। दिमाग की बिमारी है इसलिये आप किसी साकिऐट्रिसट के पास जाइये।
DOCTOR:	āpko sharīr kī bimārī nahī̃. dimāg kī bimārī hɛ. is liye āp *psychiatrist* ke pās jāiye.

DOCTOR:	*Rakesh jī, what do you eat for breakfast?*
RAKESH:	*Ten samosas.*
DOCTOR:	*And, what (do you) drink?*
RAKESH:	*I like tea a lot. (In the) morning (I) drink a lot of tea.*
DOCTOR:	*You do not have (any) physical illness. (You) have a mental illness. Therefore, you (should) go to the psychiatrist.*

शब्दावली **shabdāvalī Vocabulary**

नाश्ता	**nāshtā** (m.)	breakfast
पीना	**pīnā** (+**ne**)	to drink
चाय	**cāy** (f.)	tea
मुझे, मुझको	**mujʰe, mujʰko**	(to) me
लगना	**lagnā** (+**ko**)	to seem, to be applied
अच्छा लगना	**accʰā lagnā** (+**ko**)	to like

सवेरा	**saverā** (m.)	morning
शरीर	**sharīr** (m.)	body
बिमारी	**bimārī** (f.)	illness
दिमाग़	**dimāG** (m.)	brain
इसलिए	**isliye**	therefore, so, thus, because of this

Notes

अच्छा लगना acc^{h}ā lagnā 'to like'

You have already learned expressions (with experiential subjects) such as

मुझको	चाय	पसन्द	है।
muj^{h}ko	**cāy**	**pasand**	**hɛ.**
me-to	tea	liking	is

I like tea.

Another common way of saying the same expression is

मुझको	चाय	अच्छी	लगती	है।
muj^{h}ko	**cāy**	**acc^{h}ī**	**lagtī**	**hɛ.**
me-to	tea (f.)	good	feel	is

I like tea. (lit. Tea feels good to me.)

'Ghost' postposition

The Hindi equivalents of 'breakfast' and 'morning' are नाश्ता **nāshtā** and सवेरा **saverā** respectively.

If we attach the postposition **mẽ** 'in' to these nouns, the peer pressure exerted by the postposition makes the nouns oblique.

Unmarked masculine nouns			*Oblique singular (unmarked nouns)*		
नाश्ता	**nāsht*ā***	breakfast	नाश्ते में	**nāsht*e* mẽ**	for (in) breakfast
सवेरा	**saver*ā***	morning	सवेरे में	**saver*e* mẽ**	in the morning

However, the English expression of time 'in the morning' is सवेरे **savere** in Hindi. Although the effect of the Hindi postposition (peer pressure) is quite apparent, the postposition में **mẽ** is dropped. The oblique form indicates its presence. Therefore, this is the 'ghost' postposition.

Word-formation: derived adjectives

Do some detective work and see how English adjectives such as 'silken' are formed in Hindi:

Nouns			*Adjectives*		
रेशम	**resham**	silk	रेशमी	**reshamī**	silken
सूत	**sūt**	cotton	सूती	**sūtī**	cotton (as in cotton clothes)
नकल	**nakal**	copy	नकली	**nakalī**	fake
असल	**asal**	fact	असली	**asalī**	real, genuine
हिन्दुस्तान	**hindustan**	India	हिन्दुस्तानी	**hindustanī**	Indian
बनारस	**banāras**	Banaras	बनारसी	**banārasī**	from Banaras (lit. Banarasian)

If you think that the addition of **ī** at the end of the word makes it an adjective, you are right. Note that all the nouns (and place names) given above end in a consonant. You cannot derive an adjective by adding **ī** to the nouns ending in a vowel. For example, the expressions 'from Delhi' or 'from Agra' cannot be reduced to one-word adjectives by the addition of **ī**. Only the postposition से **se** can rescue these expressions.

Now, observe how words such as 'physical' and 'mental' are formed in Hindi:

शरीर	की	बीमारी	दिमाग	की	बिमारी
sharīr	**kī**	**bimārī**	**dimāg**	**kī**	**bimārī**
body	of	illness (f.)	brain	of	illness (f.)
Physical/bodily illness			Mental illness		

The possessive construction is used instead. Is it possible to reduce शरीर की **sharīr kī** and दिमाग की **dimāg kī** to the **ī**- type adjectives? Yes, of course.

शरीरी	बीमारी	दिमागी	बिमारी
sharīrī	**bimārī**	**dimāgī**	**bimārī**
Physical/bodily illness		Mental illness	

Always remember, though, that word-formation can sometimes be quite tricky in languages.

Go to the doctor

You have observed that the English 'to' is usually को **ko** in Hindi. However, the English expression 'go to the psychiatrist' is

साकिऐट्रिसट	के	पास	जाइये।
psychiatrist	**ke**	**pās**	**jāiye**
Psychiatrist	of	near	please go

In other words, the English expression is phrased in Hindi as 'Please go near the psychiatrist.' The compound postposition के पास **ke pās** is used instead of को **ko**. Similarly, the Hindi version of 'Please go to the doctor' is

डाक्टर	के	पास	जाइये।
dākTar	**ke**	**pās**	**jāiye**

Contractive e pronoun forms

मुझे **muj^{h}e** is the short form of मुझको **muj^{h}ko**.

अभ्यास **ab^{h}yās** Exercises

Exercise 1

Choose any word from the following four columns and form at least seven sentences. You can use a word from the columns as many times as you like.

मुझको	पढ़ने	का	शौक	है।
muj^{h}ko	paR^{h}ne	kā	shauk	hɛ
आपको	गाने	पसन्द		हैं।
āpko	gāne	pasand		hɛ̃
	क्या/kyā			
	तैरने/tɛrne			
	खाने/k^{h}āne			
	क्या–क्या/kyā–kyā			

Exercise 2

Read the following statements and then answer the question about each statement. Your answer should be in Hindi.

1 Statement: John is fond of dancing and singing. (Hint: dancing = नाचना **nācnā**)
Question: गाने के अलावा जॉन को क्या पसन्द है?
gāne ke alāvā John ko kyā pasand hɛ?
Answer: …………

2 Statement: Judy loves to write stories and poems? (Hint: poem = कविता **kavitā** (f.))
Question: जूडी को क्या क्या शौक हैं?
Judy ko kyā kyā shauk hɛ̃?
Answer: …………

3 Statement: Ramesh's likes and dislikes are given below:

Likes	*Dislikes*
समोसा खाना **samosā k^{h}ānā** to eat samosa	चिकन खाना **cikan k^{h}ānā** to eat chicken
शाकाहारी खाना **shākāhārī k^{h}ānā** vegetarian food	माँसाहारी खाना **mā̃sāhārī k^{h}ānā** non-vegetarian food
कहानियाँ **kahāniyā̃** stories	कविताएँ **kavitāyẽ** poems
भारतीय संगीत **b^{h}ārtīya saŋgīt** Indian music	देसी संगीत **desī saŋgīt** Country music

Question: रमेश को क्या क्या नापसन्द है/हैं?
Ramesh ko kyā kyā nāpasand hɛ/hɛ̃?
Answer:

Question: रमेश को क्या क्या पसन्द है/हैं?
Ramesh ko kyā kyā pasand hɛ/hɛ̃?
Answer:

Exercise 3

There are two possible interpretations of the following sentences. Uncover their ambiguity by translating them into English.

1 जॉन को खाना पसन्द है।
John ko k^{h}ānā pasand hɛ.
2 जॉन को गाना पसन्द है।
John ko gānā pasand hɛ.

Exercise 4

Write two things children do not like about their parents.

Exercise 5

How many ways can you find to say 'I like swimming' in Hindi?

Exercise 6 (CD 1; 38)

If you have the recording, circle the items which the speaker's daughter likes:

1 cats बिल्ली **billī**
2 dogs कुत्ता **kuttā**
3 spicy foods मसालेदार खाना **masāledār k^{h}ānā**
4 cricket (game) क्रिकेट **krikeT**
5 a classical Indian dance भरतनाट्यम् **b^{h}aratnāTyam**
6 rock music रॉक म्यूज़िक **rāk myuzik**

5 छुट्टियों में क्या करेंगे? c^huTTiyõ mẽ kyā karẽge?

What will you do during the break?

By the end of this unit you should be able to:

- talk about your own and others' plans
- compare people and objects
- develop paraphrasing skills
- express desires (use desiratives)
- use the future tense
- use capabilitatives
- use progressive tense forms

बातचीत **bātcīt Dialogue 1** (CD 2; 1)

मैं भारत जाना चाहता हूँ। ***mɛ̃ bʰārat jānā cāhtā hū̃*** ***I want to go to India***

Suman Kumar is planning to spend his Christmas vacation in India. He knows that December and January are excellent months to visit India. Summers are hot and they are followed by monsoons. So he goes to an ethnic travel agent in Toronto to make his travel plans.

एजेन्ट: क्या सेवा कर सकती हूँ?
AGENT: kyā sevā kar saktī hū̃?
सुमन: हिन्दुस्तान के लिये टिकट चाहिये।
SUMAN: hindustān ke liye TikaT (*ticket*) cāhiye?
एजेन्ट: सिर्फ अपने लिये?
AGENT: sirf apne liye?
सुमन: परिवार के लिये।
SUMAN: parivār ke liye.
एजेन्ट: कितने लोग हैं?
AGENT: kitne log hɛ̃?
सुमन: चार- दो बड़े और दो बच्चे।
SUMAN: cār – do baRe aur do bacce.
एजेन्ट: बच्चों की उमर बारह से कम है?
AGENT: baccõ kī umar bārā se kam hɛ?
सुमन: लड़की की उमर बारह है और लड़के की छह।
SUMAN: laRkī kī umar bārā hɛ aur laRke kī cʰe.
एजेन्ट: कब जाना चाहते हैं?
AGENT: kab jānā cāhte hɛ̃?
सुमन: क्रिसमस में।
SUMAN: *Christmas* mẽ.
एजेन्ट: पीक सीज़न है, टिकट महँगी होगी।
AGENT: *peak season* hɛ TikaT (*ticket*) mɛhɛ̃gī hogī.
सुमन: कोई बात नहीं।
SUMAN: koī bāt nahī̃.

AGENT: *What can I do (for you)* (lit. what service can I do)?
SUMAN: *I need a ticket for India.*
AGENT: *Only for yourself?*
SUMAN: *For the family.*
AGENT: *How many people are (there in the family)?*
SUMAN: *Four – two adults and two children.*

AGENT: *Is the age of the children less than twelve?*
SUMAN: *The girl is twelve and the boy (is) six.*
AGENT: *When do (you) want to go?*
SUMAN: *During Christmas.*
AGENT: *(It) is (the) peak season. The ticket will be expensive.*
SUMAN: *It does not matter* (lit. none matter).

शब्दावली **shabdāvalī Vocabulary**

सेवा	**sevā** (f.)	service
सकना	**saknā**	can, be able to
अपना	**apnā**	one's own
परिवार	**parivār** (m.)	family
उमर	**<umar>** (f.)	age
से	**se**	than, from, by
कम	**kam**	less
चाहना	**cāhnā** (+ne)	to want
में	**mẽ**	in, during
छुट्टियों में	**chuTTiyõ mẽ**	during break/vacation
महँगा	**<mɛhẽgā>** (m. adj.)	expensive
कोई	**koī**	some, any, someone, anyone

Pronunciation

The word for 'age' is pronounced and written in two ways: उमर **umar** and उम्र **umra**.

The Hindi word **mɛhẽgā** is written **mahãgā** महँगा.

Notes

सकना **saknā 'can'**

The expression 'What can I do (for you)' is expressed as

मैं	क्या	सेवा	कर	सकती	हूँ?
mɛ̃	**kyā**	**sevā**	**kar**	**saktī**	**hū̃?**
I (f. sg.)	what	service	do	can	am

Notice the placement of सकना **saknā** 'can/to be able to', which is like any other verb in Hindi. It is conjugated in different tenses.

Consider one more example.

मैं बोल सकता हूँ।
mɛ̃ bol saktā hū̃.
I (m. sg.) talk can am
I can talk.

The form सकता हूँ **saktā hū̃** agrees with the subject and the real verb बोल **bol** 'talk' precedes सकता हूँ **saktā hū̃**.

अपना apnā 'one's own'

अपना **apnā** is a possessive pronoun which means 'one's own'. The English possessive pronouns can either be translated as regular possessives or using the अपना **apnā** form. Observe the distinction Hindi makes in this regard.

मेरा नाम जान है।
merā nām John hɛ
my name John is
My name is John.

and

मैं अपना नाम लिखता हूँ।
mɛ̃ apnā nām likʰtā hū̃.
I own name write am
I write my name.

In other words, the English phrase 'my' can be said in two ways in Hindi: मेरा **merā** or अपना **apnā**. The possessive pronoun does not show any relationship to the subject of the sentence whereas अपना **apnā** shows this relationship. In the second sentence, the possessed thing मेरा नाम **merā nām** belongs to the subject of the sentence; therefore, मेरा **merā** changes to अपना **apnā**. In the first sentence, however, the subject नाम **nām** *is* part of the possessed element. The rule-of-thumb is that if in a simple clause you come across the following situation in *the same clause*, the possessive pronoun becomes अपना **apnā**.

Subject		*Possessive*		*Possessive changes to*	
मैं	mẽ	मेरा	merā	अपना apnā	
हम	ham	हमारा	hamārā	अपना apnā	
तू	tū	तेरा	terā	अपना apnā	
तुम	tum	तुम्हारा	tumhāra	अपना apnā	
आप	āp	आपका	āpkā	अपना apnā	
वह	vo	उसका	uskā	अपना apnā	(वह vo . . . उसका uskā must refer to the same person)
वे	ve	उनका	unkā	अपना apnā	(वे ve . . . उनका unkā must have the same referent)

Prediction

In Hindi मैं . . . मेरा **mẽ . . . merā** type combinations cannot be found in a simple sentence. In the third person, the वह . . . उसका **vo . . . uskā** (वे . . . उनका **ve . . . unkā**) combination cannot occur if the possessed thing and the possessor subject refer to the same person.

वह	अपना	काम	करता	है।
vo	**apnā**	**kām**	**kartā**	**hɛ**
he	own	job	do	is

He (John) does his (John's) work.

However, if in the English sentence 'he' refers to John and 'his' refers to Bill, then अपना **apnā** will not be used. When the subject possessor and the possessed thing are not identical, possessive pronouns will be used.

वह	उसका	काम	करता	है।
vo	**uskā**	**kām**	**kartā**	**hɛ**
he	his	job	do	is

He (i.e. John) does his (i.e. Bill's) work.

अपना **apnā** is the masculine singular form. Its two other number gender variants are अपने **apne** (m. pl.) and अपनी **apnī** (f.). In Dialogue 1, in

सिर्फ	अपने	लिए
sirf	**apne**	**liye**
only	own	for

the subject आप **āp** is implied. Because of the following postposition, अपना **apnā** becomes oblique.

Comparative/Superlative से se 'than'

When learning Hindi, you do not need to memorize different forms such as 'good, better, best'. Only the से **se** postposition is used with the standard of comparison.

बच्चों	की	उम्र	बारह	से	कम	है।
baccõ	**kī**	**umar**	**bārā**	**se**	**kam**	**hɛ.**
children	of	age (f.)	twelve	than	less	is

The children's age is less than twelve.

The से **se** is used after the standard/object of comparison, which is 'twelve'. Also, the adjective follows the postposition. Similarly,

जॉन	राम	से	अच्छा	है।
John	**rām**	**se**	**acc^{h}ā**	**hɛ.**
John	Ram	than	good	is

John is better than Ram.

Thus, the word of the comparative phrase 'better than Ram' is reversed in Hindi, i.e. 'Ram than good'.

The superlative degree is expressed by choosing सब **sab** 'all' as the object of comparison. The English sentence 'John is best' is expressed as 'John is good than all', as in

जॉन	सब	से	अच्छा	है।
John	**sab**	**se**	**acc^{h}ā**	**hɛ.**
John	all	than	good	is

John is the best.

Again notice the Hindi word order – all than good.

The adjective can be further modified by words indicating degree, such as ज़्यादा **zyādā** 'more':

जॉन	राम	से	ज़्यादा	अच्छा	है।
John	**rām**	**se**	**zyādā**	**acc^{h}ā**	**hɛ.**
John	Ram	than	more	good	is

John is much better than Ram.

चाहना **cāhnā 'to want'**

Note the word order of the English sentence 'You want to go.'

आप	जाना	चाहते	हैं।
āp	**jānā**	**cāhte**	**hɛ̃.**
you	to go	want	are

You want to go.

The infinitive form 'to go' precedes the verb चाहना **cāhnā** 'to want'. The verb चाहना **cāhnā** receives tense conjugation. Study one more example:

वह	नाचना	चाहती	है।
vo	**nācnā**	**cāhtī**	**hɛ.**
she	to dance	want	is

She wants to dance.

बातचीत **bātcīt** **Dialogue 2** (CD 2; 3)

भारत के बारे में सोचना ***b^{h}ārat ke bāre mẽ socnā*** ***Thinking about India***

On the same day Suman Kumar runs into his colleague Al Nasiri. They start talking about the Christmas break. Al catches him off-guard, lost in his own world. He attracts Suman's attention by saying:

अल: भई, किस दुनिया में हो? क्या सोच रहे हो?
AL: b^{h}aī, kis duniyā mẽ ho? kyā soc rahe ho?
सुमन: हिन्दुस्तान के बारे में सोच रहा था।
SUMAN: hindustān ke bāre mẽ soc rahā t^{h}ā.
अल: क्यों, सब ठीक है न?
AL: kyõ, sab T^{h}īk hɛ na?
सुमन: हाँ, क्रिसमस ब्रेक में हिन्दुस्तान जा रहे हैं।
SUMAN: hā̃, *Christmas Break* mẽ hindustān jā rahe hɛ̃.
अल: अकेले या परिवार के साथ।
AL: akele yā parivār ke sāt^{h}?
सुमन: बीबी बच्चे यानी कि पूरे कुटुम्ब के साथ।
SUMAN: bībī bacce yānī ki pūre kutumba ke sāt^{h}.
अल: हाँ भाई, नहीं तो बीबी तलाक के लिये कहेगी। कहाँ जाओगे?
AL: hā̃ b^{h}āī, nahī̃ to bībī talāk ke liye kahegī. kahā̃ jāoge?

सुमन:	दिल्ली, आगरा और जयपुर।
SUMAN:	dillī, āgrā aur jaipur.
अल:	आगरा, कैसे जाओगे?
AL:	āgrā kɛse jāoge?
सुमन:	हवाई जहाज़ से।
SUMAN:	havāī jahāz se.
अल:	हवाई जहाज़ से जाना बेकार है।
AL:	havāī jahāz se jānā bekār hɛ.
सुमन:	क्यों?
SUMAN:	kyõ?
अल:	हवाई जहाज़ से गाड़ी में कम समय लगता है।
AL:	havaī jahāz se gāRī mẽ kam samaya lagtā hɛ.

AL:	*Well, in what world are you? What are you thinking?*
SUMAN:	*I was thinking about India.*
AL:	*Why, everything is all right, isn't it?*
SUMAN:	*Yes (everything is fine); (we) are going to India during the Christmas break.*
AL:	*Alone or with the family?*
SUMAN:	*Wife, children, that is, with the whole family.*
AL:	*Yes, brother; otherwise (your) wife will ask for a divorce. Where will (you) go?*
SUMAN:	*Delhi, Agra and Jaipur.*
AL:	*How will (you) go to Agra?*
SUMAN:	*By plane.*
AL:	*(It is) useless to go (to Agra) by plane.*
SUMAN:	*Why?*
AL:	*(It) takes less time (to go to Agra) on the train than by plane.*

शब्दावली **shabdāvalī Vocabulary**

भई	**b^hai**	hey, well (excl.)
किस	**kis**	which
दुनिया	**duniyā** (f.)	world
सोचना	**socnā** (+ne)	to think
के बारे में	**ke bāre mẽ**	about, concerning
था	**t^hā**	was
सब	**sab**	all
अकेला	**akelā** (m. adj.)	alone
परिवार	**parivār** (m.)	family
के साथ	**ke sāt^h**	with, together

बीबी	**bībī** (f.)	wife
यानी	**yānī**	that is, in other words
नहीं तो	**nahī̃ to**	otherwise
कुटुम्ब	**kutumba** (m.)	family (archaic word; light-hearted humour)
तलाक	**talāk** (m.)	divorce
हवा	**havā** (f.)	air, wind
जहाज़	**jahāz** (m.)	a ship, vessel, plane
बेकार	**bekār**	useless
गाड़ी	**gāRī** (f.)	train, vehicle, cart
समय	**samaya** (m.)	time
लगना	**lagnā** (–**ne**)	to take, to cost

Notes

भई b^{h}aī 'Hey' vs भाई b^{h}āī 'Brother'

The short vs long vowel can make a considerable difference in meaning. The case in point is the contrast between भई **b^{h}aī** and भाई **b^{h}āī**. The former is used as an exclamatory marker to express surprise, happiness, etc. The latter (भाई **b^{h}āī)** is a kinship term and you will recall that it means 'brother'. However, in the Hindi-speaking community, it can be used as an address for a friend, stranger, shopkeeper, for both young and old. Sometimes, in very informal circumstances, it can even be used for women who are known to the speaker. Our advice is not to use it for women. In non-relationship situations, its main function is as an attention-getter while establishing a social relationship by using a kinship word for a person to whom one is not related. It therefore carries some sense of affection. The attention-getters such as सुनिए **suniye** and कहिए **kahiye** are neutral in terms of social relationship.

The feminine counterpart of भाई **b^{h}aī** is बहन **bɛhɛn**. The honorific particle जी **jī** is used with बहन **bɛhɛn** more frequently than with भाई **b^{h}āī**. Believe it or not, women are very much respected and cared about (sometimes more than men) in the very large segment of the South Asia Society! Of course, South Asia is not a perfect society.

क्या kyā 'what', कौन kaun 'who', and किस kis 'what, who'

किस **kis** is the oblique singular counterpart of both क्या **kyā** 'what' and कौन **kaun** 'who'. (Remember the 'peer pressure' phenomenon.)

क्या दुनिया	**kyā duniyā**	what world
किस दुनिया में	**kis duniyā mẽ**	in what world

For details see the Reference grammar section.

Compound postpositions

You have come across postpositions of one and two elements. Here is the compound postposition consisting of three elements. Remember you will not find any compound postposition with का **kā**.

के बारे में	**ke bāre mẽ**	about, concerning (lit. in regard to)

Observe the use of this postposition.

हिन्दुस्तान के बारे में	**hindustān ke bāre mẽ**	about India
कहानी के बारे में	**kahānī ke bāre mẽ**	about the story
लड़कों के बारे में	**laRkõ ke bāre mẽ**	about the boys
	(**laRkõ** = boys, oblique plural)	

Past tense: verb 'to be'

The Hindi forms of English 'was' and 'were' are the following four:

	Masculine	*Feminine*
Singular	था **tʰā** was	थी **tʰī** was
Plural	थे **tʰe** were	थीं **tʰī̃** were

As in English, these forms agree with their subject. The only difference is that in Hindi they agree in gender in addition to number.

Progressives

So far you observed that Hindi either consists of one unit (e.g. polite commands) or two units (the simple present). Now, you have an opportunity to familiarize yourself with the verb which has three units.

मैं	हिन्दुस्तान	के बारे में	सोच	रहा	था।
mẽ	**hindustān**	**ke bāre mẽ**	**soc**	**rahā**	**tʰā.**
I	India	about	think	ing	was

I was thinking about India.

The Hindi equivalent of English 'was thinking' is सोच रहा था **soc rahā t^{h}ā**. The Hindi verb is broken into three units: 'verb stem' (सोच **soc**), 'ing' (रहा **rahā**), 'was' (था **t^{h}ā**). The only difference between Hindi and English is that in Hindi '-ing' is a separate word and the auxiliary 'was' ends the verbal string. Sentences such as the above are called either 'past progressives' or 'past continuous'. We will call them *past progressive.*

Like an adjective ending in **ā**, **rahā** has three variants: रहा **rahā** (masculine, singular), रहे **rahe** (masculine, plural) and रही **rahī** (feminine).

In order to form the present progressive as in English the auxiliary 'was' is replaced by present forms such as 'am', 'is', 'are'. The same is true in Hindi. Just substitute the present 'to be' forms and you will get the present progressive verb form. For instance:

मैं	हिन्दुस्तान	के बारे में	सोच	रहा	हूँ।
mẽ	**hindustān**	**ke bāre mẽ**	**soc**	**rahā**	**hũ**
I	India	about	think	ing	am

I am thinking about India.

Future

The English future tense consists of two verbal units, whereas in Hindi it is only one. You came across an example of a Hindi future tense in Unit 3:

हम	फिर	मिलेंगे।
ham	**p^{h}ir**	**milẽge**
we	again	meet-will

We will meet again.

तुम	कहाँ	जाओगे?
tum	**kahā̃**	**jāoge?**
you	where	go-will

Where will you go?

The Hindi verb forms can be broken up in the following manner.

मिल	+ एँ	+ ग	+ ए
mil	+ **ẽ**	+ **g**	+ **e**
stem	+ person (आप **āp**)	+ future 'will'	+ number-gender (m. pl.)

जा + ओ + ग + ए
jā + **o** + **g** + **e**
stem + person (तुम **tum**) + future 'will' + number-gender (m. pl.)

जा + ऊँ + ग + ई
jā + **ū̃** + **g** + **ī**
stem + person (मैं **mɛ̃**) + future 'will' + number-gender (f. sg./pl.)

The ghost postposition को ko 'to' with locations

आप	क्रिसमस	ब्रेक	में	हिन्दुस्तान	जा	रहे	हैं।
āp	**Christmas**	**break**	**mẽ**	**hindustān**	**jā**	**rahe**	**hɛ̃.**
you	Christmas	Break	in	India	go	ing	are

You are going to India during the Christmas break.

Although the postposition को **ko** is dropped in Hindi, this is the ghost postposition we referred to in the previous chapter. Recall the discussion of the phrase 'in the morning' सवेरे **savere**. If we place, say, अपना **apnā** 'own' before India, the ghost postposition will change it to its oblique form – अपने **apne**.

बातचीत bātcīt Dialogue 3 (CD 2; 5)

आगरा की गाड़ी ***āgrā kī gāRī*** ***The train to Agra***

Al Nasiri and Suman Kumar continue to discuss the best ways of getting to Agra. Finally, Al Nasiri convinces Suman Kumar to take a train to Agra.

अल: आगरा के लिये सब से अच्छी गाड़ी ताज ऐक्सप्रेस है।
AL: āgrā ke liye sab se acc[h]ī gāRī Taj Express hɛ.
सुमन: ताज ऐक्सप्रेस कहाँ से चलती है?
SUMAN: Taj Express kahā̃ se caltī hɛ?
अल: नयी दिल्ली से, सवेरे सात बजे।
AL: nayī dillī se, savere sāt baje.
सुमन: और आने के लिए?
SUMAN: aur āne ke liye?
अल: वही गाड़ी शाम को वापस आती है।
AL: vahī gāRī shām ko vāpas ātī hɛ.
सुमन: लेकिन हम लोग रात को ताजमहल देखना चाहते हैं।
SUMAN: lekin ham log rāt ko tāj mɛhɛl dek[h]nā cāhte hɛ̃.

अल: हाँ, ताज रात को और भी सुन्दर लगता है।
AL: hā̃, tāj rāt ko aur b^{h}ī sundar lagtā hɛ.
सुमन: तो एक रात आगरा रुकेंगे, अगले दिन दिल्ली लौटेंगे।
SUMAN: to ek rāt āgrā rukẽge, agle din dillī lauTẽge.
अल: चाँदनी रात, ताज महल और बीबी साथ. . . . मज़ा कीजिये।
AL: cā̃dnī rāt, tāj mɛhɛl aur bībī sāt^{h} . . . mazā kījiye.

AL: *The best train for Agra is the Taj Express.*
SUMAN: *Where does the Taj Express leave from?*
AL: *From New Delhi, (at) seven o'clock in the morning.*
SUMAN: *And to come (back)?*
AL: *The same train comes back (to New Delhi) in the evening.*
SUMAN: *But we people want to see the Taj Mahal at night.*
AL: *Yes, Taj looks even more beautiful at night.*
SUMAN: *Then, we will stay (for a) night (in) Agra; the next day (we) will return to Delhi.*
AL: *The moonlit night, Taj Mahal and with (your) wife . . . (you) enjoy (both).*

शब्दावली **shabdāvalī Vocabulary**

नया	**nayā** (m. adj.)	new
सात बजे	**sāt baje**	seven o'clock
आना	**ānā** (–**ne**)	to come
वह	**vah <vo>**	that, he, she
वही	**vahī (vah+hī)**	same, that very
शाम	**shām** (f.)	evening
वापस	**vāpas**	back
वापस आना	**vāpas ānā** (–**ne**)	to come back
रात	**rāt** (f.)	night
ताज	**tāj** (m.)	crown
महल	**mɛhɛl** (m.)	palace
ताजमहल	**tāj mɛhɛl**	the Taj Mahal
और भी	**aur b^{h}ī**	even more
लगना	**lagnā** (+**ko**)	to seem, to appear
रुकना	**ruknā** (–**ne**)	to stop
अगला	**aglā** (adj.)	next
दिन	**din** (m.)	day
लौटना	**lauTnā** (–**ne**)	to return, to come back
चाँद	**cā̃d** (m.)	moon
चाँदनी	**cā̃dnī** (f.)	moonlit
मज़ा करना	**mazā karnā** (+**ne**)	to enjoy

Pronunciation

mɛhɛl is written as **mahal** महल.

Notes

Time expressions

सवेरे	**savere**	in the morning
दोपहर को	**dopɛhɛr ko**	at noon
शाम को	**shām ko**	in the evening
रात को	**rāt ko**	at night

With the exception of सवेरे **savere**, the को **ko** postposition is uniformly used with other time adverbs. सवेरे **savere** takes the ghost postposition को **ko**.

Emphatic particle ही hī 'only, right, very'

The particle of exclusion is ही **hī** 'only.' The English word 'same' is equivalent to 'that very' in Hindi. It can be used with nouns, pronouns and adverbs. It is usually used as a separate word except with those pronouns and adverbs which end in **-h**. It undergoes contraction with **-h** ending pronouns and adverbs.

Pronouns			*Particle*		*Emphatic pronoun*	
वह		+	ही	=	वही	
vo	he/she/that	+	**hī**	=	**vahī**	that very, same
यह		+	ही	=	यही	
ye	this	+	**hī**	=	**yahī**	this very
Adverbs			*Particle*		*Emphatic adverb*	
वहाँ		+	ही	=	वहीं	
vahā̃	there	+	**hī**	=	**vahī̃**	right there
यहाँ		+	ही	=	यहीं	
yahā̃	here	+	**hī**	=	**yahī̃**	right here

Irregular commands

Recall that polite commands are formed by adding **-iye** to a stem. The following four stems are irregular because they undergo a change with **-iye**.

Stem			*Irregular stem*		*Polite command*		
कर	**kar**	do	कीज	**kīj**	कीजिए	**kīj-iye**	Please do
दे	**de**	give	दीज	**dīj**	दीजिए	**dīj-iye**	Please give
ले	**le**	take	लीज	**līj**	लीजिए	**līj-iye**	Please take
पी	**pī**	drink	पीज	**pīj**	पीजिए	**pīj-iye**	Please drink

पढ़ने का अभ्यास १ paR^hne kā ab^hyās 1 Reading practice 1 (CD 2; 7)

एक लोक कथा: हवाई किले बनाना
ek lok kathā: havāī kile banānā
An ancient folk tale: 'To build castles in the air'

This is a folk story of a poor Brahmin from ancient times. He was a miser and used to save the flour that he got from his client in a ceramic pitcher. He used to guard the pitcher jealously and keep it next to his bed. One day he began to day-dream.

1 एक दिन देश में अकाल पड़ेगा।
ek din desh mẽ akāl paRegā.
2 मैं आटा बेचूँगा।
mɛ̃ āTā becū̃gā.
3 और कुछ जानवर ख़रीदूँगा।
aur kuc^h jānvar xarīdū̃gā.
4 तो मैं अमीर बनूँगा।
to mɛ̃ amīr banū̃gā.
5 एक दिन मेरी शादी होगी।
ek din merī shādī hogī.
6 फिर मेरा बच्चा होगा।
p^hir merā baccā hogā.

7 अब मैं आराम से किताबें पढ़ूँगा।
ab mɛ̃ ārām se kitābẽ paR^hū̃gā.
8 बच्चा मेरे पास आयेगा।
baccā mere pās āyegā.

(At this point he continues to dream that he will ask his wife to take away the child. Because she is busy she won't be able to hear him; he will therefore kick her. Thinking this, he actually kicks out and hits the pitcher with his leg. The pitcher falls down and breaks. With this, the castle he built in the air vanishes.)

1 *One day (there) will be a famine in the country.*
2 *I will sell the flour.*
3 *And I will buy some animals.*
4 *Then I will become rich.*
5 *One day my marriage will occur.* (lit. my marriage will take place)
6 *Then I will have a child.*
7 *Now I will read books comfortably.*
8 *The child will come to me.* (lit. come near me).

शब्दावली **shabdāvalī** **Vocabulary**

देश	**desh** (m.)	country
अकाल पड़ना	**akāl paRnā** (–**ne**)	famine to occur
आटा	**āTā** (m.)	flour
बेचना	**becnā** (+**ne**)	to sell
कुछ	**kuc^h**	some
जानवर	**jānvar** (m.)	animal
ख़रीदना	**xarīdnā** (+**ne**)	to buy
अमीर	**amīr**	rich
बनना	**bannā** (–**ne**)	to become
आराम	**ārām** (m.)	comfort
पढ़ना	**paR^hnā** (–**ne**)	to study, to read

Web resources

http://www.ncsu.edu/project/hindi_lessons/

For the sights and sounds of Indian monuments, Units 2 and 9 are particularly recommended

अभ्यास abʰyās Exercises

Exercise 1

You land at New Delhi airport and, on arrival at immigration, the officer asks you the following questions in Hindi. First, translate the questions into English in the space given next to the question, and then answer the questions in Hindi.

OFFICER: आपका नाम? ________
āpkā nām?

YOU: ________

OFFICER: आप भारत में कितने दिन रहेंगे? ________
āp bʰārat mẽ kitne din rahẽge?

YOU: ________

OFFICER: कहाँ–कहाँ जायेंगे? ________
kahā̃-kahā̃ jāẽge?

YOU: ________

OFFICER: हिन्दुस्तान में पता क्या है? ________
hindustān mẽ patā kyā hɛ?

YOU: ________

OFFICER: वापस कब जायेंगे? ________
vāpas kab jāẽge?

YOU: ________

OFFICER: कोई इल्लीगल सामान है? ________
koī *illegal* sāmān hɛ?

YOU: ________

Exercise 2

There are a few incorrect verbs in the following passage. Pick them out and replace them with the right verbs.

मैं आप के लिए क्या करना सकता है? हम आगरा जा चाहता है। आगरा कितनी दूर हैं? बहुत दूर नहीं, लेकिन आप कब जा रहा है? हम कल जायेगा। गाड़ी सुबह दिल्ली से चलते है। आप गाड़ी से जा चाहता हैं।

mɛ̃ āp ke liye kyā karnā saktā hɛ? ham āgrā jā cāhtā hɛ. āgrā kitnī dūr hɛ̃? bahut dūr nahī̃, lekin āp kab jā rahā hɛ? ham kal jāegā. gāRī subā dillī se calte hɛ. āp gāRī se jā cāhtā hɛ̃?

Exercise 3

The sentences in the following letter are in the wrong order. Rearrange them in the right order.

प्रिय राकेश

तुम्हारा मिला खत। पढ़ कर खुशी हुई। तुम रहे कब आ हो? कल मैं शिकागो हूँ जा रहा। शिकागो बहुत शहर है बड़ा । मैं शिकागो से हवाई जहाज़ जाऊँगा। लेकिन मैं जाना चाहता हवाई जहाज़ से नहीं हूँ। गाड़ी मुझे पसन्द है से ज्यादा हवाई जहाज़। बाकी सब है ठीक।

तुम्हारा दोस्त,
राजीव

Priya Rakesh:

tumhārā milā xat. paR^{h} kar xushī huī. tum rahe kab ā ho? kal mɛ̃ *Chicago* hū̃ jā rahā. *Chicago* bahut shɛhɛr hɛ baRā. mɛ̃ *Chicago* se hawāī jahāz (airplane) jāū̃gā. lekin mɛ̃ jānā cāhtā hawāī jahāz se nahī̃ hū̃. gāRī muj^{h}e pasand hɛ se zyāda hawāī jahāz. bākī sab hɛ T^{h}īk.

tumhārā dost,
Rājīv.

Exercise 4

Here are the answers. What were the questions? (Wherever needed, the object of the inquiry is underlined.)

Q: ________________
A: मैं शिकागो जा रही हूँ।
mɛ̃ Chicago jā rahī hū̃.

Q: ________________
A: मैं यहाँ सात दिन रहूँगी।
mɛ̃ yahā̃ sāt din rahū̃gī.

Q: ________________
A: मैं अपना काम कर रही हूँ।
mɛ̃ apnā kām kar rahī hū̃.

Q: ________________
A: जी हाँ, चाय बहुत पसन्द है।
jī hā̃, cāy bahut pasand hɛ.

Q: ________________
A: मेरे चार भाई हैं।
mere cār b^{h}āī hɛ̃.

Exercise 5

If you won a million dollars, what would you do? Use the following words or phrases:

king
queen
buy a yacht, Rolls Royce
travel around the world
become crazy with happiness
buy diamonds for my wife/girlfriend
return to work

Exercise 6

This fast-talking robot is programmed for the 'me' generation. Could you change his speech to suit the 'we' generation? Note the gender of 'robot' is masculine in Hindi.

मैं *रोबाट* हूँ। मैं *कालिफ़ोनिया* से हूँ। मै हिन्दी बोल सकता हूँ। मैं हिन्दी समझ भी सकता हूँ। मैं हिन्दी गाने गा सकता हूँ । मेरी *मैमोरी* बहुत बड़ी है। मैं हर सवाल पूछ सकता हूँ और हर जवाब दे सकता हूँ। यानी हर काम कर सकता हूँ। मैं हमेशा काम कर सकता हूँ। मैं कभी नहीं थकता हूँ। मेरे पास हर सवाल का ज़वाब है। लेकिन मसालेदार खाना नहीं खा सकता।

mẽ *robot* hū̃. mẽ *California* se hū̃. mẽ hindī bol saktā hū̃. mẽ hindī samaj^h b^hī saktā hū̃. mẽ hindī gāne gā saktā hū̃. merī *memory* bahut baRī hɛ. mẽ har savāl puc^h saktā hū̃ aur har javāb de saktā hū̃. yānī har kām kar saktā hū̃. mẽ hameshā kām kar saktā hū̃. mẽ kab^hī nahī̃ t^haktā hū̃. mere pās har savāl kā javāb hɛ. lekin masāledār k^hānā nahī̃ k^hā saktā.

Exercise 7

Listen to Mr Smith's comments about a forthcoming visit to North America and then answer the following questions in Hindi:

1 मि॰ स्मिथ *अमरीका* कब जायेंगे?
Mr Smith *America* kab jāẽge?
2 वे कौन सी *एयरलाइन* से *न्यू यार्क* जायेंगे?
ve kaun sī *airline* se *New York* jāẽge?
3 क्या वे अपने परिवार के साथ *न्यू यार्क* पहुँचेंगे?
kyā ve apne parivār ke sāt^h *New York* pahũcẽge?
4 वे *डिज़्नी वर्ड* क्यों जाना चाहते हैं?
ve *Disney World* kyõ jānā cāhte hẽ?
5 वे *डिज़्नी वर्ड* में कितने दिन रहेंगे?
ve *Disney World* mẽ kitne din rahẽge?

6 कल क्या किया?
kal kyā kiyā?
What did you do yesterday?

By the end of this unit you should be able to:

- talk about past events/actions
- use time adverbials with full clauses
- talk about topics dealing with 'lost and found'
- learn to express sequential actions
- learn more about paraphrasing devices
- employ some more very common expressions

बातचीत **bātcīt Dialogue 1** (CD 2; 9)

क्या बात है? ***kyā bāt hɛ? What is the matter?***

Aditi Chatterjī is coming to America for graduate study. She lands at Kennedy Airport. As she is cleared through customs and is ready to take her flight to Chicago, she makes the horrifying discovery that her passport and traveller's cheques have been stolen. She calls her family in Calcutta (now Kolkatta), reversing the charges. She gets in touch with her father, Suman Chatterjī, who is anxiously waiting for news of her arrival in the USA.

सुमन: हैलो।
SUMAN: hɛllo.
अदिति: हैलो, डैड, मैं अदिति बोल रही हूँ।
ADITI: hɛllo, DɛD, mɛ̃ Aditi bol rahī hū̃.
सुमन: कहाँ से बोल रही हो?
SUMAN: kahā̃ se bol rahī ho?
अदिति: न्यू यॉर्क से।
ADITI: New York se.
सुमन: क्यों, अभी शिकागो नहीं पहुँची।
SUMAN: kyõ, ab^{h}ī Chicago nahī̃ pahū̃cī?
अदिति: नहीं।
ADITI: nahī̃.
सुमन: क्या बात है? परेशान लग रही हो। सब ठीक-ठाक है न?
SUMAN: kyā bāt hɛ? pareshān lag rahī ho. sab T^{h}īk-T^{h}āk hɛ na?
अदिति: मैं तो ठीक हूँ, लेकिन मेरा पासपोर्ट, मेरे पैसे और (ट्रैवलरज़) चैक्स गुम हो गये।
ADITI: mɛ̃ to T^{h}īk hū̃, lekin merā *passport*, mere pɛse aur Trɛvlars (*traveller's*) *cheques* gum ho gaye.
सुमन: क्या!
SUMAN: kyā!
अदिति: किसी ने मेरी जेब काटी – ऐसा लगता है।
ADITI: kisī ne merī jeb kāTī – ɛsā lagtā hɛ.
सुमन: सच!
SUMAN: sac!
अदिति: हाँ।
ADITI: hā̃.

ADITI: *Hello, Dad, this is Aditi calling.* (lit. I am Aditi speaking)
SUMAN: *Where are you calling from?*
ADITI: *From New York.*
SUMAN: *Hey, haven't you reached Chicago yet?* (lit. why, you did not reach Chicago yet?)

ADITI: *No.*
SUMAN: *What is the matter? (You) seem to be upset. Everything is fine, isn't it?*
ADITI: *As regards me, I am fine, but my passport, money and traveller's cheques are lost.*
SUMAN: *What!* (lit. What! I do not believe it!)
ADITI: *Someone picked my pocket – it seems.*
SUMAN: *Is that right!* (lit. Truth!)
ADITI: *Yes.*

शब्दावली **shabdāvalī** Vocabulary

हैलो	**hɛllo**	hello
अभी	**ab^hī**	right now
पहुँचना	**pahũcnā** (–**ne**)	to reach, arrive
बात	**bāt** (f.)	matter
क्या बात है?	**kyā bāt hɛ?**	what is the matter?
परेशान	**pareshān** (adj.)	troubled
सब	**sab**	all
ठीक-ठाक	**T^hīk-T^hāk**	fine, hale and hearty
तो	**to** (particle)	then, as regards
गुमना	**gumnā** (–**ne**)	to be lost
गए/गये	**gaye** (m. pl)	went
क्या	**kyā!**	what! I do not believe it!
किसी	**kisī**	someone
ने	**ne**	agent marker in the past tense
जेब	**jeb** (f.)	pocket
काटना	**kāTnā** (+**ne**)	to cut
जेब काटना	**jeb kāTnā**	to pickpocket
ऐसा	**ɛsā**	such, it
सच	**sac!**	Truth! It can't be true!

Notes

The perfective form (the simple past)

We introduced the simple past tense forms of the verb 'to be'. Now, note the Hindi equivalent of the English 'Didn't (you) reach Chicago?':

तुम	अभी	शिकागो	नहीं	पहुँचीं?
(tum)	**ab^hī**	**Chicago**	**nahī̃**	**pahũcī̃?**
you	right now	Chicago	not	reached (f. pl.)

Although the Hindi verb पहुँचीं **pahũcĩ̄** is translated as 'reached', it has no intrinsic tense reference like words such as है **hɛ** 'is' and था **tʰā** 'was'. It simply shows that the action or situation is completed. The act may be completed in the present, past or future tense. Usually adverbs such as 'yesterday' and 'tomorrow' and the form of the verb 'to be' provide the tense information.

Now recall the suffixes given in Magic Key 1 and do some detective work regarding the feminine forms.

Verb stem		*Perfective form*	
पहुँच **pahũc**	reach	पहुँचा **pahũcā**	masculine singular
		पहुँचे **pahũce**	masculine plural
		पहुँची **pahũcī**	feminine singular
		पहुँचीं **pahũcĩ̄**	feminine plural

Yes, for the first time feminine plural forms compete with masculine forms and have their own distinct plural identity. The Hindi pronoun तुम **tum** always takes the plural form.

Now note another perfective form from the above dialogue:

किसीने	मेरी	जेब	काटी।
kisī-ne	**merī**	**jeb**	**kāTī**
someone-agent	my	pocket (f.)	cut (f. sg.)

Someone picked my pocket. (lit. someone cut my pocket)

You will notice two things different that are from the previous sentence: (1) the use of the postposition ने **ne**, and (2) the verb agreement. The postposition ने **ne** occurs with those subjects that have transitive verbs in the perfective form. Notice verbs such as 'come', 'go', and 'reach' are intransitive, whereas verbs such as 'cut', 'write', 'do', and 'buy' are transitive. The Hindi word for the English 'someone' is कोई **koī**. Because of the postposition ने **ne**, the subject pronoun कोई **koī** becomes किसी **kisī**. In other words, peer pressure makes it oblique. Also, remember that the verb does not agree with those subjects followed by a postposition. Therefore, the verb does not agree with the subject; instead it agrees with the object जेब **jeb** 'pocket', which is feminine singular in Hindi. For details about perfective forms see the Reference grammar section.

Because the perfectives mark a situation or action as completed, they are usually associated with the past tense.

गया 'Went' – an exception in verb form

The English verb 'to go' is an exception in the past tense form – 'went' rather than 'goed'. Similarly, it is also irregular in Hindi in the perfective form. Here are the Hindi equivalents of the English verb form 'went':

Verb stem	*Perfective form*			
जा **jā** *go*	गया	**gayā**	went	(masculine singular)
	गये/गए	**gaye**	went	(masculine plural)
	गयी/गई	**gayī**	went	(feminine singular)
	गयीं/गईं	**gayī̃**	went	(feminine plural)

Because Hindi and English belong to the same language family, what is remarkable is that the English 'g' of the verb stem 'go' shows up in the Hindi irregular form and then takes the Hindi perfective suffixes. The sound 'y' intervenes in the two vowels which is quite common, occurring in many languages.

The other three important verbs that are irregular in the past tense are the following: लेना **lenā** 'to take', देना **denā** 'to give' and पीना **pīnā** 'to drink'.

Stem		*Masculine*		*Feminine*	
		Singular	*Plural*	*Singular*	*Plural*
ले **le**	take	लिया **liyā**	लिये/लिए **liye**	ली **lī**	लीं **lī̃**
दे **de**	give	दिया **diyā**	दिये/दिए **diye**	दी **dī**	दीं **dī̃**
पी **pī**	drink	पिया **piyā**	पिये/पिए **piye**	पी **pī**	पीं **pī̃**

Compound verbs: word-for-word translation

मेरे	पैसे	और	ट्रैवलरज़	चैक्स	गुम	गये।
mere	**pɛse**	**aur**	***traveller's***	***cheques***	**gum**	**gaye.**
my	money	and	traveller's	cheques	lost	went

My money and traveller's cheques (are) lost.

Notice the clustering of the two verbs गुम **gum** 'be lost' and गये **gaye** 'went' (m. pl.). This clustering of the real verbs is a special property of Hindi and other South Asian languages. They are called 'compound verbs'. We will deal with this class of verbs later on in this book. For the time being note this verb clustering and memorize the sentence given above.

Echo-words

You have already come across the word ठीक **Tʰīk** 'fine, correct'. In the phrase ठीक–ठाक **Tʰīk Tʰāk**, the second word ठाक **Tʰāk** does not have any meaning of its own. It just echoes the first word by making a slight vowel change. The meaning added by the echo word is 'etc.', 'and all that' or 'other related things/properties'. Therefore, ठीक–ठाक **Tʰīk Tʰāk** means 'fine, etc.'. Very often the first consonant sound is changed in Hindi echo words, e.g. काम-वाम **kām vām** 'work, etc.', नाम-वाम **nām vām** 'name etc.'. The preferred consonant change is by means of व **v**.

बातचीत **bātcīt** Dialogue 2 (CD 2; 11)

मेरा पासपोर्ट गुम गया है ***merā pāsporT gum gayā hɛ*** ***My passport is lost***

Aditi Chatterjii continues to talk with her father, Suman Chatterjii about the incident. She informs her father that she filed a report at the airport and that American Express will issue her new traveller's cheques but not without her passport. So, she needs some money by telegram, and in the meanwhile she needs to go to the Indian Consulate Office in New York. At the consulate, she talks with an officer.

अदिति: मेरा पासपोर्ट गुम गया है। नया पासपोर्ट चाहिये।
ADITI: merā pāsporT (*passport*) gum gayā hɛ. nayā pāsporT (*passport*) cāhiye.
अफ़सर: कब गुमा?
OFFICER: kab gumā?
अदिति: आज, करीब पाँच घंटे पहले।
ADITI: āj, karīb pā̃c gʰanTe pɛhle.
अफ़सर: आपको मालूम है कि कहाँ गुमा?
OFFICER: āpko mālūm hɛ ki kahā̃ gumā?
अदिति: जी हाँ, कैनेडी हवाई अड्डे में।
ADITI: jī hā̃, *Kennedy* havāī aDDe mẽ.
अफ़सर: कैसे?
OFFICER: kɛse?
अदिति: जब इम्मिग्रेशन से बाहर आई, तो मेरे पास था। फिर, शिकागो की फ़्लाइट के लिये दूसरे टर्मिनल गयी, तब भी था। जब काउन्टर पर पहुँची, तो देखा, पासपोर्ट, टिकट, पैसे, और ट्रैवलरज़ चैक्स पर्स में नहीं थे।

ADITI: jab *immigration* se bāhar āyī, to mere pās tʰā. pʰir, Chicago kī *flight* ke liye dūsre Tarminal (*terminal*) gayī, tab bʰī thā. jab kāunTar (*counter*) par pahũcī, to dekʰā, pāsporT, *ticket*, pɛse, aur *traveller's cheques purse* mẽ nahī̃ tʰe.
अफ़सर: पुलिस में रिपोर्ट की।
OFFICER: police mẽ riporT (report) kī?
अदिति: जी हाँ, ये देखिए।
ADITI: jī hā̃, ye dekʰiye.
अफ़सर: अच्छा ये फार्म भरिये, एक–दो महीने में नया पासपोर्ट आपको मिल जायेगा।
OFFICER: accʰā ye *form* bʰariye, ek-do mahīne mẽ nayā pāsporT āpko milegā.
अदिति: इससे जल्दी नहीं मिल सकता?
ADITI: isse jaldī nahī̃ mil saktā?
अफ़सर: जी नहीं, पहले रिपोर्ट हिन्दुस्तान जायेगी और क्लियरैन्स के बाद ही पासपोर्ट मिल सकता है।
OFFICER: jī nahī̃, pɛhɛle *report* hindustān jayegī aur *clearance* ke bād hī pāsporT mil saktā hɛ.
अदिति: शुक्रिया।
ADITI: shukriyā
अफ़सर: कोई बात नहीं।
OFFICER: koī bāt nahī̃.

ADITI: *My passport is lost? (I) need a new passport.*
OFFICER: *When was (it) lost?*
ADITI: *About five hours ago today.*
OFFICER: *Do you know where (it) was lost?*
ADITI: *Yes, at Kennedy Airport.*
OFFICER: *How?*
ADITI: *When I came out of Immigration, I had (it).* (lit. then (it) was near me) *Then (I) went to the other terminal for the flight to Chicago; even then I had (it).*
When I reached the counter, then (I) noticed the passport, ticket, money and the traveller's cheques were not in (my) handbag.
OFFICER: *(Did you) report (this) to* (lit. in) *the police?*
ADITI: *Yes, look at this* (referring to the police report).
OFFICER: *Okay. Fill out this form. In one or two months you will get a new passport.*
ADITI: *Can't (I) get (it) earlier than that?*
OFFICER: *No, first the report will go to India and only after clearance (you) can get (it).*

ADITI: *Thanks.*
OFFICER: *You are welcome* (or do not mention it).

शब्दावली **shabdāvalī Vocabulary**

नया	**nayā** (m. adj.)	new
करीब	**karīb**	about, approximately
घंटा	**g^{h}anTā** (m.)	hour
पहला	**pɛhɛlā** (m. adj.)	first
पहले	**pɛhɛle**	(at) first, ago, previously
मालूम होना	**mālūm honā** (+ko)	to know, to be known
हवाई अड्डा	**havāī aDDā** (m.)	airport
जेब	**jab** (relative pronoun)	when
बाहर	**bāhar**	out, outside
आना	**ānā** (–ne)	to come
आयी/आई	**āyī** (f. sg.)	came
दूसरा	**dūsrā** (m. adj.)	second, other, another
तो	**to**	then
देखना	**dek^{h}nā** (+ne)	to see, to look at, to notice
देखिये/देखिए	**dek^{h}iye**	please see, look at, notice
भरना	**b^{h}arnā** (+ne)	to fill
भरिये/भरिए	**b^{h}ariye**	please fill, please fill out
एक–दो	**ek-do**	one or two
महीना	**mahīnā**	month
मिलना	**milnā** (–ne, +ko)	to meet, to get, to be available
मिलेगा	**milegā** (m. sg.)	will get
जल्दी	**jaldī**	quickly
के बाद	**(ke) bād**	after, later
शुक्रिया	**shukriyā**	thanks

Pronunciation

dūsre is written as **dūsare** दूसरा. The vowel **a** is dropped in colloquial pronunciation (see Script Unit 4).

Notes

मालूम होना **mālūm honā vs** जानना **jānnā 'to know'**

Consider the word-for-word translation of the Hindi equivalent of the English expression 'Do you know . . . ?' in our dialogue.

आपको मालूम है?
āpko mālūm hɛ?
you-to known is
Do you know . . . ?

The Hindi sentence is similar to the English 'Is it known to you . . . ?' The only difference is that in Hindi आपको **āpko** is still the subject but the non-volitional subject. Remember the discussion of dative/experiential subjects in Unit 3: in Hindi there is a distinction between non-volitional and volitional verbs. The verb मालूम होना **mālūm honā** suggests the type of knowing or knowledge which is non-volitional or unintentional in nature. The verb जानना **jānnā** can also be translated as 'to know' but the difference is that जानना **jānnā** refers to an act of knowing that is volitional and where some effort or research has gone into that knowledge. As I pointed out earlier, the volitional verbs do not take dative को **ko** marking with their subjects. Observe the following volitional counterpart of मालूम होना **mālūm honā**.

आप जानती हैं?
āp jāntī hɛ̃ . . . ?
you (f.) know are
Do you know . . . ?

Notice that the verb agrees with the subject आप **āp** which is feminine in our dialogue. In the former sentence आपको **āpko** is the subject and the verb does not agree with it. We will detail the question of agreement again in this chapter. In the former sentence the verb agrees with the implied object यह **ye** 'this', which is masculine singular, and that is why the verb takes the singular form है **hɛ**.

Similarly, you have already come across two different usages of the verb मिलना **milnā** 'to meet' and मिलना **milnā** 'to get, to obtain.'

हम मिलेंगे।
ham milẽge
we meet-will
We will meet.

The understood subject in the Hindi expression of the English 'you will get the passport' is supplied below:

आपको पासपोर्ट मिलेगा।
āpko passport milegā
you-to passport get-will
You will get the passport.

English verbs such as 'to get' or 'to obtain' are treated as unintentional acts in Hindi and many other South Asian languages. That explains why the Hindi subject is followed by the postposition को **ko**. Can you predict the element which the verb मिलेगा **milegā** agrees with? No more suspense: it agrees with the object passport which is masculine singular in Hindi.

The ने ne construction

If we fill in the understood subjects in the following two expressions from the above dialogue –

तो	देखा।
to	**dek^{h}ā**
then	saw

and

पुलिस	को	रिपोर्ट	की?
police	**ko**	**reporT**	**kī?**
police	to	report	did

the complete sentences will be

तो	मैंने	देखा।
to	**mẽne**	**dek^{h}ā**
then	I-agent	saw

Then I saw.

and

आपने	पुलिस	को	रिपोर्ट	की?
āpne	**police**	**ko**	**reporT**	**kī?**
you agent	police	to	report (f.)	did (f. sg.)

Did you report to the police?

The ने **ne** postposition is attached to the subject. Without the postposition the sentences would be ungrammatical. However, observe the following sentences:

जब	मैं	इम्मिग्रेशन	से	बाहर	आई।
jab	**mẽ**	**immigration**	**se**	**bāhar**	**āyī.**
when	I (f. sg.)	immigration	from	out	came (f. sg.)

When I came out of immigration.

and

मैं	दूसरे	टर्मिनल	गयी।
mẽ	**dūsre**	**Tarminal**	**gayī.**
I (f. sg.)	other	terminal	went (f. sg.)

I went to the other terminal.

The above two sentences do not require the ने **ne** postposition. But why not? The difference is that verbs such as 'come' and 'go' are intransitive. The ने **ne** postposition is restricted to the transitive verbs in the perfective form. Verbs such as 'to see' and 'to report' are transitive and are used in the perfective form; so the postposition ने **ne** with the subject is required. This type of construction is called 'the ergative' construction in linguistic literature. Many languages of the world, such as Basque and some Australian Aboriginal languages, have this property.

The pronominal forms with the ने **ne** postposition are as follows:

Nominative pronouns		*The* ने ***ne*** *pronouns*		
मैं	**mẽ**	मैंने	**mẽne**	I
हम	**ham**	हमने	**hamne**	we
तू	**tū**	तूने	**tūne**	you (singular)
तुम	**tum**	तुमने	**tumne**	you (plural)
आप	**āp**	आपने	**āpne**	you (honorific)
वह	**vo**	उसने	**usne**	she, he, it, that
वे	**ve**	उन्होंने	**unhõne**	they, those
यह	**ye**	इसने	**isne**	this
ये	**ye**	इन्होंने	**inhõne**	these

Note that the third person pronouns show peer group pressure as a result of ने **ne**. If you are learning the script, it is written as one word with the third person plural pronoun.

The ने **ne** forms of the question pronoun are: किसने **kisne** 'who' (singular) and किन्होंने **kinhõne** 'who' (plural).

Complex verbs

As in English, in Hindi a noun can be turned into a verb. The only difference is that the noun has to be anchored in verbs such as करना **karnā** 'to do' and होना **honā** 'to be'. This is a very productive process which allows Hindi to take nouns from languages such as Sanskrit and Persian and turn them into verbs. English has not been spared either. So you can take English nouns such as the following and turn them into verbs:

English noun	*Hindi verb*	*Complex verb*		
report	**karnā** करना	रिपोर्ट करना	report	**karnā** 'to report'
telephone	**karnā** करना	टेलीफोन करना	telephone	**karnā** 'to telephone'
pay	**karnā** करना	पे करना	pay	**karnā** 'to pay'
complain	**karnā** करना	कम्पलेन करना	complain	**karnā** 'to complain'

As a matter of fact, even English adjectives and verbs can be used to generate Hindi complex verbs:

English adjective/verb	*Hindi verb*	*Complex verb*	
better	**honā** होना	better	**honā** 'to recover'
choose	**karnā** करना	choose	**karnā** 'to choose'

This construction can be extremely useful in those situations where one fails to recall the Hindi verb. For example, if you fail to recall the Hindi verb पढ़ना **paR^{h}nā** 'to read/study', do not give up the idea: you can custom-make the verb **study karnā** from the English word 'study'. We will nickname Hindi anchor verbs such as **karnā** and **honā** 'transformer'.

The omission of 'to'

We pointed out earlier the use of the preposition in English in expressions such as 'I went to the other terminal.' In Hindi no postposition is used with the target; therefore, it is not appropriate to substitute Hindi को **ko** for English 'to'.

Approximation by compounding

एक–दो महीने में
ek-do mahīne mẽ
one-two month in
In one or two months.

दो–एक महीने में
do-ek mahīne mẽ
is also fine.

बातचीत **bātcīt Dialogue 3** (CD 2; 13)

ज्योतिषी के पास जाना ***jyotishi ke pās jānā*** ***Visiting an astrologer***

John Kearney has visited India several times and he loves Indian philosophy. The concept of reincarnation fascinates him, and therefore he never misses a chance to visit an astrologer or a fortune-teller. An international fair is being held in London. John visits the Indian pavilion and there he finds an astrologer and palmist. He shows the palmist his hand in order to learn about his past. The palmist looks at his hand and makes some general remarks about him, and finally asks about the purpose of John's visit.

जॉन	मैं अपने भूत के बारे में जानना चाहता हूँ।
JOHN:	mɛ apne bʰūt ke bāre mẽ jānnā cāhtā hū̃.
ज्योतिषी	अपने फ़रिश्ते के बारे में पूछिये, भूत के बारे में क्यों?
PALMIST:	apane farishte ke bāre mẽ pūcʰiye, bʰūt ke bāre mẽ kyõ?
जॉन	मेरा मतलब है कि पिछले जन्म के बारे में।
JOHN:	merā matlab hɛ ki picʰle janma ke bāre mẽ.
ज्योतिषी	पत्रे के बिना मुश्किल है।
PALMIST:	patre ke binā mushkil hɛ.
जॉन	तो मेरे बचपन के बारे में बताइये।
JOHN:	to mere bacpan ke bāre mẽ batāiye.
ज्योतिषी	ये लाइनें बताती हैं कि आपका बचपन बहुत अच्छा था . . . सुन्दर परिवार . . . बड़ा घर . . . ये ठीक है?
PALMIST:	ye lāinẽ batātī hɛ̃ ki āpkā bacpan bahut accʰā tʰā . . . sundar parivār . . . baRā gʰar . . . ye Tʰīk hɛ?
जॉन	जी हाँ, . . . लेकिन. . . .
JOHN:	jī hā̃, . . . lekin . . .
ज्योतिषी	लेकिन पिछले पाँच साल अच्छे नहीं थे।
PALMIST:	lekin picʰle pā̃c sāl accʰe nahī̃ tʰe.
जॉन	पिता जी के मरने के बाद परिवार पर बहुत मुश्किलें आईं।
JOHN:	pitā jī ke marne ke bād parivār par bahut mushkilẽ āyī̃.
ज्योतिषी	यह बड़े अफ़सोस की बात है।
PALMIST:	ye baRe afsos kī bāt hɛ.

JOHN:	*I want to know about my past/ghost.**
PALMIST:	*Please ask about your angels; why ask about (your) ghost?*
JOHN:	*I mean about my last birth.*
PALMIST:	*It is difficult (to tell) without the astrological chart.*

JOHN: *Then, tell me about my childhood.*

PALMIST: *These lines (on your hand) tell me that your childhood was very good . . . beautiful family . . . a big house . . . is this right?*

JOHN: *Yes, . . . but . . .*

PALMIST: *But (your) last five years were not good.*

JOHN: *After the death of (my) father, (our) family faced a lot of difficulties.* (lit. very many difficulties came on the family)

PALMIST: *I am sorry (to hear) this.* (lit. this is a matter of great sorrow)

(*The word **b^{h}ūt** is ambiguous. The palmist interprets it as 'ghost' just for fun.)

शब्दावली **shabdāvalī** **Vocabulary**

भूत	**b^{h}ūt** (m.)	ghost, past
फ़रिश्ता	**farishtā** (m.)	angel
पूछना	**pūc^{h}nā** (–ne)	to ask
पूछिये/पूछिए	**pūc^{h}iye**	please ask
मतलब	**matlab** (m.)	meaning
जन्म	**janma** (m.)	birth
पत्रा	**patrā** (m.)	astrological chart
के बिना	**(ke) binā**	without
मुश्किल	**mushkil** (f.)	difficult, difficulty
बचपन	**bacpan** (m.)	childhood
बताना	**batānā** (+ne)	to tell
बताइये/बताइए	**batāiye**	please tell
साल	**sāl** (m.)	year
मरना	**marnā** (–ne)	to die
के बाद	**(ke) bād**	after
आना	**ānā** (–ne)	to come
अफ़सोस	**afsos** (m.)	sorrow

Notes

Very frequent expressions: word-for-word translation

Consider how the following three very frequent English expressions are phrased in Hindi:

English	*Hindi*
1 I mean.	मेरा मतलब है। **merā matlab hɛ** my meaning is
2 I am glad to hear this.	ये ख़ुशी की बात है। **ye xushī kī bāt hɛ.** this happiness of matter (f.) is This is a matter of happiness.
3 I am sorry to hear this.	ये अफ़सोस की बात है। **ye afsos kī bāt hɛ.** this sorrow of matter (f.) is This is a matter of sorrow.

लाइनें **lāinẽ 'lines'**

आपकी लाइनें बताती हैं।
āpkī lāinẽ batātī hɛ̃.
you of lines tell are
Your lines tell (me).

Note that the English word 'line' takes the feminine gender in Hindi.

अभ्यास **ab^{h}yās Exercises**

Exercise 1

Rearrange the following words to make correct sentences in Hindi.

मेरे दोस्त, वे थे अच्छे कितने दिन! मैं सोचा ने वे रहेंगे दिन हमेशा। वे बचपन दिन के थे। मैं था हमेशा खेलता और नाचता था हर सुन्दर चीज़ थी। हर था दिन नया और हर रात अन्दाज़ का था। दिन वे अब नहीं रहे।

mere dost, ve t^{h}e acc^{h}e kitne din! mɛ̃ socā ne ve rahẽge din hameshā. ve bacpan din ke t^{h}e. mɛ̃ t^{h}ā hameshā k^{h}eltā aur nāctā t^{h}ā. har sundar cīz t^{h}ī. har t^{h}ā din nayā aur har rāt andāz kā t^{h}ā. din ve ab nahī̃ rahe.

Exercise 2

Underline the correct form of the subject and the verb in the following sentences. (Hint: the gender of the English word 'report' is feminine.):

1 (मैंने/मैं) वहाँ (गये/गयी)।
(mɛ̃ne/mɛ̃) vahā̃ (gaye/gayī).
2 (वह/उसने) मुझको (बताया/बताये)।
(vo/usne) muj^hko (batāyā/batāye).
3 (हम/हमने) घर (आया/आये)।
(ham/hamne) g^har (āyā/āye).
4 (तुम/तुमने) घर देर से (पहुँचे/पहुँचा)।
(tum/tumne) g^har der se (pahũce/pahũcā).
5 (वे/वेने /उन्होंने) पुलिस को रिपोर्ट (की/किया/किये)।
(ve/vene/unhõne) *police* ko *reporT* (kī/kiyā/kiye).
6 (आप/आपको/आपने) ये किताब कब (मिला/मिले/मिली)।
(āp/āpko/āpne) ye kitāb kab (milā/mile/milī).

Exercise 3

Activity: asking about your family histories

First talk about your family history making use of the cues to make questions. Use the same method to ask your friends or partners questions about their family.

Examples: परिवार/कहाँ से/आ **parivār** 'family'/**kahā̃ se/ā** 'come'
आपका परिवार कहाँ से आया?
āpkā parivār kahā̃ se āyā?

माता-पिता/जन्म/हो **mātā-pitā** 'mother-father'/**janma** 'birth'/**ho** 'be, happen'
आपके माता-पिता का जन्म कहाँ हुआ?
āp ke mātā- pitā kā janma kahā̃ huā?

Hint: use the English word for 'arranged marriage'.
The verb 'to be married' = marriage to take place/happen.
younger/older = small/big

1 parents/where/ born
2 parents/when/ born
3 rich or poor
4 marriage/when/happen
5 how old
6 arranged marriage /love marriage
7 mother younger than your father.

Exercise 4

Make questions from the following statements. The object of an inquiry is indicated by the underlined words in the statements:

Examples: शादी के बाद मेरे माता-पिता इंग्लैंड गये।
shādī ke bād mere mātā-pitā England gaye.

शादी के बाद मेरे माता-पिता कहाँ गये?
shādī ke bād mere mātā-pitā kahā̃ gaye?

मेरा परिवार दस साल पहले यहाँ आया।
merā parivār das sāl pɛhɛle yahā̃ āyā

आपका परिवार कितने साल पहले यहाँ आया?
āpkā parivār kitne sāl pɛhɛle yahā̃ āyā?

1 कल जॉन का जन्म दिन था।
kal John kā janma din tʰā.
2 जॉन कके परिवार ने एक पार्टी की।
John ke parivār ne ek party kī.
3 वो पार्टी शाम को हुई।
vo *party* shām ko huī.
4 जॉन को पार्टी के बारे में मालूम नहीं था?
John ko *party* ke bāre mẽ mālūm nahī̃ tʰā?
5 ये सरप्राइस पार्टी थी।
ye *surprise party* tʰī.
6 कल जॉन का जन्म दिन था।
kal John kā janma din tʰā.

Exercise 5: पुराना ज़माना purānā zamānā 'Old days' (CD 2; 15)

Indians, like most of us, have nostalgic feelings about the past. The past is good and glorious. But the present . . . If you have the recording, listen to the passage. After the beep, answer each statement either by saying सच **sac** (true) or झूठ **jʰūTʰ** (false).

Circle true (सच **sac**) or false (झूठ **jʰūTʰ**) for each statement:

1	आजकल लोग लव मैरिज करते हैं।	स (सच)	झू (झूठ)
	āj-kal log *love marrige* karte hɛ̃.	**s** (true)	**jʰ** (false)

2	पुराने ज़माने में आदमी घर में काम करते थे। purāne zamāne mẽ ādmī g^h^ar mẽ kām karte t^h^e.	स (सच) **s** (true)	झू (झूठ) **j^h^** (false)
3	आज-कल सिर्फ आदमी टीवी देखते हैं। āj-kal sirf ādmī TV dek^h^te hɛ̃.	स (सच) **s** (true)	झू (झूठ) **j^h^** (false)
4	आज-कल सिर्फ आदमी खाना बनाते हैं। āj-kal sirf ādmī k^h^ānā banāte hɛ̃.	स (सच) **s** (true)	झू (झूठ) **j^h^** (false)
5	पुराने ज़माने में परिवार अच्छा था। purāne zamāne mẽ parivār acc^h^ā t^h^ā.	स (सच) **s** (true)	झू (झूठ) **j^h^** (false)
6	पुराने ज़माने में टीवी नहीं था। purāne zamāne mẽ TV nahī̃ t^h^ā.	स (सच) **s** (true)	झू (झूठ) **j^h^** (false)
7	और आज-कल समय नहीं है। aur āj-kal samay nahī̃ hɛ.	स (सच) **s** (true)	झू (झूठ) **j^h^** (false)

Now write sentence corrections of the false statements.

7 क्या आप हिन्दी बोल सकते हैं? kyā āp hindī bol sakte hɛ̃?

Can you speak Hindi?

By the end of this unit you should be able to:

- talk about your skills
- give advice
- use obligatives
- form purpose clauses
- observe compound verbs
- use emphatic and persuasive forms

बातचीत **bātcīt Dialogue 1** (CD 2; 16)

क्या आप हिन्दी बोल सकते हैं? ***kyā āp hindī bol sakte hẽ? Can you speak Hindi?***

Vijay Mishra lives in Vancouver, Canada and he takes a bus from the University of British Columbia to downtown Vancouver. The bus is not crowded. He puts his money into the fare box slot. The bus driver, who is a white blue-eyed Canadian, utters something and Vijay Mishra understands it as 'downtown eh', and he replies 'yes' and sits down. As he settles down, he thinks that what he heard was not English but Hindi. A bit puzzled, he does not want to rule out that what he actually heard was the Hindi language. In fact, the driver had asked, 'downtown ***jānā hɛ****'. So Vijay Mishra asks:*

विजय: माफ कीजिये, आपने क्या कहा?
VIJAY: māf kījiye, āpne kayā kahā?
ड्राइवर: मैंने पूछा कि डाउनटाउन जाना है।
DRIVER: mẽne pūc^{h}ā ki *downtown* jānā hɛ.
विजय: अरे आप तो बहुत अच्छी हिन्दी बोल सकते हैं।
VIJAY: are! āp to bahut acc^{h}ī hindī bol sakte hẽ.
ड्राइवर: हाँ, थोड़ी-थोड़ी हिन्दी बोल लेता हूँ।
DRIVER: hā̃, t^{h}oRī t^{h}oRī hindī bol letā hū̃.
विजय: हिन्दी आपने कहाँ सीखी?
VIJAY: hindī āpne kahā̃ sīk^{h}ī?
ड्राइवर: दूसरी वर्ल्ड वार के समय मैं ब्रिटिश आर्मी में सैनिक था। उस समय हिन्दुस्तान में सीखी।
DRIVER: dūsrī *World War* ke samaya mẽ *British Army* mẽ sɛnik t^{h}ā. us samaya hindustān mẽ sīk^{h}ī.
विजय अभी भी अच्छी हिन्दी आती है।
VIJAY: ab^{h}ī b^{h}ī acc^{h}ī hindī ātī hɛ.
ड्राइवर: काफ़ी समय से योग और मैडीटेशन सीख रहा हूँ इसलिये हिन्दी नहीं भूली।
DRIVER: kāfī samaya se yoga aur *meditation* sīk^h rahā hū̃ isliye hindī nahī̃ b^{h}ūlī.
विजय ये तो बहुत अच्छा है, नहीं तो यहाँ हिन्दुस्तानी भी हिन्दी भूल जाते हैं।
VIJAY: ye to bahut acc^{h}ā hɛ nahī̃ to yahā̃ hindustānī b^{h}ī hindī b^{h}ūl jāte hẽ.
ड्राइवर: यह बात तो सच है।
DRIVER: ye bāt to sac hɛ.

VIJAY: *Excuse me, what did you say?*
DRIVER: *I asked if you need to go downtown.*

VIJAY: *Hey, you can speak Hindi very well.*
DRIVER: *Yes, (I) can speak a little Hindi.*
VIJAY: *Where did you learn Hindi?*
DRIVER: *At the time of World War II, I was a soldier in the British Army. During that time (I) learned (it) in India.*
VIJAY: *Even now you know Hindi well.*
DRIVER: *For a long time I have been learning yoga and meditation; therefore, (I) did not forgot Hindi.*
VIJAY: *This is very good; otherwise even Indians forget Hindi here.*
DRIVER: *This is true.*

शब्दावली **shabdāvalī Vocabulary**

तो	**to**	as regards (particle)
थोड़ा	**t^{h}oRā**	little, few
बोलना	**bolnā** (+/–**ne**)	to speak
बोल लेना	**bol lenā** (+**ne**)	to speak for one's benefit
बोल लेता हूँ	**bol letā hū̃**	(I can) speak
सीखना	**sīk^{h}nā** (+**ne**)	to learn
समय	**samaya** (m.)	time
सैनिक	**sɛnik** (m.)	soldier
अभी भी	**ab^{h}ī b^{h}ī**	even now
काफ़ी	**kāfī**	enough, sufficient
भूलना	**b^{h}ūlnā** (+/–**ne**)	to forget
नहीं तो	**nahī̃ to**	otherwise
यहाँ	**yahā̃**	here

Notes

Linguistic attitudes and hyper-politeness

The linguistic attitudes of Indians are very interesting. A foreigner with minimal linguistic competence (even limited to just a few words) in Indian languages will be showered with compliments such as 'you speak excellent Hindi' and 'you speak beautiful Hindi'. This is more of a welcome gesture than a faithful reflection of one's linguistic competence. So try to understand the main intention behind such compliments. Also, do not be quick to judge your complimenter with suspicion. They are not mocking your linguistic competence.

Formulaic expression: माफ़ कीजिये māf kījiye 'forgive me/excuse me'

The English expression 'excuse me' ('I beg your pardon' in British English) is ambiguous in a number of ways. We pointed out earlier, in Unit 2, that when the main function of 'excuse me' is to get attention, then it is paraphrased as 'please say' or 'please listen'. In this dialogue, Vijay did not hear the driver at first and then asked him to repeat his statement; this calls for an apology. Thus Vijay appropriately uses माफ़ कीजिये **māf kījiye**. The first part of the expression माफ़ **māf**, 'pardoned' is the short adjectival form of the noun माफ़ी **māfī** 'forgiveness', which is used with the verb करना **karnā** 'to do'. (Remember the 'transformer' verbs outlined in the last unit.) Thus, this expression is like other conjunct verbs you have encountered in earlier dialogues:

Noun	*Verb*
माफ़	करना
māf	karnā
पसन्द	करना
pasand	karnā
रिपोर्ट	करना
riporT	karnā

The polite imperative form of माफ़ करना **māf karnā** is माफ़ कीजिये **māf kījiye**. You guessed it right; the subject आप **āp** and the object मुझको **muj^{h}ko** 'me' are implied.

The internal obligative (one's inner need): मुझको जाना है muj^{h}ko jānā hɛ 'I need to go'

The Hindi counterpart of the English expression 'you need to go downtown' is

आपको	डाउनटाउन	जाना	है।
āpko	**downtown**	**jānā**	**hɛ**
you-to	downtown	to go	is

You need to go downtown.

The internal obligation is expressed by the infinitive form followed by the 'to be' verb form. The subject is always the experiencer subject with the को **ko** postposition. In the above sentence the 'to be' verb is in the present tense form. In short, the internal obligatives have the following structure:

subject	*infinitive verb*	*'to be' verb*
+ को **ko**	जाना **jānā**	है **hɛ** is था **t^hā** was होगा **hogā** will be

Examples: आपको डाउनटाउन जाना है।
āpko downtown jānā hɛ.
You need to go downtown.

आपको डाउनटाउन जाना था।
āpko downtown jānā t^hā.
You needed to go downtown.

आपको डाउनटाउन जाना होगा।
āpko downtown jānā hogā.
You will need to go downtown.

In the case of an intransitive verb, the verb always stays masculine singular. This is because the verb cannot agree with a subject because it has to be followed by the postposition को **ko** and there is no object to agree with either.

Three types of capabilitatives

In the dialogue, you will have noticed the three different ways of saying 'one can speak Hindi'. This is the first:

आप	हिन्दी	अच्छी	बोल	सकते	हैं।
āp	**hindī**	**acc^hī**	**bol**	**sakte**	**hɛ̃**
you	Hindi	good	speak	can-present	are

You can speak Hindi well.

Notice the placement of सकना **saknā** in the Hindi sentence. The subject is just plain nominative as in English. The verb agrees with the subject. It is सकना **saknā** which receives the tense conjugation and it is preceded by the plain stem form of the verb.

The second way is:

मैं	थोड़ी	थोड़ी	हिन्दी	बोल	लेता	हूँ।
mɛ̃	**t^{h}oRī**	**t^{h}oRī**	**hindī**	**bol**	**letā**	**hū̃.**
I	little	little	Hindi	speak	take-present	am

I can speak Hindi a little.

When one does not have native-like or full competence in a skill, this construction is used. In other words, this type of expression is used to express 'partial competence' and it usually has quantifiers such as थोड़ा **t^{h}oRā** 'a little/few' with it. Notice the clustering of the two verbs – **bol** बोल 'to speak' and लेना **lenā** 'to take'. It is the second verb which carries the tense/aspect form. These types of verb are called 'compound' verbs. We will discuss this class of verbs in detail later on. For the time being just memorize this expression.

The third way is like saying 'Hindi comes to you' as in

आपको	अभी	भी	हिन्दी	आती	है।
āpko	**ab^{h}ī**	**b^{h}ī**	**hindī**	**ātī**	**hɛ**
you-to	now	even	Hindi	come-present	is

You even now know Hindi, or You even now know (how to speak) Hindi. (lit. Hindi even now comes to you)

In this construction the verb is आना **ānā** 'to come' and the subject is an experiential/dative subject. Remember that dative subjects are marked with the postposition को **ko**. The verb agrees with 'Hindi', which is feminine singular. Unless otherwise modified with a quantifier denoting meagreness, this construction expresses 'full' or 'near complete' competence in a skill, to the extent that a skill comes to a person without any conscious effort.

This construction – 'Hindi comes to you' – is restricted to skills such as swimming, playing the sitar or any other musical instrument. It cannot be used in expressions such as 'I know John.'

Compare the following two sentences:

उसको	तैरना	आता	है।
usko	**tɛrnā**	**ātā**	**hɛ**
he/she-to	to swim	come-present	is

(S)he knows (how to) swim. (lit. Swimming/to swim comes to him/her)

The verb agrees with the infinitive form तैरना **tɛrnā** which is masculine singular.

मैं	जॉन	को	जानता	हूँ।
mɛ̃	**John**	**ko**	**jāntā**	**hū̃.**
I	John	object	know-present	am

I know John.

However, one cannot say 'John comes to me.'

Focus, emphasis and word order

In the dialogue, Vijay asks the driver

हिन्दी	आपने	कहाँ	सीखी?
hindī	**āpne**	**kahā̃**	**sīkʰī?**
Hindi	you agent	where	learned

Where did you learn Hindi?

Normal word order is as follows:

आपने	हिन्दी	कहाँ	सीखी?
āpne	**hindī**	**kahā̃**	**sīkʰī?**
you agent	Hindi	where	learned

Where did you learn Hindi?

Since Hindi is the subject of the discussion, 'Hindi', which is the object of the sentence, is moved to the beginning of the sentence. If you have the recording, you will hear a slight emphasis on the word, 'Hindi'. In other words, an element of a sentence can be pulled out of its normal place in a sentence and placed at its beginning to express focus or emphasis.

The particle तो to 'as regards'

We came across the use of तो **to** in the sense of 'then'. However, observe that in the following two examples तो **to** follows a constituent rather than appearing in the clause-initial position in a 'when–then' type of sentence.

आप	तो	बहुत	अच्छी	हिन्दी	बोल	सकते	हैं।
āp	**to**-particle	**bahut**	**accʰī**	**hindī**	**bol**	**sakte**	**hɛ̃.**
you	as regards	very	good	Hindi	speak	can-present	are

As regards you, you can speak very good Hindi.

ये	तो	बहुत	अच्छा	है।
ye	**to**-particle	**bahut**	**acc^{h}ā**	**hɛ**
this	as regards	very	good	is

As regards this, this is very good.

The particle तो **to** is another way of expressing emphasis but implies some sense of exclusion. The first sentence says ‘As regards you, you can speak very good Hindi’ and implies that ‘others (from your group) cannot speak very good Hindi’.

Compound verb भूल जाना b^{h}ūl jānā ‘to forget’

Observe another example of a compound verb in dialogue:

यहाँ	हिन्दुस्तानी	भी	हिन्दी	भूल	जाते	हैं।
yahā̃	**hindustānī**	**b^{h}ī**	**hindī**	**b^{h}ūl**	**jāte**	**hɛ̃.**
here	Indians	also	Hindi	forget	go-present	are

Here even Indians forget Hindi.

The two verbs are clustered together – भूल **b^{h}ūl** and जाना **jānā**. They share the chore of expressing meaning. भूल **b^{h}ūl**, the first verb, is in the form of a stem and conveys the main meaning, whereas जाना **jānā** carries the tense form but does not convey its literal meaning of ‘going’. As promised, we will detail this class of verb later. For the time being satisfy yourself with the ‘sharing’ nature of Hindi compound verbs.

बातचीत **bātcīt** **Dialogue 2** (CD 2; 18)

क्या आपको हिन्दी लिखनी आती है? ***kyā āpko hindī lik^{h}nī ātī hɛ? Can you write Hindi?***

Vijay and the driver continue to talk to each other. The topic of discussion continues to be the Hindi language.

विजय: क्या आपको हिन्दी लिखनी आती है?
VIJAY: kyā āpko hindī lik^{h}nī ātī hɛ?
ड्राइवर: ज़्यादा नहीं। आर्मी में कभी-कभी लिखनी पड़ती थी लेकिन अब कोई जरूरत नहीं।

DRIVER: zyādā nahī̃. *army* mẽ kab^{h}ī-kab^{h}ī lik^{h}nī paRtī t^{h}ī lekin ab koī zarūrat nahī̃.
विजय: हिन्दी में क्यों लिखना पड़ता था?
VIJAY: hindī mẽ kyõ lik^{h}nā paRtā t^{h}ā?
ड्राइवर: सन्देश कोड और सन्देशों के लिये – ख़ासकर यूरोप जाने वाले सन्देशों के लिये। डाउनटाउन में कुछ काम है?
DRIVER: *secret codes* aur sandeshõ ke liye – xāskar Europe jāne vāle sandeshõ ke liye. Downtown mẽ kuc^{h} kām hɛ?
विजय: बिजली का बिल देना था। आज फ़ुरसत मिली, तो सोचा कि ख़ुद वहाँ जाऊँ।
VIJAY: bijlī kā bill denā t^{h}ā. āj fursat milī, to socā ki xud vahā̃ jāū̃.
ड्राइवर: तो वह दफ़्तर आने वाला है ... असल में अगला स्टाप है।
DRIVER: to vo daftar āne vālā hɛ . . . asal mẽ aglā *stop* hɛ.
विजय: अच्छा, नमस्कार।
VIJAY: acc^{h}ā, namaskār.
ड्राइवर: नमस्कार।
DRIVER: namaskār.

VIJAY: *Do you know (how to) write Hindi?* (lit. does to write Hindi come to you?)
DRIVER: *Not much. In the army I had to write sometimes but now (there) is no need (to write in Hindi).*
VIJAY: *Why did (you) have to write in Hindi?*
DRIVER: *For secret codes and messages, especially for messages going to Europe. Do (you) have some work downtown?*
VIJAY: *(I) needed to pay the electric bill* (lit. I need to give the electricity bill). *Today (I) had (some) free time so I thought I would go myself* (i.e. in person).
DRIVER: *Then (in that case), that office is about to come up . . . in fact, (it) is the next stop.*
VIJAY: *Okay. Goodbye.*
DRIVER: *Bye.*

शब्दावली **shabdāvalī Vocabulary**

लिखना	**lik^{h}nā** (+ne)	to write
ज़्यादा	**zyādā** (invariable)	more
कभी	**kab^{h}ī**	ever
कभी-कभी	**kab^{h}ī-kab^{h}ī**	sometimes
पड़ना	**paRnā**	to fall, to lie down; in compound verbs 'to have to'
ज़रूरत	**zarūrat** (f.)	need, necessity
संदेश	**sandesh** (m.)	message

ख़ासकर	**xāskar**	especially, particularly
जाने वाले	**jāne vāle**	going
काम होना	**kām honā (+ko)**	to have work
बिजली	**bijlī** (f.)	electricity, lightning
फ़ुरसत	**fursat** (f.)	free time, spare time, leisure
ख़ुद	**xud**	oneself
जाना	**jānā (–ne)**	to go
जाऊँ	**jāū̃**	should go (subjunctive)
दफ़्तर	**daftar** (m.)	office
आने वाला	**āne vālā**	about to come
असल में	**asal mẽ**	in fact, in reality
अगला	**aglā** (m. adj.)	next

Notes

Variation: हिन्दी लिखनी आती है Hindi lik^{h}nī āti hɛ or हिन्दी लिखना आता है Hindi lik^{h}nā ātā hɛ

In the Standard-Hindi-speaking area, the verb and the preceding infinitive form agree with the object in number and gender, whereas in the Eastern-Hindi-speaking area both remain invariable, i.e. masculine singular.

Standard Hindi	*Eastern Hindi*
आपको हिन्दी लिखनी आती है। **āpko hindī** (f.) **lik^{h}nī ātī hɛ.** you know how to write Hindi.	आपको हिन्दी लिखना आता है। **āpko hindī lik^{h}nā ātā hɛ.** you know how to write Hindi.
आपको ख़त लिखने हैं। **āpko xat lik^{h}ne hɛ̃.** you-to letters to write are (m. pl.)	आपको ख़त लिखना है। **āpko xat lik^{h}nā hɛ.** you-to letters to write is (m. sg.)

However, the following sentence in our dialogue

बिजली	का	बिल	देना	था।
bijlī	**kā**	***bill***	**denā**	**t^{h}ā.**
electricity	of	bill (m. sg.)	to give	was

(I) needed to pay the electric bill.

remains the same in both dialects because in Standard Hindi the agreement is with ***bill*** which is masculine singular.

The external obligative (compulsion): मुझको जाना पड़ता है mujʰko jānā paRtā hɛ 'I have to go'

The only difference between the internal and the external obligative is that in the latter the infinitive is followed by the verb पड़ना **paRnā** 'to lie down' instead of the verb होना **honā** 'to be'. The external obligative expresses 'an external pressure/compulsion to do something' rather than 'one's own internal need to do something'. Compare the two types of obligatives:

Internal obligative (inner need)

आपको	हिन्दी	लिखनी	है।
āpko	**hindī**	**likʰnī**	**hɛ.**
you-to	Hindi (f. sg.)	write (f. sg.)	is

You need to write Hindi.

External obligative (compulsion)

आपको	हिन्दी	लिखनी	पड़ती	है।
āpko	**hindī**	**likʰnī**	**paRtī**	**hɛ.**
you-to	Hindi (f. sg.)	to write (f. sg.)	lie down (f. sg.)	is

You have to write Hindi.

In Eastern Hindi the infinitive and the verb form are in the masculine singular form, i.e. लिखना है **likʰnā hɛ** and लिखना पड़ता है **likʰnā paRtā hɛ**, respectively.

Now, take a look at the use of the external obligative in our dialogue:

आर्मी	में	कभी-कभी	लिखनी	पड़ती	थी।
army	**mẽ**	**kabʰī-kabʰī**	**likʰnī**	**paRtī**	**tʰī.**
Army	in	sometimes	to write (f. sg.)	lie down (f. sg.)	was

I had to write sometimes in the Army. (lit. I used to have to write sometimes in the Army)

The omitted subject मुझको **mujʰko** 'to me' is experiential and the object is Hindi. The tense form chosen is the past habitual. If the act of compelled writing was carried out only once, the verb पड़ना **paRnā** would have to be in the simple past form, i.e. पड़ी. **paRī** and the adverb कभी-कभी **kabʰī-kabʰī** would have to be dropped.

There is a striking similarity between the verb पड़ना **paRnā** 'to lie down' and पढ़ना **paRʰnā** 'to read/study'.

Negative-incorporated words: 'nobody', 'nowhere', 'never', etc.

Have a look at the Hindi expression 'now (I have) no need of Hindi writing':

अब	कोई	जरूरत	नहीं।
ab	**koī**	**zarūrat**	**nahī̃.**
now	some	need	not

Now (I have) no need.

Negative words such as 'nobody', 'nowhere', 'never' are simply derived from their positive Hindi counterparts and the negative particle नहीं **nahī̃** is placed in its original position, i.e. right before the verb.

कोई **koī**	someone	नहीं **nahī̃**	=	no one, nobody
कहीं **kahī̃**	somewhere	नहीं **nahī̃**	=	nowhere
कभी **kab^{h}ī**	ever	नहीं **nahī̃**	=	never

The immediate future: the वाला vālā construction

वाला **vālā** is quite notorious for the meaning it renders and the behaviour it exhibits. It has many facets. Here, we will examine the cases in which वाला **vālā** follows an infinitive verbal form and thus marks the 'immediate future' tense.

वह	दफ्तर	आने	वाला	है।
vo	**daftar**	**āne**	**vālā**	**hɛ**
that	office (m. sg.)	to come	about	is

That office is about to come up (i.e. the next stop is that office).

The many facets of वाला **vālā** become evident from the following two facts: (1) it acts like a postposition and exercises peer pressure on the preceding infinitive form, and consequently the infinitive form becomes oblique; and (2) it agrees with the subject in number and gender in the way that is typical of an adjective ending in **-ā**. Now, observe one more example of such usage:

गाड़ी	जाने	वाली	थी।
gāRī	**jāne**	**vālī**	**t^{h}ī.**
train (f. sg.)	to go	about (f. sg.)	was (f. sg.)

The train was about to go/leave.

It might be puzzling to see how वाला **vālā** can still be considered an example of the 'immediate future'. However, in this example, वाला **vālā** still renders the 'immediate future' with reference to the past. In short, the structure of the 'immediate future' construction in Hindi is as follows:

subject (nominative)	stem + ने **ne**	वाला **vālā**	verb 'to be'
		वाली **vālī**	
		वाले **vāle**	

The agentive वाला vālā construction

In comparison with the above examples, observe the position of वाला **vālā** in the following phrase. Here, its best literal translation is the English agentive suffix '-er'.

यूरोप	जाने	वाले	सन्देशों	के लिये
Europe	**jāne**	**vāle**	**sandeshõ**	**ke liye**
Europe	to go	-er	messages	for

For the Europe-going messages. (lit. for the Europe go-er messages)

Can you guess the meaning of the following the phrases?

खेलने वाला **k^helne vālā** and पढ़ने वाली **paR^hne vālī**

The meaning is 'player' and 'reader', respectively. In the former a masculine singular head (e.g. 'boy') is implied whereas the feminine singular head (e.g. 'girl') is implied in the latter.

The meaning of the वाला **vālā** phrase is often contextually governed. For example, the phrase

दिल्ली	वाला
dillī	**vālā**
Delhi	-er

means 'the person who lives in Delhi'. However, if the phrase is used in the context of a train or vehicle, it can mean either 'the train which goes/is going to Delhi' or 'a vehicle which is made in Delhi'.

Formulaic expressions: 'I have some work' and 'Are you free?'

क्या	आपको	डाउन टाउन	में	कुछ	काम	है?
kyā	**āpko**	***downtown***	**mẽ**	**kuc^h**	**kām**	**hɛ?**
what	you-to	downtown	in	some	work	is

Do you have some work downtown?

आज	मुझको	फुरसत	मिली।
āj	**muj^{h}ko**	**fursat**	**milī.**
today	me-to	free/spare time (f.)	got

Today I was free.

The English expressions such as 'I am busy' and 'I am free' are paraphrased as 'to me the work is' and 'to me the free/leisure/spare time is'. Similarly, the best way to ask 'Are you free?' is

आपको	फुरसत	है?
āpko	**fursat**	**hɛ?**

and 'are you busy?' is

आपको	काम	है?
āpko	**kām**	**hɛ?**

The subjunctive

The subjunctive expresses the idea of a possibility. Expressions with words such as 'perhaps' and suggestion (e.g. 'Shall we go?'), or permission (e.g. 'May I come in?') usually employ the subjunctive.

मैंने	सोचा	कि	खुद	वहाँ	जाऊँ।
mɛ̃ne	**socā**	**ki**	**xud**	**vahā̃**	**jāū̃**
I-agent	thought	that	self	there	go (subjunctive)

I thought that (I) myself would go there.

Verbs such as चाहना **cāhnā** 'to want', सोचना **socnā** 'to think' (which are called non-factive verbs) and जानना **jānnā** 'to know' (which belongs to the class of factive verbs) select a subjunctive verb form in their subordinate clause, i.e. जाऊँ **jāū̃**.

The subjunctives are very simple to form. The magic trick is to take any future form and just drop the future ending, i.e. गा **gā**, गे **ge** and गी **gī**. For instance, the corresponding subjunctive forms of हम मिलेंगे **ham milẽge** 'we will meet', तुम जाओगे **tum jāoge** 'you will go' and मैं जाऊँगी **mɛ̃ jāũgī** 'I will go' are: हम मिलें **ham milẽ** 'we shall meet', तुम जाओ **tum jāo** 'you would go', and मैं जाऊँ **mɛ̃ jāũ** (with rising intonation) 'may I go?', respectively.

The emphatic reflexive: ख़ुद xud 'oneself'

The emphatic pronoun ख़ुद **xud** is very similar to English emphatic pronouns, with the difference that the Hindi form ख़ुद **xud** remains invariable whereas the English emphatic pronouns vary according to their subject. In

मैंने	सोचा	कि	मैं	ख़ुद	वहाँ	जाऊँ ।
mɛ̃ne	**socā**	**ki**	**mɛ̃**	**xud**	**vahā̃**	**jāũ**

the emphatic form will always remain unchanged even if the subject of the (subordinate) clause changes.

बातचीत bātcīt Dialogue 3 (CD 2; 20)

मेरी तबीयत बहुत खराब है। merī tabīyat bahut xarāb hɛ I am very sick

Professor John Ryder is on his first research trip to rural India. He reached his village at the beginning of the Monsoon season. Although he took all precautions and vaccinations before leaving for India, he awakens one night with a high fever and diarrhoea. He calls Dr Naim's residence. Dr Naim's wife picks up the phone.

जॉन:	हैलो, क्या डा॰ नाइम हैं?
JOHN:	hello, kyā Dr. Naim hɛ̃?
नाइम की पत्नी:	जी नहीं, कोई ज़रूरी बात है?
NAIM'S WIFE:	jī nahī̃, koī zarūrī bāt hɛ?
जॉन:	मेरी तबीयत बहुत खराब है।
JOHN:	merī tabīyat bahut xarāb hɛ.
नाइम की पत्नी:	एक मरीज को देखने गये हैं।
NAIM'S WIFE:	ek marīz ko dek^{h}ne gaye hɛ̃.
जॉन:	कितनी देर में लौटेंगे?
JOHN:	kitnī der mẽ lauTẽge?

नाइम की पत्नी:	मेरे ख़्याल से जल्दी आ जायेंगे। मुझे अपना टैलिफ़ोन नम्बर और पता दे दीजिये। आते ही उन्हें भेज दूँगी।
NAIM'S WIFE:	mere xyāl se jaldī ā jāyẽge. muj^{h}e apnā Telīfon (*telephone*) *number* aur patā de dījiye. āte hī unhẽ b^{h}ej dū̃gī.
जॉन:	बहुत–बहुत धन्यवाद।
JOHN:	bahut-bahut d^{h}anyavād.

JOHN:	*Hello, is Dr Naim (there)?*
NAIM'S WIFE:	*No, is (there) something urgent?*
JOHN:	*(I) am very sick.* (lit. my condition/health is very bad)
NAIM'S WIFE:	*He went to see a patient.*
JOHN:	*When will he return?* (lit. in how much period of time will he return?)
NAIM'S WIFE:	*I think (he) will come (back) soon.* (lit. with my opinion [he] will come soon) *Please give me your phone number and address. As soon as (he) returns, (I) will send him (to your place).*
JOHN:	*Thanks a lot.*

शब्दावली **shabdāvalī Vocabulary**

ज़रूरी	**zarūrī**	important, urgent, necessary
तबीयत	**tabīyat** (f.)	health, disposition
ख़राब	**xarāb**	bad
मरीज़	**marīz** (m.)	patient
देर	**der** (f.)	delay, time (period of, slot of)
लौटना	**lauTanā** (–**ne**)	to return
लौटेंगे	**lauTẽge**	will return
ख़्याल	**xyāl** (m.)	opinion, thought
जल्दी	**jaldī**	quickly
आ जाना	**ā jānā** (–**ne**)	to come (compound verb)
आ जायेंगे	**ā jāyẽge**	will come (compound verb)
मुझे	**muj^{h}e**	to me
पता	**patā** (m.)	address
दे देना	**de denā** (+**ne**)	to give (compound verb)
दे दीजिये	**de dījiye**	please give (compound verb)
आते ही	**āte hī**	as soon as (he) comes
उन्हें	**unhẽ**	him (honorific)
भेजना	**b^{h}ejnā** (+**ne**)	to send
भेज देना	**b^{h}ej denā** (+**ne**)	to send (compound verb)
भेज दूँगी	**b^{h}ej dū̃gī**	will send (compound verb)
धन्यवाद	**d^{h}anyavād**	thanks

Notes

Variation

tabīyat can also be spelled with a short **i** (i.e. **tabiyat** तबियत).

Present and past perfective forms

वे	एक	मरीज़	को	देखने	गये	हैं।
ve	**ek**	**marīz**	**ko**	**dek^{h}ne**	**gaye**	**hɛ̃.**
he (hon.)	one	patient	obj.	to see (obl.)	gone	are

He went to see a patient. (lit. he has gone to see a patient)

क्या	आप	कभी	आगरा	गये	हैं?
kyā	**āp**	**kab^{h}ī**	**āgrā**	**gaye**	**hɛ̃?**
what	you	ever	Agra	went	are

Have you ever been (lit. gone) to Agra?

हाँ,	मैं	गया	हूँ।
hā̃,	**mɛ̃**	**gayā**	**hū̃.**
yes	I	went	am

Yes, I have been (there). (lit. Yes, I have gone there.)

हाँ,	दो	साल	पहले	मैं	गया	था।
hā̃,	**do**	**sāl**	**pɛhɛle**	**mɛ̃**	**gayā**	**t^{h}ā.**
yes	two	years	ago	I	went	was

Yes, two years ago I went (there). (lit. Yes, two years ago, I had gone (there).)

By adding the present forms (हूँ **hū̃** 'am', है **hɛ** 'is', हैं **hɛ̃** 'are' and हो **ho** 'are' (you)) and past forms (था **t^{h}ā** 'was', थे **t^{h}e** 'were', थी **t^{h}ī** 'was' and थीं **t^{h}ī̃** 'were') of the verb 'to be' to the perfective form, one can get present and past perfective forms, respectively. The present perfect indicates the completed action which has relevance for the present situation and the past perfective shows relevance to the past. That is why the present perfective and past perfective are called 'recent past' and 'remote past'. What is notable is that in the first sentence and the last sentence English will use the simple perfective form but Hindi will use the present and the past perfective, respectively. The past perfect in English is viewed with reference to an event in the past, as in 'When I was in Agra, he had already come.'

Compound verbs

We have already mentioned compound verbs in Hindi. Observe another example from our dialogue:

मेरे	ख़्याल	से	वे	जल्दी	आ	जायेंगे।
mere	**xyāl**	**se**	**ve**	**jaldī**	**ā**	**jāyẽge**
my	opinion	with	he (hon.)	soon	come	go-will

I think he will come (back) soon.

Note the two verbs आ **ā** 'come' and जा **jā** 'go' are clustered in the verb phrase. The meaning of the sentence is not merely an accumulative or conjunctive meaning rendered by the verbs. In other words, the sentence does not mean 'he will come and go'. On the contrary, the action of coming is being described and the verb जाना **jānā** 'to go' is only a responsible carrier of the tense information. It also loses its literal meaning and adds some related but new overtone or emphasis to the first verb. In the case of capabilitative construction with सकना **saknā**, the helping verb adds a clear (literal) meaning; however, as you will see below, this is usually not the case with helping verbs such as आना **ānā** and जाना **jānā**.

You can view compound verbs as people married to each other or romantically in love with one another, with both willing to cooperate to the extent of being dependent on each other in some ways. The compound verb

आ	जायेंगे।
ā	**jāyẽge**

is composed of two units: (1) the main verb आ **ā** 'come', which is in its stem form and is totally dependent on the second unit, i.e. (2) the helping verb – जा **jā** 'go' – for tense information. In addition to supplying tense information, the other roles played by the helping verb are described below:

जाना **jānā** as a helping verb

As we already know, the literal meaning of **jānā** जाना is 'to go'. As a helping verb, it refers to the 'transformation of a state or action, completeness or finality'.

Simple verbs			*Compound verbs*		
आना	**ānā**	to come	आ जाना	**ā jānā**	to come back, arrive
खाना	**k^{h}ānā**	to eat	खा जाना	**k^{h}ā jānā**	to eat up
पीना	**pīnā**	to drink	पी जाना	**pī jānā**	to drink up
समझना	**samaj^{h}nā**	to understand	समझ जाना	**samaj^{h} jānā**	to understand fully
होना	**honā**	to be	हो जाना	**ho jānā**	to become
भूलना	**b^{h}ūlnā**	to forget	भूल जाना	**b^{h}ūl jānā**	to forget completely

देना **denā** as a helping verb

The literal meaning of देना **denā** is 'to give'. When one gives something, the beneficiary of the action is someone other than the subject. That is exactly what is added to the main verb by the helping verb देना **denā**, i.e. to do an action for others. In Dialogue 3, the doctor's wife first asks for John's address and telephone number. The expression she uses is as follows:

मुझे अपना टेलीफोन नम्बर और पता दे दीजिये।
muj^{h}e apnā *telephone number* aur patā de dījiye.
Give me your telephone number and address.

She then says:

आते ही उन्हें भेज दूँगी।
āte hī unhẽ b^{h}ej dū̃gī.
As soon as he comes, I will send him.

The compound verbs दे देना **de denā** and भेज देना **b^{h}ej denā** are used to highlight the beneficiary of the actions. The simple corresponding verbs देना **denā** 'to give' and भेजना **b^{h}ejnā** 'to send' are unable to emphasize the beneficiary. In the first sentence, the direct beneficiary of the action is the wife herself and in the second sentence John is the beneficiary of the wife's action of sending Dr Naim to his house.

लेना **lenā** as a helping verb

The verb लेना **lenā** means 'to take'. You can now predict its meaning as a helping verb. It conveys 'doing for oneself', i.e. for the benefit of the subject. For example, in answer to the request for the telephone number and address, John could have answered as follows:

अच्छा लिख लीजिए।
acc^{h}ā, lik^h līјiye
OK write take-imp.
Please, write (it) down for your benefit.

The compound verb लिख लेना **lik^h lenā** stresses that Dr Naim's wife is the direct beneficiary of the action of writing down the address and telephone number.

In the previous dialogue, we saw the other meaning (i.e. partial competence) of लेना **lenā** when used as a helping verb with skill verbs.

-ते ही -te hī 'as soon as'

The addition of -ते ही **-te hī** to the verbal stem renders the meaning of 'as soon as', as in

आते ही	उन्हें	भेज	दूँगी।
āte hī	**unhẽ**	**b^{h}ej**	**dū̃gī.**
come-as soon as	him (hon.)	send	give-will

(I) will send him as soon as (he) comes (back).

The pitfalls:

'I think'

Compare and contrast the Hindi phrase with its English translation.

मेरे ख्याल से **mere xyāl se . . .** I think . . .

The Hindi equivalent is either मेरे ख्याल से **mere xyāl se** 'with my opinion' or मेरे ख्याल में **mere xyāl mẽ** 'in my opinion'. The Hindi verb सोचना **socnā** 'to think' is not acceptable in this context, as in the following sentence:

मैं	सोचता	हूँ।
mẽ	**soctā**	**hū̃**
I	think-present	am

The English verb 'to think' is ambiguous: (1) it refers to the process of thinking, as in 'I will think of something', and (2) it expresses an opinion, as in 'I think he is a nice man.' In the latter sense, it is paraphrased as 'In my opinion he is a nice man.' The failure to distinguish between the two types of 'think' is the most common source of errors on the part of English learners of Hindi as a second language.

Compound verbs

Failure to understand the shades in meaning conveyed by compound verbs can take a toll on communication. For example, if a student goes to a professor and requests a letter of recommendation, it makes a significant difference whether the student uses

recommendation letter	लिखिये	**likʰiye**
recommendation letter	लिख दीजिये	**likʰ dījiye**
recommendation letter	लिख लीजिये	**likʰ lījiye**

Even though the polite forms are used in all three expressions, the only appropriate choice is the second. The first and last have the potential to offend the professor. The first is polite, but still a command, and the last claims the professor to be the direct beneficiary of the act of writing a letter of recommendation.

Similarly, be gentle and sensitive with the use of obligatives and capabilitatives.

Coping skills

If you are unsure which form to use, compound or simple verb, the best thing you can do is to spell out the beneficiary मेरे लिए **mere liye** 'for me' with simple verbs. By doing this, you cannot totally eliminate the ill-effects of making a bad choice, but you can reduce the damage considerably.

अभ्यास abʰyās Exercises

Exercise 1

Underline the appropriate choice of subject in the following sentences and then translate the sentences into English:

1 (मैं/मुझको/मैंने) सितार आती है।
(mɛ̃/mujʰko/mɛ̃ne) sitār ātī hɛ.
2 क्या (आप/आपको/आपने) तैर सकते हैं?
kyā (āp/āpko/āpne) tɛr sakte hɛ̃?

3 (उसको/वह/उसने) कहाँ जाना है?
(usko/vo/usne) kahā̃ jānā hɛ?
4 (वे/उन्होंने/उनको) संगीत कब सीखा?
(ve/unhõne/unko) saŋgīt kab sīk^{h}ā?
5 वह सेल्समैन है। (उसको/उसने/वहे) बाहर जाना पड़ता है।
vo *salesman* hɛ. (usko/usne/vo) bāhar jānā paRtā hɛ.
6 जॉन को बहुत काम है। इसलिए (वे/उसको/उसने) कुछ फुरसत नहीं है।
John ko bahut kām hɛ. isliye (ve/usko/usne) kuc^h fursat nahī̃ hɛ.

Exercise 2

Complete the following sentences by supplying the missing parts of the verb:

1 बिल को जल्दी है क्योंकि उसकी गाड़ी दस मिनट में जा ____ ________ है।
Bill ko jaldī hɛ kyõki uskī gāRī das minute mẽ jā ___ ____ hɛ.
2 ड्राइवर जल्दी करो, मेरे दोस्त की फ़्लाइट आ ___ ___ है।
Driver jaldī karo, mere dost kī *flight* ā ____ ___ hɛ.
3 सर्दी का मौसम था, जल्दी बर्फ गिर ___ ____ थी।
sardī kā mausam t^{h}ā, jaldī barf gir ___ ____ t^{h}ī.
4 पार्टी के लिए मेहमान पहुँच ____ ______ हैं।
party ke liye mɛhmān pahũc ______ ________ hɛ̃.
5 शाम का समय था, अंधेरा हो ____ ______ था।
shām kā samay t^{h}ā, and^{h}erā ho ___ ______ t^{h}ā.
6 आप कभी हिन्दुस्तान ग __ हैं।
āp kab^{h}ī hindustān ga __ hɛ̃.

Exercise 3

Match the duties given on the left with the professions given on the right:

1	अध्यापक ad^{h}yāpak	उसको कार चलानी है। usko kār calānī hɛ.
2	डॉक्टर *doctor*	उसको कपड़े धोने हैं। usko kapRe d^{h}one hɛ̃.
3	गायक gāyak	उसको पढ़ाना है। usko paR^{h}ānā hɛ.
4	ड्राइवर *driver*	उसको लिखना है। usko lik^{h}nā hɛ.
5	धोबी d^{h}obī	उसको मरीज को देखना है। usko marīz ko dek^{h}nā hɛ.

6 लेखक उसको गाना है।
lek^{h}ak usko gānā hɛ.

Exercise 4

Underline the appropriate helping verb(s) in the following sentences:

1 क्या आप मेरे लिए *रिकोमैंडेशन लैटर* लिख लेंगे/देंगे?
kyā āp mere liye *recommendation letter* lik^{h} (lẽge/dẽge)?
2 रात आयी और अंधेरा हो (गया/आया) था।
rāt āyī aur and^{h}erā ho (gayā/āyā) t^{h}ā.
3 मैं हिन्दी नहीं पढ़ सकता, आप ये खत पढ़ (लीजिये/दीजिये)
mɛ̃ hindī nahī̃ paR^{h} saktā, āp ye xat paR^{h} (lījiye/dījiye).
4 वो थोड़ा थोड़ा तैर (सकता/लेता/आता) है।
vo t^{h}oRā t^{h}oRā tɛr (saktā/letā/ātā) hɛ.
5 उसको बहुत अच्छा नाचना (सकता/लेता/आता) है।
usko bahut acc^{h}ā nācnā (saktā/letā/ātā) hɛ.
6 मैं आपकी बात बिल्कुल भूल (आया/गया)।
mɛ̃ āpkī bāt bilkul b^{h}ūl (āyā/gayā).

Exercise 5

Write five sentences about the things you hated but had to do during your childhood. The following sentence can serve as a model for your answers.

बचपन	में	मुझे	पालक	खानी	पड़ती	थी।
bacpan	**mẽ**	**muj^{h}e**	**pālak**	**k^{h}ānī**	**paRtī**	**t^{h}ī.**
childhood	in	to me	spinach (f.)	eat-to	lay-present	was

During childhood, I had (lit. used) to eat spinach.

Exercise 6 (CD 2; 22)

If you have the recording, listen to the recorded passage. After the beep, answer each statement either by saying सच **sac** (true) or झूठ **j^{h}ūT^{h}** (false).

Now circle either सच **sac** (true) or झूठ **j^{h}ūTh** (false) for each statement.

1 सोमवार को मैंने काम किया।	स (सच)	झू (झूठ)
somvār ko mɛ̃ ne kām kiyā.	**s** (true)	**j^{h}** (false)
2 मंगलवार को मैं अपने दोस्त से मिला।	स (सच)	झू (झूठ)
maŋgalvār ko mɛ̃ apne dostõ se milā.	**s** (true)	**j^{h}** (false)

3 बुधवार को घर से बाहर नहीं गया। स (सच) झू (झूठ)
bud^{h}vār ko g^{h}ar se bāhar nahī̃ gayā. **s** (true) **j^h** (false)
4 गुरुवार को लन्दन में ही रहा। स (सच) झू (झूठ)
guruvār ko Londan mẽ hī rahā. **s** (true) **j^h** (false)
5 शुक्रवार को मेरी तबीयत ठीक नहीं थी। स (सच) झू (झूठ)
shukravār ko merī tabīyat T^{h}īk nahī̃ t^{h}ī. **s** (true) **j^h** (false)
6 शनिवार को मैंने काम किया। स (सच) झू (झूठ)
shanivār ko mẽne kām kiyā. **s** (true) **j^h** (false)
7 रविवार को मैंने आराम किया। स (सच) झू (झूठ)
ravivār ko mẽne ārām kiyā. **s** (true) **j^h** (false)

8 मुझे चैक कैश करवाने हैं।

muj^{h}e *cheque cash* karvāne hɛ̃

I need to get cheques cashed

By the end of this unit you should be able to:

- understand causatives
- use the present participial forms
- understand more about compound verbs, subjunctives and obligatives
- understand about auxiliary verb deletion with negation
- use conditionals
- highlight contrast
- persuade someone
- advise and caution someone

बातचीत **bātcīt Dialogue 1** (CD 2; 23)

कुछ परहेज़ कीजिये ***kuc^h parhez kījiye Be careful what you eat***

Finally, Dr Naim reaches John Ryder's house. It is about eleven o'clock at night. Indian doctors still make house calls!

जॉन: आदाब अर्ज, डाक्टर नाइम।
JOHN: ādād arz, Dr Naim.
डॉक्टर: आदाब, रायडर साहिब। इस बार कई साल के बाद मुलाकत हुई।
DR NAIM: ādāb, Ryder sāhib. is bār kaī sāl ke bād mulākāt huī.
जॉन: जी हाँ, कोई पाँच साल बाद।
JOHN: jī hā̃, koī pā̃c sāl bād.
डॉक्टर: तशरीफ रखिए . . . अच्छा, पहले बताइये, तबीयत कैसी है?
DR NAIM: tashrīf rak^{h}iye . . . acc^{h}ā, pɛhle batāiye, tabīyat kɛsī hɛ?
जॉन: तबीयत तो अच्छी नहीं, नहीं तो इतनी रात को आपको तकलीफ़ न देता।
JOHN: tabīyat to acc^{h}ī nahī̃, nahī̃ to itnī rāt ko āpko taklīf na detā.
डॉक्टर: तकलीफ की बात क्या है? ये तो मेरा फर्ज़ है। ख़ैर बुख़ार कितना है?
DR NAIM: taklīf kī bāt kyā hɛ? ye to merā farz hɛ. xɛr, buxār kitnā hɛ?
जॉन: जब एक घंटे पहले मैंने थर्मामीटर लगाया, तो एक सौ दो डिग्री था अब शायद कुछ ज़्यादा हो।
JOHN: jab ek g^{h}anTe pɛhle mɛ̃ne *t^{h}ermometer* lagāyā, to ek sau do *degree* t^{h}ā ab shāyad kuc^h zyādā ho.
डॉक्टर: अच्छा, जरा फिर थर्मामीटर लगाइये।
DR NAIM: acc^{h}ā, zarā p^{h}ir *t^{h}ermometer* lagāiye.
(Dr Naim takes John's pulse and temperature)
डॉक्टर: बुखार थोड़ा बढ़ गया है। दस्त भी हैं?
DR NAIM: buxār t^{h}oRā baR gayā hɛ. dast b^{h}ī hɛ̃?
जॉन: जी हाँ, दो घंटे में सात-आठ बार बाथरूम गया।
JOHN: jī hā̃, do g^{h}anTe mẽ sāt-āT^h bār bathroom gayā.
डॉक्टर: पिछली बार आपने बहुत समोसे खाये थे, और इस बार?
DR NAIM: pic^{h}lī bār āpne bahut samose k^{h}āye t^{h}e, aur is bār?
जॉन: शाम को कुछ आम खाये।
JOHN: shām ko kuc^h ām k^{h}āye.
डॉक्टर: मेरी सलाह मानिये . . . एक-दो महीने तक आप कुछ परहेज़ कीजिये, समोसे और आम बन्द । मैं एक टीका लगाता हूँ और यह दवाई लीजिये। दो गोलियाँ हर दो घंटे । तो कल सुबह अपनी तबीयत के बारे में बताइये । अच्छा, अब आराम कीजिये । मैं आपके टेलीफोन का इंतज़ार करूँगा । खुदा हाफ़िज़।

DR NAIM: merī salāh māniye . . . ek-do mahīne tak āp kuc^h parhez kījiye, samose aur ām banda. mɛ̃ ek Tīkā lagātā hū̃ aur ye davāī lījiye. do goliyā̃ har do g^hanTe. to kal subā apnī tabīyat ke bāre mẽ batāiye. acc^hā ab ārām kījiye. mɛ̃ āpke Telifon kā intzār karū̃gā. xudā hāfiz.

जॉन: बहुत बहुत शुक्रिया, डाक्टर साहिब, खुदा हाफ़िज़।

JOHN: bahut bahut shukriyā, Doctor sāhib, xudā hāfiz.

JOHN: *Greetings, Dr Naim.*

DR NAIM: *Greetings, Ryder sir, (we) meet again after several years.*

JOHN: *Yes, after about five years.*

DR NAIM: *Please be seated . . . OK. First, tell (me), how you are feeling?* (lit. how is (your) disposition?)

JOHN: *As regards my disposition, I am not feeling well; otherwise I would not have bothered you so late at night.*

DR NAIM: *Why talk about trouble. This is my duty. Well, how high is the fever?*

JOHN: *An hour ago when I took my temperature, it was one hundred and two degrees. Now it might be slightly higher.*

DR NAIM: *Okay, again (let's) take (your) temperature.*

(Dr Naim takes John's pulse and temperature)

DR NAIM: *The fever has increased slightly; (do you) have diarrhoea too?*

JOHN: *Yes, (I) went to the bathroom about seven or eight times in the past two hours.*

DR NAIM: *The last time you ate many samosas and this time?*

JOHN: *In the evening (I) ate some mangoes.*

DR NAIM: *Please take my advice. For about one or two months exercise some caution* (lit. do some abstinence). *No more samosas and mangoes* (lit. samosas and mangoes closed). *I (will) give you an injection and (you) take this medicine Two pills every two hours. Then tell me tomorrow morning how you feel. I will wait for your call. Okay. Now get some rest. Goodbye.*

JOHN: *Many many thanks, doctor. Goodbye.*

शब्दावली **shabdāvalī Vocabulary**

आदाब	**ādāb** (m.)	salutation, greetings
अर्ज़	**arz** (f.)	request
इस बार	**is bār**	this time
साल	**sāl** (m.)	year

के बाद	**ke bād**	after
मुलाकात	**mulākāt** (f.)	meeting
मुलाकात होना	**mulākāt honā (–ne)**	to meet
तशरीफ़	**tashrīf** (f.)	(a term signifying respect)
तशरीफ़ रखना	**tashrīf rak^{h}nā** (+ne)	to be seated
तशरीफ़ लाना	**tashrīf lānā** (–ne)	to grace one's place, welcome, come
पहले	**pɛhle**	first
इतना	**itnā** (m. adj.)	so much/many, this much/many
रात	**rāt** (f.)	night
तकलीफ	**taklīf** (f.)	trouble, bother
तकलीफ़ देना	**taklīf denā** (+ne)	to bother
फ़र्ज़	**farz** (m.)	duty
लगाना	**lagānā** (+ne)	to fix, apply
शायद	**shāyad**	perhaps
बढ़ना	**baR^{h}nā** (–ne)	to increase, advance
दस्त	**dasta** (m.)	diarrhoea
आम	**ām**	mango; as adj. common, general
सलाह	**salāh** (f.)	advice
सलाह मानना	**salāh mānnā** (+ne)	to accept/take advice
सलाह लेना	**salāh lenā** (+ne)	to seek/take advice
महीना	**mahīnā** (m.)	month
परहेज़	**parhez** (m.)	abstinence
x से परहेज़ करना	**x se parhez karnā** (+ne)	to abstain, avoid
बन्द	**banda**	to be closed
बन्द करना	**banda karnā** (+ne)	closed
बन्द होना	**banda honā** (–ne)	to close
टीका लगाना	**Tīkā lagānā** (+ne)	to give an injection/a shot
दवाई /दवा	**davāī/davā** (f.)	medicine
गोली	**golī** (f.)	tablet, pill; bullet
इंतज़ार	**intzār** (m./f.)	wait
x (का/की) इंतज़ार करना	**x (kā/kī) intzār karnā** (+ne)	to wait for x
आराम	**ārām** (m.)	comfort, rest
आराम करना	**ārām karnā** (+ne)	to rest
खुदा हाफ़िज़	**xudā hāfiz**	goodbye

Notes

'We meet again after several years'

Another way of saying 'we meet again after several years' in Hindi is something like 'our meeting took place after several years'.

कई	साल	(के) बाद	हमारी	मुलाकात	हुई।
kaī	**sāl**	**(ke) bād**	**hamārī**	**mulākāt**	**huī.**
several	years	after	our	meeting (f.)	happened.

The politeness bug

Note the use of तशरीफ रखिए **tashrīf rak^{h}iye** instead of बैठिए **bɛT^{h}iye** 'please sit'. As in English, when receiving a guest, we will usually say 'Please have a seat', or 'Please be seated', rather than 'please sit'. Similarly, it is more polite and much friendlier to use तशरीफ रखिए **tashrīf rak^{h}iye** than बैठिए **bɛT^{h}iye**, particularly if the listener is a Muslim. In English if the verb 'sit' is used, it is modified in some form, e.g. 'Please sit down for a while'; the same is true of the Hindi verb बैठ **bɛT^h** 'sit'. If it is used, it needs to precede the polite form of the verb आ **ā** 'to come' (e.g. आइए, बैठिए **āiye, bɛT^{h}iye** 'Please come (and) sit') or be followed by a question tag (e.g. बैठिए न **bɛT^{h}iye na** 'Please sit down, won't you?').

x का इंतज़ार करना 'To wait for x'

The Hindi equivalent of the English 'I was waiting for you' turns out to be

मैं	आपका	इंतज़ार	कर	रहा	था।
mɛ̃	**āpkā**	**intzār**	**kar**	**rahā**	**t^{h}ā.**
I	your	wait (m.)	do	ing	was

i.e. I was doing your wait

The conditional: counter-factive

The Hindi sentence in our dialogue is as follows:

इतनी	रात	को	मैं	आपको	तकलीफ	न	देता।
itnī	**rāt**	**ko**	**mɛ̃**	**āp-ko**	**taklīf**	**na**	**detā.**
so much	night	at	I	you-to	bother	not	give-would have

The previous sentence is a part of the 'if' clause which is implied.

अगर	तबीयत	ठीक	होती	तो . . .
agar	**tabīyat**	**T^{h}īk**	**hotī**	**to** . . .
if	disposition	fine	were	then . . .

If my condition were fine . . .

Note that the simple present form without the auxiliary verb is used in such counter-factive sentences. The 'if' clause implies that the condition has not been fulfilled; therefore, the action expressed by the 'then' clause did not take place. Consider another example of counter-factives:

अगर	वह	आता	तो	मैं	जाता।
agar	**vo**	**ātā,**	**to**	**mɛ̃**	**jātā**
if	he	come-pres.	then	I	go-pres.

If he had come, I would have come.

अगर	वह	किताबें	लिखती	तो	हम	बहुत	खुश	होते।
agar	**vo**	**kitābẽ**	**lik^{h}tī,**	**to**	**ham**	**bahut**	**xush**	**hote.**
if	she	books	write-present	then	we	very	happy	be-pres.

Had she written books, we would have been very happy.

Thus, the English verb forms such as 'had come' and 'would have gone' are translated, not as a past tense form, but with the present imperfective without an auxiliary verb.

Formulaic expression

The Hindi expression

तकलीफ	की	बात	क्या	है?
taklīf	**kī**	**bāt**	**kyā**	**hɛ**
bother	of	matter	what	is

is not a question sentence. It is equivalent to the English expressions 'do not bother' and 'do not mention'. Thus, the Hindi question word क्या **kyā** is like 'not' in the expression in question. The verb form is always in the simple present rather than in the imperative form as in English.

Negative particle: न na

We have already come across नहीं **nahĩ** 'not'. Another Hindi negative particle is न **na**, which occurs in constructions such as 'neither . . . nor', counter-factives and polite imperatives. (See the Grammar section for more details.)

The subjunctive

अब	बुखार	कुछ	ज्यादा	हो।
ab	**buxār**	**kuc**^{h}	**zyādā**	**ho**
now	fever (m.s.)	some	more	be-subjunctive

The fever might be slightly more.

Since the context is the probable increase in fever, the Hindi verb 'to be' is in the subjunctive form. The verb agrees with बुखार **buxār** 'fever'. Although the verb हो **ho** might appear to be in the simple present tense form, it is not because तुम **tum** is not the subject in the above sentence.

Compound verb with the helping verb: जाना jānā

In the expression

बुखार	थोड़ा	बढ़	गया	है।
buxār	**t**^{h}**oRā**	**baR**^{h}	**gayā**	**hɛ**
fever	little	increase	went	is

The fever has shot up a little.

the compound verb बढ़ जाना **baR**^{h} **jānā** is employed for the reasons explained in the previous unit.

मेरी सलाह मानिये meri salāh māniye 'Accept my advice'

Hindi paraphrases the English expression 'Take my advice' as 'Accept my advice'.

मेरी	सलाह	मानिये।
merī	**salāh**	**māniye.**
my	advice (f.)	accept-imperative

Please accept my advice.

The substitution of the verb लेना **lenā** 'take' produces an odd sentence in Hindi.

बातचीत **bātcīt Dialogue 2** (CD 2; 25)

दिल्ली में गुम जाना ***dillī mẽ gum jānā Lost in Delhi***

Philip Rosenberg is lost in downtown Delhi. He knows that somewhere in the vicinity there is an American Express office where he could cash some traveller's cheques. In fact, he visited that office just two days ago. He does not remember its address either. He inquires from a stranger about its location:

फ़िलिप: यहाँ पास कोई अमरीकन ऐक्सप्रैस का दफ़्तर है। मैं दो दिन पहले वहाँ गया था, लेकिन आज नहीं मिल रहा।
PHILIP: yahā̃ pās koī *American Express* kā daftar hɛ. mɛ̃ do din pɛhɛle vahā̃ gayā tʰā, lekin āj nahī̃ mil rahā.
अजनबी: आपको पता मालूम है?
STRANGER: āpko patā mālūm hɛ?
फ़िलिप: मैं पता तो भूल गया।
PHILIP: mɛ̃ patā to bʰūl gayā.
अजनबी: मेरे ख़्याल से अगली सड़क पर अमरीकन ऐक्सप्रैस का दफ़्तर है।
STRANGER: mere xyāl se aglī saRak par *Amercian Express* kā daftar hɛ.
(pointing to the street)
फ़िलिप: (*seemingly puzzled*) वह सड़क तो सुन्दर है, लोग उसे अगली सड़क क्यों कहते हैं?
PHILIP: (*seemingly puzzled*) vo saRak to sundar hɛ, log use aglī saRak kyõ kɛhte hɛ̃?
अजनबी: अगली हिन्दी का शब्द है अंग्रेजी का नहीं। 'अगली' का मतलब अंग्रेज़ी में 'next' है।
STRANGER: aglī hindī kā shadba hɛ angrezī kā nahī̃. 'aglī' kā matlab angrezī mẽ 'next' hɛ.
फ़िलिप: बहुत ख़ूब।
PHILIP: bahut xūb.
(Philip goes to the cashier's window at the American Express office)
फ़िलिप: मुझे कुछ ट्रैवलरज़ चैक कैश करवाने हैं।
PHILIP: mujʰe kucʰ *traveller's cheque cash* karvāne hɛ̃.
कैशियर: कौन-सी करन्सी में हैं?
CASHIER: kaun sī *currency* mẽ hɛ̃?

फ़िलिप: अमेरिकन डालर। ऐक्सचेंज रेट क्या है?
PHILIP: amrīkan *dollars. Exchange rate* kyā hɛ?
कैशियर: एक अमेरिकन डालर चालीस रूपये का है।
CASHIER: ek amrīkan dollar cālīs rupaye kā hɛ.
(Philip signs the cheques and the cashier gives him the equivalent amount in rupees)
कैशियर: कुल दो सौ डालरज़। ये रहे आप के आठ हज़ार रूपये। गिन लीजिये।
CASHIER: kul do sau *dollars*. ye rahe āpke āT^h hazār rupaye. gin lījiye.
फ़िलिप: ठीक है। धन्यवाद।
PHILIP: T^hīk hɛ. d^hanyavād.

PHILIP: *(There) is an American Express office nearby. Two days ago I went there. But today I cannot find (it).*
STRANGER: *Do you know the address?*
PHILIP: *I forgot the address.*
STRANGER: *I think the American Express office is on the next* (i.e. **aglī**) *street.*
(pointing to the street)
PHILIP: (Seemingly puzzled) *That street is a beautiful one. Why do people call it 'ugly'?*
STRANGER: *'aglī' is a Hindi word, not English. In English the meaning of 'aglī' is 'next'.*
PHILIP: *(That's) great!*
(Philip goes to the cashier's window at the American Express office)
PHILIP: *I need to get some traveller's cheques cashed.*
CASHIER: *In which currency are they?*
PHILIP: *In American dollars. What is the exchange rate?*
CASHIER: *One American dollar to forty rupees.*
(Philip signs the cheques and the cashier gives him the equivalent amount in rupees.)
CASHIER: *A total of two hundred dollars. Here are your eight thousand rupees. Please count it (for your own sake).*
PHILIP: *That's fine* (lit. they are fine). *Thanks.*

शब्दावली **shabdāvalī Vocabulary**

दफ़्तर	**daftar** (m.)	office
मिलना	**milnā (+ko)**	to find, to receive
अगला	**aglā** (m. adj.)	next
शब्द	**shabda** (m.)	word

अंग्रेज़ी	**angrezī** (f.)	the English language
अंग्रेज़	**angrez** (m.)	an English man
मतलब	**matlab** (m.)	meaning
बहुत ख़ूब	**bahut xūb**	great! splendid!
कैश करना	***cash* karnā** (+**ne**)	to cash
कैश करवाना	***cash* karvānā**	to get someone to cash (+**ne**)
कुल	**kul**	total
सौ	**sau**	hundred
रहना	**<rɛhnā>**	to live
रहे	**rahe**	lived, are
हज़ार	**hazār**	thousand
गिनना	**ginnā** (+**ne**)	to count
गिन लेना	**gin lenā** (+**ne**)	to count (for one's benefit)
धन्यवाद	**d^{h}anyavād**	thanks

Notes

नहीं मिल रहा milnā 'I cannot find it'

In the preceding units we came across three important usages of the verb मिलना **milnā** – namely 'to meet', 'to run into' and 'to be available'. Now observe another use of this verb in the following sentence from the dialogue. Also, note its word-for-word translation.

लेकिन	आज	नहीं	मिल	रहा।
lekin	**āj**	**nahī̃**	**mil**	**rahā.**
but	today	not	find	ing

But today (I) cannot find (it). (lit. but today I am not finding it)

When the verb मिलना **milnā** is used to express the meaning 'find', it takes the experiencer subject. If we insert the implied subject in the above sentence, the form of the Hindi subject will not be the nominative मैं **mɛ̃**, but the experiential subject मुझको **muj^{h}ko** or मुझे **muj^{h}e**.

लेकिन	आज	मुझे	दफ्तर	नहीं	मिल	रहा।
lekin	**āj**	**mujhe**	**daftar** (m.)	**nahī̃**	**mil**	**rahā.**

Note that the verb does not agree with the subject. Instead it agrees with an object, which is दफ्तर **daftar** 'office' in the above sentence. The gender of दफ्तर **daftar** is masculine. Did you notice the missing element of the verb phrase?

Negation and auxiliary verb deletion

Notice the missing element of the verb in the above sentence.

लेकिन	आज	मुझे	दफ्तर	नहीं	मिल	रहा	है।
lekin	**āj**	**muj^he**	**daftar**	**nahī̃**	**mil**	**rahā**	**hɛ.**

The auxiliary verb है **hɛ** can be optionally deleted in negative sentences. Only the auxiliary verbs of the simple present and present progressive tenses are subject to this optional deletion. Note some examples:

Positive sentences	*Negative sentences*
मैं जाता हूँ। **mɛ̃ jātā hū̃** I go	मैं नहीं जाता हूँ। **mɛ̃ nahī̃ jātā hū̃** I do not go मैं नहीं जाता। **mɛ̃ nahī̃ jātā** I do not go
मैं जा रहा हूँ। **mɛ̃ jā rahā hū̃** I am going	मैं नहीं जा रहा हूँ। **mɛ̃ nahī̃ jā rahā hū̃** I am not going मैं नहीं जा रहा। **mɛ̃ nahī̃ jā rahā** I am not going
तुम जाती हो। **tum jātī ho** you (f.) go	तुम नहीं जाती हो। **tum nahī̃ jātī ho** you (f.) do not go तुम नहीं जाती। **tum nahī̃ jātī** you (f.) do not go
तुम जा रही हो। **tum jā rahī ho** you (f.) are going	तुम नहीं जा रही हो। **tum nahī̃ jā rahī ho** you (f.) are not going तुम नहीं जा रही। **tum nahī̃ jā rahī** you (f.) are not going

Causative verbs

We came across the following related verbs in our earlier dialogues. Note the slight change in form and meaning.

Verb	*Causative-I*	*Causative-II*
पढ़ **paR^h** study, read	पढ़ा **paR^hā** teach	पढ़वा **paR^hvā** have someone teach
कर **kar** do	——	करवा **karvā** have someone do
लग **lag** seem	लगा **lagā** attach	लगवा **lagvā** cause to be attached

You might already have observed the same base stem in the three verb forms. For the time being, we will omit the more intricate details of verb forms – such as the presence of the two verbs of करना **karnā** but three forms of the other two verbs – and proceed to the fundamental points. At first glance it becomes clear that the verb forms in columns two and three share the verb stem in column one, adding either the suffix आ **ā** or वा **vā** as in

पढ़	+	आ	=	पढ़ा	
paR^{h}	+	ā	=	paR^{h}ā	cause someone to read, teach
पढ़	+	वा	=	पढ़वा	
paR^{h}	+	vā	=	paR^{h}vā	to have x to teach y

The two suffixes आ **-ā** and वा **-vā** form the causative verbs. The meaning they express can be translated as follows: आ **-ā** expresses 'make someone do something', whereas वा **-vā** means 'have x make y do something'. The English verb 'teach' is a causative verb in Hindi, but in most cases the causative verbs cannot be translated into English that easily. Note the following examples:

मैं	कहानी	पढ़ता	हूँ।
mẽ	**kahānī**	**paR^{h}tā**	**hū̃.**
I	story	read-pres.	am

I read a story.

मैं	जॉन	को	कहानी	पढ़ाता	हूँ।
mẽ	**John**	**ko**	**kahānī**	**paR^{h}ātā**	**hū̃**
I	John	to	story	read-caus. **ā**-pres.	am

I make John read a story *or* I teach John a story

मैं	जॉन	को	राम	से	कहानी	पढ़वाता	हूँ।
mẽ	**John**	**ko**	**Rām**	**se**	**kahānī**	**paR^{h}vātā**	**hū̃**
I	John	to	Ram	by	story	read-caus. **vā**-pres.	am

I have Ram make John read a story.

Notice that the causative verbs with वा **-vā** always have an indirect agent (e.g. राम से **Ram se** 'by Ram').

Did you notice the use of the causative verb in our dialogue? The following sentence contains a causative verb.

मुझे	कुछ	ट्रैवलस	चैक्स	कैश	करवाने	हैं।
muj^{h}e	**kuc^{h}**	***traveller's***	***cheques***	***cash***	**karvāne**	**hẽ.**
me	some	traveller's	cheques	cash	do-caus.**vā**-inf.	are

I need to (have someone) get some traveller's cheques cashed.

In this sentence the indirect agent (by someone) is implied because of the causative verb with the suffix वा **-vā**.

लेना **lenā** as a helping verb

When the cashier hands over the rupees to Philip, he says

गिन लीजिये
gin lījiye
count take-imp.
Please (you) count (for your own benefit).

Had he used the simple verb form instead of the compound verb (i.e. गिनिए **giniye**), the beneficiary of the action of counting would have remained unspecified. The helping verb ले **le** indicates the subject as the beneficiary.

पढ़ने का अभ्यास १ paR^{h}ne kā ab^{h}yās 1 Reading practice 1 (CD 2; 27)

एक लोक-कथा ek lok-kat^{h}ā A folk tale

1 एक गाँव में चोर जेल से भाग गया।
ek gā̃v mẽ ek cor jail se b^{h}āg gayā.
2 पुलिस वाला उसको पकड़ने के लिये दौड़ा।
pulis (police) vālā usko pakaRne ke liye dauRā.
3 इतने में गाँव वालों ने भागते चोर को पकड़ लिया।
itne mẽ gā̃v vālõ ne b^{h}āgte cor ko pakaR liyā.
4 पुलिस वाला ज़ोर ज़ोर से चिल्ला रहा था, 'पकड़ो, मत जाने दो।'
pulis vālā zor zor se cillā rahā t^{h}ā, 'pakRo, mat jāne do'.
5 ये सुनते ही गाँव वालों ने चोर को छोड़ दिया।
ye sunte hī gā̃v vālõ ne cor ko c^{h}oR diyā.
6 जब पुलिस वाला गाँव वालों के पास पहुँचा।
jab pulis vālā gā̃v vālõ ke pās pahũcā.
7 तो उसको बहुत गुस्सा आया।
to usko bahut gussā āyā.
8 गुस्से में उसने गाँव वालों से पूछा।
gusse mẽ usne gā̃v vālõ se pūc^{h}ā,
9 'तुमने चोर को क्यों छोड़ दिया?'
'tumne cor ko kyõ c^{h}oR diyā'
10 गाँव वालों ने जवाब दिया,
gā̃v vālõ ne javāb diyā,

11 आपने ही कहा 'पकड़ो मत, जाने दो।'
āpne hī kahā, 'pakRo mat, jāne do'.

1 *In a* (lit. one) *village, a thief ran away* (i.e. escaped) *from jail.*
2 *A policeman ran to catch him.* (lit. ran for catching)
3 *In the meanwhile the villagers caught the escaping* (lit. running) *thief.*
4 *The policeman was screaming very loudly, 'catch (him), do not let (him) go'.*
5 *As soon as the villagers heard this, they left the thief.*
6 *When the policeman reached the villagers* (lit. reached near the villagers)
7 *he became very angry.*
8 *Angrily* (lit. in anger) *he asked the villagers* (lit. asked from the villagers)
9 *'Why did you leave the thief?'* (i.e. why did you let the thief go?)
10 *The villagers answered.*
11 *You yourself said, 'Don't catch (him); let (him) go.'*

शब्दावली **shabdāvalī Vocabulary**

लोक	**lok**	people
कथा	**kat^{h}ā** (f.)	story
लोक-कथा	**lok-kat^{h}ā** (f.)	folk tale
गाँव	**gā̃v** (m.)	village
भागना	**b^{h}āgnā (–ne)**	to run
भाग गया	**b^{h}āg gayā** (compound verb)	to run away
पुलिस वाला	**pulis vālā** (m.)	policeman
पकड़ना	**pakaRnā (+ne)**	to catch
दौड़ना	**dauRnā (–ne)**	to run
इतने में	**itne mẽ**	in the meanwhile
गाँव वाला	**gā̃v vālā** (m.)	villager
भागते	**b^{h}āgte** (present participle)	running
चोर	**cor** (m.)	thief
पकड़ना	**pakaRnā (+ne)**	to catch
पकड़ लिया	**pakaR liyā** (compound verb)	to catch (for one's benefit)
ज़ोर से	**zor se**	loudly
चिल्लाना	**cillānā (–ne)**	to scream
मत	**mat**	not (see notes)
जाने दो	**jāne do** (compound verb)	let (someone) go
सुनते ही	**sunte hī (sun + te hī** participle)	as soon as (someone) heard
छोड़ना	**c^{h}oRnā (+ne)**	to leave

छोड़ दिया	**c^h^oR diyā** (compound verb)	left (for someone else's sake)
गुस्सा	**gussā** (m.)	anger
पूछना	**pūc^h^nā** (–**ne**)	to ask
जवाब	**javāb** (m.)	answer
जवाब देना	**javāb denā** (+**ne**)	to answer, to reply

Pronunciation

Compare the pronunciation of the stem पकड़ **pakaR** 'catch' in the following three verbal forms. Note the presence of the stem-final vowel अ **a** in the first two forms and its absence in the third form, which is written as पकड़ो **pakaRo** but is pronounced as पक्ड़ो **pakRo**. For further details about when the vowel अ **a** is retained and under what conditions it is dropped, see Script Unit 4 in this book.

pakaRne ke liye	पकड़ने के लिये	in order to catch
pakaR liyā	पकड़ लिया	caught (for their own benefit)
pakRo	पकड़ो	catch!

Notes

Present participle

In the third line we came across the expression

इतने	में	गाँव	वालों	ने	भागते	चोर	को
itne	**mẽ**	**gā̃v**	**vālõ**	**ne**	**b^h^āgte**	**cor**	**ko**
this much	in	village-er	(agent)		running	thief	to

पकड़	लिया।
pakaR	**liyā.**
catch	took

In the meantime (lit. in this much (time)), the villagers caught the thief.

The phrase **b^h^āgte cor ko** भागते चोर को is in the oblique form of the simple present participial phrase.

भागता	(हुआ)	चोर
b^h^āgtā	**(huā)**	**cor**
run + present participle	happened	thief (m. sg.)

The running thief *or* The thief who is/was/will be running.

The composition of the first element is as follows:

भाग	+	त	+	ा
b^{h}āg	+	**t**	+	**ā**
run	+	present	+	masculine singular

You have probably guessed by now that this is the same form that we came across in the formation of the simple present tense. The only difference is that the auxiliary verb is absent.

The second element is the same form as the simple past tense form of the verb होना **honā**. Recall the forms हुआ **huā**, हुए **hue**, हुई **huī** and हुईं **huī̃**. The last form (i.e. the feminine plural हुईं **huī̃**) does not appear in the participial construction. Why? The reason is clarified by the explanation that this element is optional and it acts as an adjective. So it can easily be omitted in conversation. That is the case in our story.

Now compare the participial form with the present tense verb form.

Present participle	*Simple present tense*
भागता चोर **b^{h}āgtā cor** The running thief.	चोर भागता है **cor b^{h}āgtā hɛ** The thief runs.

In the present participial form the verb form ceases to function like a real verb and begins to behave like an adjective. Therefore, the verbal adjectives which are drawn from the simple present tense are called 'present participles'. In other words, they are like adjectives ending in आ **-ā** (i.e. participial adjective), the only difference being that they are derived from verbs.

Like the adjectives ending in आ **-ā**, these agree in number or gender with the following noun. For example:

भागता	लड़का	**b^{h}āgt*ā***	**laRk*ā***	the running boy
भागती	लड़की	**b^{h}āgt*ī***	**laRk*ī***	the running girl
भागते	लड़के	**b^{h}āgt*e***	**laRk*e***	the running boys
भागती	लड़कियाँ	**b^{h}āgt*ī***	**laRk*i*yā̃**	the running girls

The main function of the present participial clause is to denote '*action in progress*'.

Note that, like adjectives, present participles do not have any inherent tense reference to time, as is clear from the English translation. The tense is usually supplied by the main verb form in the sentence. If in the third line the verb 'caught' is changed to the present or the future tense, the tense reference of the participial form 'running' will change to the present or the future correspondingly. That is why the alternative English translation of भागता चोर **b^{h}āgtā cor** contains three possible tense references.

Ambiguity and pausing

पकड़ो	मत	जाने	दो।
pakRo	**mat**	**jāne**	**do**
catch	not	go-oblique infinitive	give

The translation of the verb phrase जाने दो **jāne do** is 'to allow to go' or 'to let go'. The familiar imperative form of the verb पकड़ना **pakaRnā** is पकड़ो **pakRo**, which means 'catch'. Depending upon the pause, the meaning changes. The pause is indicated by the comma.

पकड़ो	मत,	जाने	दो।
pakRo	**mat,**	**jāne**	**do**
catch	not,	go-oblique infinitive	give

Don't catch (him); let (him) go.

But the pause is immediately after पकड़ो **pakRo**; then the negative particle मत **mat** negates the second verb, as in

पकड़ो,	मत	जाने	दो।
pakRo,	**mat**	**jāne**	**do.**
catch,	not	go-oblique infinitive	give

Catch, don't let (him) go.

The negative particle मत mat

We encountered two negative particles – नहीं **nahī̃** and न **na** – in the earlier conversation. The third negative marker मत **mat** is primarily restricted to familiar and non-honorific imperatives. In prohibitives, the use of मत **mat** is particularly noteworthy.

Word order and contrastive negation

We mentioned earlier that the negative particle is usually placed before the verb. So usually the Hindi equivalent of the English 'Do not catch' is

मत पकड़ो ।
mat pakRo
not catch-imperative (familiar)
Don't catch.

However, the contrastive function is highlighted by the placement of the negative particle in the postverbal position (i.e. after the verb). This is the reason that मत **mat** is placed after पकड़ो **pakRo** in the expression

पकड़ो मत, जाने दो।
pakRo mat, jāne do
Don't catch (him); let (him) go.

The other reading, 'Catch, do not let (him) go,' has conjunctive rather than contrastive force. Therefore the negative particle appears in its normal preverbal position.

पढ़ने का अभ्यास २ **paR^{h}ne kā ab^{h}yās 2 Reading practice 2**

गाना gānā Song

Here is a sample of the opening lines of an old Hindi romantic song. In the song, the lover is imploring his beloved never to forget him. However, the approach is an indirect one (remember the politeness bug!). Therefore, rather than asking directly not to forget him, he says:

ये रातें, ये मौसम, ये हँसना, हँसाना
ye rātẽ, ye mausam, ye hãsnā, hãsānā
मुझे भूल जाना, इन्हें न भुलाना
muj^{h}e b^{h}ūl jānā, inhẽ na b^{h}ulānā.

These nights, this weather, this laughter and making (each other) laugh,
(You may) forget me, but never make them forget.

शब्दावली **shabdāvalī Vocabulary**

रात	**rāt** (f.)	night
मौसम	**mausam** (m.)	weather

हँसना	**hãsnā (–ne)**	to laugh
हँसाना	**hãsānā (+ne)**	to make someone laugh
भूलना	**b^hūl (–ne)**	to forget
भूल जाना	**b^hūl jānā** (compound verb)	to forget fully
भुलाना	**b^hulānā (+ne)**	to make someone forget

अभ्यास ab^hyās Exercises

Exercise 1

Match the words or phrases given in the following three columns to make appropriate Hindi sentences.

आइये	की बात क्या	रखिए
तकलीफ	तशरीफ	है
शायद	आपका इंतजार	काम ज्यादा हो
वो	अर्ज	है
आदाब	आपको दफ़्तर में	कर रही थी

āiye	kī bāt kyā	rak^hiye
taklīf	tashrīf	hɛ
shāyad	āpkā intazār	kām zyādā ho
vo	arz	hɛ
ādāb	āpko dafter mẽ	kar rahī t^hī.

Exercise 2

Circle the approprate form of the verb in each of the following sentences:

1 माफ कीजिये, मैं चैक भेजना (भूल लिया/भूल गया/भूल दिया)
māf kījiye, mɛ̃ cheque b^hejnā (b^hūl liyā/b^hūl gayā/b^hūl diyā).
2 मैने खाना (खा लिया/खा पड़ा/खा दिया)
mɛ̃ne k^hānā (k^hā liyā/k^hā paRā/k^hā diyā).
3 आपका बुखार (बढ़ लिया/बढ़ गया/बढ़ दिया)
āpkā buxār (baR^h liyā/baRh gayā/baR^h diyā).
4 आपने कुछ ज़वाब नहीं (लिया/दिया/आया/गया)
āpne kuc^h javāb nahī̃ (liyā/diyā/āyā/gayā).
5 आप मेरी सलाह मान (लीजिये/दीजिये/आइये)
āp merī salāh mān (lījiye/dījiye/āiye).

Exercise 3

Which job description matches the job?

1	अध्यापक ad^hyāpak	इमारतें बनवाता है। imāratẽ banvātā hɛ.
2	डॉक्टर DākTar (doctor)	कपड़े बनाता है। kapRe banātā hɛ.
3	कैशियर *cashier*	खाना बनाता है। k^hānā banātā hɛ.
4	दर्जी darzī 'tailor'	टीका लगाता है। Tīkā lagātā hɛ.
5	खानसामा k^hānsāmā 'cook'	चैक कैश करता है। *cheque cash* kartā hɛ.
6	ड्राइवर *driver*	छात्रों को पढ़ाता है। c^hātrõ ko paR^hātā hɛ.
7	सिविल इन्जीनियर *civil engineer*	कार चलाता है। kār calātā hɛ.

Exercise 4

Ram and Shyam are brothers. Ram believes in self-help and does everything on his own. Shyam, on the other hand, gets someone to do his work. Write about Shyam according to the model given below:

राम ने अपना काम किया।
rām ne apanā kām kiyā.
Ram did his work.

शाम ने हिलडा से अपना काम करवाया।
shyām ne hildā se apnā kām karvāyā.
Shyam had Hildā do his work.

1 राम: राम ने अपनी कार चलाई।
श्याम: ______________________
Ram: rām ne apnī kār calāī.
Shyam: ______________________

2 राम: राम अपना खत लिखेगा।
श्याम: ______________________
Ram: rām apnā xat lik^hegā.
Shyam: ______________________

3 राम: राम अपना घर बना रहा है।
श्याम: ____________________
Ram: rām apnā g^{h}ar banā rahā hɛ.
Shyam: ____________________

4 राम: राम अपनी कहानी सुना रहा था।
श्याम: ____________________
Ram: rām apnī kahānī sunā rahā t^{h}ā.
Shyam: ____________________

5 राम: राम अपनी लड़की को पढ़ाता है।
श्याम: ____________________
Ram: rām apnī laRkī ko paR^{h}ātā hɛ.
Shyam: ____________________

Exercise 5

Fill out the appropriate present participial form according to the model given below:

चलना:	मैं	*चलती*	गाड़ी	में	चढ़ा।
calnā:	mɛ̃	*caltī*	gāR^{h}ī	mẽ	caR^{h}ā.
भागना:	मैंने	भागते	कुत्ते	को	देखा।
b^{h}āgnā:	mɛ̃ne	b^{h}āgte	kutte	ko	dek^{h}ā.

1 हँसना: मुझे वो __________ लड़की बहुत पसन्द है।
2 खेलना: __________ बच्चे बहुत सुन्दर लग रहे थे।
3 गाना: __________ चिड़िया उड़ रही थी।
4 सितार बजाना: __________ आदमी बहुत अच्छा है।
5 तैरना: __________ मछलियों को देखो।
6 रोना: डॉक्टर ने __________ बच्चे को टीका लगाया।

1 hãsnā: muj^{h}e vo __________ laRkī bahut pasand hɛ.
2 k^{h}elnā: __________ bacce bahut sundar lag rahe t^{h}e.
3 gānā: __________ ciRiyā uR rahī t^{h}ī.
4 sitār bajānā: __________ ādmī bahut acc^{h}ā hɛ.
5 tɛrnā: __________ mac^{h}aliyõ ko dek^{h}o.
6 ronā: DākTar ne __________ bacce ko Tīkā lagāyā.

Exercise 6

Pac-Man has attacked the following text and, some elements have been chewed up. Your task is to supply the postpositions or the missing parts of the verb in those places where Pac-Man has left three bullets behind.

मैं रेलवे स्टेशन पर अपने दोस्त • • • इंतज़ार कर रहा था। थोड़ी देर बाद गाड़ी आयी और मेरा दोस्त गाड़ी से उतरा। हम बहुत खुश हो कर मिले। इस बार पाँच साल के बाद हमारी मुलाकात • • •। थोड़ी देर बाद मैंने कहा, 'इस बार बहुत देर के बाद यहाँ आये हो'। उसने जवाब • • •, अच्छी बात थी कि अगर गाड़ी देर से न • • •, तो मैं आज भी न • • •।

mɛ̃ *railway station* par apne dost • • • intzār kar rahā tʰā. tʰoRī der bād gāRī āyī aur merā dost gāRī se utrā. ham bahut xush ho kar mile. is bār pā̃c sā̃l ke bād hamārī mulākāt • • •. tʰoRī der bād mɛ̃ne kahā, 'is bār bahut der ke bād yahā̃ āye ho.' usne javāb • • •, 'accʰī bāt tʰī ki agar gāRī der se na • • •, to mɛ̃ āj bʰī na • • •.

9 फार्चून कुकी में क्या लिखा है? 'fortune cookies' mẽ kyā likʰā hɛ?

What's written in the fortune cookie?

By the end of this unit you should be able to:

- use past participials
- understand how to say 'no' in socially sensitive situations
- use the participial forms as adverbials
- use the construction 'neither . . . nor'
- understand hidden assumptions
- form purpose clauses
- learn more about Indian and Chinese food (particularly curries).
- use the passive construction
- understand more on reduplication
- use idiomatic expressions

पढ़ने का अभ्यास १ paR^{h}ne kā ab^{h}yās 1 Reading practice 1 (CD 2; 28)

जल्दी पैसा आने वाला है। ***jaldī pɛsā āne vālā hɛ*** ***Money will come soon***

सीन: अमरीका में एक चीनी रैस्टोरैन्ट
Scene: Chinese restaurant in the US

1 एक दिन दो दोस्त खाना खाने एक चीनी रैस्टोरैन्ट गये।
ek din do dost k^{h}ānā k^{h}āne ek cīnī *restaurant* gaye.
2 खाने के बाद बैरा 'फार्चून कुकीज़' लाया।
k^{h}āne ke bād bɛrā '*fortune cookies*' lāyā.
3 दोनों ने अपनी-अपनी 'फार्चून कुकी' को खोला और अपनी-अपनी किस्मत के बारे में पढ़ा।
donõ ne apnī-apnī '*fortune cookie*' ko k^{h}olā aur apnī-apnī kismat ke bāre mẽ paR^{h}ā.
4 फिर एक दोस्त ने दूसरे से पूछा, 'कागज़ पर क्या लिखा है?'
p^{h}ir ek dost ne dūsre se pūc^{h}ā, 'kāgaz par kyā lik^{h}ā hɛ?'
5 लिखा है – 'जल्दी पैसा आने वाला है।'
lik^{h}ā hɛ – 'jaldī pɛsā āne vālā hɛ.'
6 यह तो बड़ी ख़ुशी की बात है।
ye to baRī xushī kī bāt hɛ.
7 तो कोई लाटरी ख़रीदी है?
to koī lāTrī (*Lottery*) xarīdī hɛ?
8 नहीं, लेकिन कल अपना जीवन बीमा करवाया है।
nahī̃, lekin kal apnā jīvan bīmā karvāyā hɛ.

1 *One day two friends went to eat in a Chinese restaurant.*
2 *After eating (i.e. after they had finished eating), the waiter brought (them) fortune cookies.*
3 *(They) both opened their fortune cookie(s) and read about their fortune(s).*
4 *Then one friend asked the other, 'What is written on the paper?'*
5 *(It) is written – 'Money is about to come soon.'*
6 *This is a matter of great happiness.*
7 *Did (you) buy a lottery ticket?*
8 *No, but yesterday, I bought life-insurance.* (lit. I have caused the life insurance to be done)

शब्दावली **shabdāvalī** **Vocabulary**

दोस्त	**dost** (m.)	friend
खाना	**k^hānā** (m.)	food
खाना	**k^hānā** (+ne)	to eat
खाने (के लिये)	**k^hane (ke liye)**	(in order) to eat
चीन	**cīn**	China
चीनी	**cīnī**	Chinese
बैरा	**bɛrā** (m.)	waiter
लाना	**lānā** (–ne)	to bring
दोनों	**donõ**	both
खोलना	**k^holnā** (+ne)	to open
किस्मत	**kismat** (f.)	fortune, fate
काग़ज़	**kāgaz** (m.)	paper
लिखना	**lik^hnā** (+ne)	to write
लिखा है	**lik^hā hɛ**	is written
जल्दी	**jaldī**	quickly, hurry
पैसा	**pɛsā** (m.)	money; one hundredth of a rupee
आने वाला	**āne vālā**	about to come
जीवन	**jīvan** (m.)	life
बीमा	**bīmā** (m.)	insurance

Notes

Cultural

Chinese food in India has a distinct Indian (spicy) taste and is very popular. However, Chinese restaurants in India don't usually offer fortune cookies.

Purpose clauses and deletion

In the last chapter, we came across the following expression:

पुलिस	वाला	उसको	पकड़ने	के लिये	दौड़ा।
pulis	**vālā**	**usko**	**pakaRne**	**ke liye**	**dauRā.**
police	one/man	him	to catch-obl.	for	ran

The policeman ran to catch him.

Now compare this Hindi expression with the opening line:

एक	दिन	दो	दोस्त	खाना	खाने	एक	चीनी
ek	**din**	**do**	**dost**	**k^{h}ānā**	**k^{h}āne**	**ek**	**cīnī**
one	day	two	friends	food	to eat-obl.	one	Chinese

रैस्टोरैन्ट	गये।
restaurant	**gaye.**
restaurant	went

One day two friends went to a Chinese restaurant to eat food.

You must have observed by now that the underlined infinitive phrases in English, such as 'to catch' and 'to eat', are not translated as plain infinitives like पकड़ना **pakaRnā** and खाना **k^{h}ānā**. The plain (simple) infinite phrase will yield an ungrammatical sentence in Hindi. As is clear from the Hindi expression पकड़ने के लिए **pakaRne ke liye** 'to catch', the Hindi equivalent of the English purpose clause 'to catch' is paraphrased as 'in order to catch', and therefore the postposition के लिए **ke liye** 'for, in order to' follows the infinitive phrase पकड़ना **pakaRnā**. Recall the peer pressure influence of the postposition on the noun that makes the noun oblique and, thus, पकड़ना **pakaRnā** changes to पकड़ने **pakaRne**. The postposition can be described as the ghost postposition – के लिए **ke liye**.

What determines the retention or deletion of the postposition in purpose clauses such as those discussed here? The answer lies in the main verb of each sentence, i.e. दौड़ा **dauRā** 'ran' and गए **gaye** 'went'. If the main verb is a motion verb, it is possible optionally to drop the postposition as खाने **k^{h}āne**. Similarly, it is possible to drop के लिए **ke liye** in the first sentence:

पुलिस	वाला	उसको	पकड़ने	दौड़ा।
pulis (police)	**vālā**	**usko**	**pakaRne**	dauRā.

If we replace the main verb in the above sentence with a stative (non-motion) verb, the postposition must be retained, as in

पुलिस वाला	उसको	पकड़ने के लिये	है।
pulis vālā	**usko**	**pakaRne ke liye**	hɛ.

The police are (there) to catch him.

The deletion of the postposition is ungrammatical; therefore, the following sentence is unacceptable:

पुलिस	वाला	उसको	पकड़ने	है।
pulis (police)	**vālā**	**usko**	**pakaRne**	**hɛ.**

Reduplication and distributive meaning

In Unit 4, we demonstrated that repetition expresses intensity. In sentence 3 the feminine form of the reflexive pronoun अपना **apnā** is repeated:

दोनों ने	अपनी–अपनी	'फ़ाचूर्न कुकी'	को	खोला।
donõ ne	**apnī-apnī**	**'fortune cookie'**	**ko**	**k^{h}olā**
both-agent	self self	fortune cookie	obj.	opened

Both opened their fortune cookie(s).

अपनी **apnī** is repeated to convey that both opened their respective cookies.

Past participle (expressing states): adjectival and adverbial use

In Unit 8 we introduced present participles. Compare the phrase भागते चोर को **b^{h}āgte cor ko** 'the running thief' with भागे चोर को **b^{h}āge cor ko**. The latter form is called the past participial form and can be translated into English as 'the escaped thief'.

Now compare the present forms with their corresponding past participial forms, and the difference in meaning rendered by the two forms:

Present participle	*Past participle*
भागता चोर **b^{h}āgtā cor** the running thief	भागा चोर **bhāgā cor** the escaped thief
बोलती लड़की **boltī laRkī** the speaking girl	बोली बात **bolī bāt** the spoken matter
लिखते लड़के **lik^{h}te laRke** the writing boys (boys who are/were/will be writing)	लिखे शब्द **lik^{h}e shabda** the written words

Note the composition of the past participial form:

Stem			+	*past participial marker*
भाग	**b^{h}āg**	run	+	आ **ā** past-masculine singular
बोल	**bol**	speak	+	ई **ī** past-feminine singular
लिख	**lik^h**	write	+	ए **e** past-masculine plural

You have probably guessed by now that the past participle is the same form that we came across in the simple past tense formation.

The only difference is that the feminine singular form is used for both singular and plural forms.

The second element (optional) remains the same in both the present and past participial forms, i.e. हुआ **huā**, हुए **hue** and हुई **huī**.

As stated earlier, in the participle the verb form ceases to function like a real verb and begins to behave like an adjective, so the verbal adjectives which are drawn from the simple past tense are called 'past participles'. In other words, they are like adjectives ending in आ **ā** with the difference being that they are derived from verbs.

Like the adjectives ending in आ **ā**, they agree in number or gender with the following noun. Note the gender number agreement in the above examples.

Unlike the present participle which denotes '*action in progress*', the past participle indicates a *state*.

Note the difference in meaning between the present participle and its corresponding past participial form:

Present participle	*Past participle*
बैठता लड़का **bɛTʰtā laRkā** The boy who is (in the process of) sitting.	बैठा लड़का **bɛTʰā laRkā** The seated boy.
सोती लड़कियाँ **sotī laRkiyā̃** The girls who are in the process of sleeping.	सोई लड़कियाँ **soī laRkiyā̃** The sleeping girls. (state)

The present participial form सोती **sotī** indicates the dozing off stage prior to sound sleep whereas the corresponding past participle indicates the state of sound sleep.

Adverbials

So far we have discussed the adjectival use of participles. Participial forms when placed before a verb mark adverbial usage. Note the translation of the quoted sentence given in sentence 4 of the reading passage.

कागज़	पर	क्या	लिखा	है?
kāgaz	**par**	**kyā**	**likʰā**	**hɛ?**
paper	on	what	written	is

What is written on the paper?

Superficially it appears as if लिखा है **likʰā hɛ** is the present perfect form of the verb लिख **likʰ**, which should be translated as 'has written', but this is not the case. The main verb is है **hɛ**, while लिखा **lik^hā** is the past participial form used as an adverb without the optional element हुआ **huā**. In short,

लिखा है।	=	लिखा (हुआ) है।
lik^hā hɛ	=	**lik^hā (huā) hɛ**

Since the main verb is है **hɛ** and लिखा **lik^hā** is the past participle, the translation is 'is written' rather than 'has written'. The insertion of the optional element disambiguates it from the present perfect form of the verb लिख **lik^h**. In passing, it should be mentioned that the verb phrase in sentence 7 of the passage ख़रीदी **xarīdī hɛ** is a real present perfect form of the verb ख़रीद **xarīd** 'buy'; therefore, its literal translation is 'has bought'.

बातचीत **bātcīt** Dialogue 1 (CD 2; 29)

मेरा पेट भर गया है। *merā peT b^har gayā hɛ*
I am full

Bill Hassett and his wife, who are visiting India for the first time, are invited to dinner by Bill's Indian partner. Bill's partner's wife, Jyotsna Singh, asks her guests about the type of food they would prefer. Bill suggests to his wife 'Honey, as is said in English: "Spice up your life." Why don't we both spice up our lives in the literal sense and try some spicy food?' So, with the intention of enjoying spicy food, he tells Jyotsna Singh:

बिल:	हिन्दुस्तानी 'करी' अभी तक हमने नहीं खायी।
BILL:	hindustānī *curry* ab^hī tak hamne nahī̃ k^hāyī.
ज्योत्सना:	आपको मसालेदार खाना पसन्द है या 'करी'?
JYOTSNA:	āpko masāledār k^hānā pasand hɛ yā *curry*?
बिल:	दोनों में फ़र्क क्या है?
BILL:	donõ mẽ farka kyā hɛ?
ज्योत्सना:	अमरीका में करी एक डिश का नाम है लेकिन हिन्दुस्तान में ऐसी बात नहीं।
JYOTSNA:	amrīkā mẽ *curry* ek *dish* kā nām hɛ lekin hindustān mẽ ɛsī bāt nahī̃.
बिल:	हमारे यहाँ 'करी' का मतलब कोई मसालेदार हिन्दुस्तानी डिश है।
BILL:	hamāre yahā̃ *curry* kā matlab 'koī masāledār hindustanī dish' hɛ.

ज्योत्सना: हिन्दुस्तान में न तो 'करी' हमेशा मसालेदार होती है और न ही 'करी पाउडर' अक्सर बिकता है। 'करी' अकसर तरी वाली होती है और माँस, सब्जी, मछली या फल की बनी होती है।

JYOTSNA: hindustān mẽ na to *curry* hameshā masāledār hotī hɛ aur na hī hindustān mẽ *curry powder* aksar biktā hɛ. *curry* aksar tarī vālī hotī hɛ aur ye mā̃s, sabzī, macc^{h}lī yā p^{h}al kī banī hotī hɛ.

बिल: अरे! बिना मसाले की करी। यह तो हमने कभी नहीं सुना था।

BILL: are! binā masāle kī *curry*. ye to hamne kab^{h}ī nahī̃ sunā t^{h}ā.

ज्योत्सना: तो अब आपको कौन सी करी पसन्द है?

JYOTSNA: to ab āpko kaun sī *curry* pasand hɛ?

ज्योत्सना: आम के आम और गुठलियों के दाम। 'करी' के बारे में पता लग गया और असली 'करी' चखने का मौका भी मिल जायेगा। अच्छा, हमको तेज़ मसालेदार माँस की 'करी' बहुत पसन्द है।

BILL: ām ke ām aur guT^{h}līyõ ke dām. *curry* ke bāre mẽ patā lag gayā aur aslī curry cak^{h}ne kā maukā b^{h}ī mil jāyegā. acc^{h}ā, hamko tez masāledār mā̃s kī curry bahut pasand hɛ.

(They laugh at the unexpected turn of the conversation; the proverb has added a lighter touch to the conversation and they continue to talk . . .)

ज्योत्सना: अरे, बात ही करेंगे या कुछ स्नैक्स भी खायेंगे।

JYOTSNA: are, bāt hī karẽga yā kuc^h snɛks b^{h}i k^{h}āyẽge

(Even after Bill has eaten a couple of snacks, and he is full, she insists on giving him more. Bill puts his hands over his plate.)

बिल: बस, और नहीं खा सकूँगा। मेरा पेट भर गया है।

BILL: bas, aur nahī̃ k^{h}ā sakū̃ga, merā peT b^{h}ar gayā hai.

बिल: बस, और बिल्कुल नहीं। बहुत खा लिया है। नहीं तो बीमार हो जाऊँगा।

BILL: bas, aur bilkul nahī̃. bahut k^{h}ā liya hai. nahī̃ to bimār ho jāū̃gā.

BILL: *So far, in India, we have not eaten curry.*

JYOTSNA: *Do you like spicy food or curry?*

BILL: *What is the difference between the two?*

JYOTSNA: *In America, curry is the name of a dish but this is not the case in India.*

BILL: *In our place (i.e. in America) curry is (called) a spicy Indian dish.*

JYOTSNA: *In India, curry is not always spicy nor is curry powder usually sold (commercially). Curry is usually liquified and (it) is made of meat, vegetables, fish or fruit.*

BILL: *Wow! Curry without spices. This we have* (lit. had) *never heard of (before).*

JYOTSNA: *So, which curry do you like?*

BILL: *(This is like) earth and heaven's joy combined. (Now) I have came to know about curry and will get an opportunity to taste a genuine curry. Well, we very much like the very spicy meat curry.*

(They laugh at the unexpected turn of the conversation; the proverb has added a lighter touch to the conversation and they continue to talk . . .)

JYOTSNA: *Hey, would you (like to) continue to talk or eat some (more) snacks?*

(Even after Bill has eaten a couple of snacks, and he is full, she insists on giving him more. Bill puts his hands over his plate.)

BILL: *Enough. (I) won't be able to eat more.*

BILL: *Enough, absolutely no more, otherwise I will get sick.*

शब्दावली **shabdāvalī** **Vocabulary**

करी/कढ़ी	**curry** (f.)	curry (*see Notes)
मसाला	**masālā** (m.)	spice
मसालेदार	**masāledār** (adj.)	spicy
या	**yā**	or
फर्क	**farka** (m.)	difference
हमारे यहाँ	**hamāre yahā̃**	at our place (house, country, etc.)
न . . . न	**na . . . na**	neither . . . nor
मतलब	**matlab** (m.)	meaning
हमेशा	**hameshā**	always
अकसर	**aksar**	often, usually
तर	**tar**	wet
तरी	**tarī** (f.)	liquid
माँस	**mā̃s** (m.)	meat
सब्जी	**sabzī** (f.)	vegetable
मछली	**macc^{h}lī** (f.)	fish
फल	**p^{h}al** (m.)	fruit
बनना	**bannā** (–**ne**)	to be made
बनी	**banī**	made
बिना	**binā**	without
कभी	**kab^{h}ī**	ever
कभी नहीं	**kab^{h}ī nahī̃**	never
आम	**ām** (m. adj.)	mango (n.); common (adj.)
गुठली	**guT^{h}lī** (f.)	stone (of a fruit)
दाम	**dām** (m.)	price
आम के आम और . . . गुठलियों के दाम	**ām ke ām aur . . . guT^{h}ilyõ ke dām**	earth's joy and heaven's combined

पता लगाना	**patā lagānā** (+ko)	to come to know
असली	**aslī**	real, genuine
चखना	**cak^{h}nā** (+ne)	to taste
मौका	**maukā** (m.)	opportunity
तेज़	**tez**	fast, quick, sharp, strong
स्नैक्स	**snɛks** (m.)	snacks
बस	**bas**	enough
सकना	**saknā**	to be able to, can
खाना	**k^{h}ānā**	food, to eat

Pronunciation

The English word 'curry' is a derivative of the Hindi word कढ़ी **kaR^{h}ī**. Note the presence of the retroflex ढ़ **R^h** in the Hindi word.

Notes

Eating etiquette: how to say 'no'

Indians are very hospitable. One of the expressions of their hospitality is to insist on giving more food to their guests. This results in one of the most embarrassing situations that guests can encounter. In addition to the linguistic strategies given in the dialogue, here are some other important expressions to refuse food. Don't keep on eating more!

आपने तो पहले ही बहुत दे दिया है।
āpne to pɛhle hī bahut de diyā hɛ
You have already given so much food.

खाना तो बहुत अच्छा है, लेकिन मेरी तबियत ठीक नहीं है।
k^{h}ānā to bahut acc^{h}ā hɛ, lekin merī tabiyat T^{h}īk nahī̃ hɛ.
The food is very good, but I am not feeling well.

Curry powder/curry

In the authentic Indian tradition, the English word 'curry' simply does not exist. It is part of the vocabulary of English-educated bilinguals. The Hindi word कढ़ी **kaR^{h}i** is restricted to a vegetarian curry which is made out from chick-pea flour. The chances are Hindi speakers will not use the term 'curry' to refer to the dishes mentioned in the dialogue, so, do not be surprised if this term is not understood in the native Indian context. Indians will express this concept by specifying the degree of spiciness and by qualifying a dish with words such as तरी वाली सब्जी **tarī vālī sabzī** or तरी वाला माँस/गोश्त **tarī vālā mās/goshta**. Curry is actually a blend of ground herbs and spices adapted by British settlers in India from the traditional spice mixtures of Indian cuisine. The basic ingredients of commercial curry powder are turmeric (which imparts the characteristic yellow colour), cumin, coriander, and cayenne pepper. Curry powder is primarily targeted at foreign consumption. English 'curry' is said to be derived from Tamil 'kari'.

Focus and word order

The normal word order of the opening sentence of the above dialogue is as follows:

हमने	हिन्दुस्तानी	'करी'	अभी तक	नहीं	खायी।
hamne	**hindustānī**	**curry**	**ab^hī tak**	**nahī̃**	**k^hāyī.**
we-agent	Indian	curry	yet	not	ate

We have not eaten Indian curry yet.

The two elements of the above sentence – time adverb and object – are placed in the sentence in the initial position as they are being singled out for emphasis.

हिन्दुस्तानी	'करी'	अभी तक	हमने	नहीं	खायी।
hindustānī	**curry**	**ab^hī tak**	**hamne**	**nahī̃**	**k^hāyī.**
Indian	curry	yet	we-agent	not	ate

As yet, it is the Indian curry (that) we have not eaten.

'Neither . . . nor' न . . . न na . . . na and emphatic particles

Note the use of the emphatic particles with न . . . न **na . . . na** 'neither . . . nor'. Also, observe the placement of the phrase हिन्दुस्तान में **hindūstān mẽ** in the 'neither . . . nor' clause:

हिन्दुस्तान	में	न	तो	'करी'	हमेशा	मसालेदार
hindustān	**mẽ**	**na**	**to**	***curry***	**hameshā**	**masāledār**
India	in	not	emp. part.	curry	always	spicy
होती	है					
hotī	**hɛ**					
be-present	is (aux.)					

और	न	ही	हिन्दुस्तान	में	करी पाउडर	अकसर
aur	**na**	**hī**	**hindustān**	**mẽ**	***currypowder***	**aksar**
and	not	emp. part	India	in	curry powder	often

बिकता	है।
biktā	**hɛ.**
be sold-pres.	is

As regards curry in India, it is neither always spicy nor is curry powder often sold in India.

The emphatic particles तो **to** and ही **hī** are more intimately tied to curry and curry powder, respectively, as shown:

हिन्दुस्तान	में	न	करी	तो	हमेशा	मसालेदार
hindustān	**mẽ**	**na**	**curry**	**to**	**hameshā**	**masāledār**
India	in	not	curry	emp. part.	always	spicy

होती	है
hotī	**hɛ**
be-present	is (aux.)

और	न	हिन्दुस्तान	में	करी	पाउडर	ही	अकसर
aur	**na**	**hindustān**	**mẽ**	**curry**	**powder**	**hī**	**aksar**
and	not	India	in	curry	powder	emp. part.	often

बिकता	है।
biktā	**hɛ.**
be sold-pres.	is

The movement of the emphatic particles from their original position after the negative particle न **na** renders the emphatic counterpart of the normal न . . . न **na . . . na** 'neither . . . nor' construction.

Past participle: adverbial

The verb होती है **hotī hɛ** is the generic construction explained in Unit 4. Can you find the past participle in the following sentence?

ये	माँस	सब्जी	मछली	या	फल	की	बनी
ye	**mā̃s**	**sabzī,**	**macc^{h}lī**	**yā**	**p^{h}al**	**kī**	**banī**
this	meat	vegetable	fish	or	fruit	of	make-past. ppl.

होती	है।
hotī	**hɛ.**
be-pres.	is (aux.)

Yes, बनी **banī** is the past participial form of the verb बनना **bannā** 'to be made.' It can be followed by the optional element हुई **huī**. However, in the following sentence

हमने	कभी	नहीं	सुना	था।
hamne	**kab^{h}ī**	**nahī̃**	**sunā**	**t^{h}ā.**
We-agent	ever	not	heard	was

We had never heard of (it).

सुना **sunā** is not a past participle. In combination with the auxiliary था **t^{h}ā**, it renders the past perfect form of the verb सुनना **sunnā** 'to hear/listen to'.

Compound verbs with जाना jānā 'to go'

As explained in Unit 7, the helping verb जाना **jānā** expresses 'transformation' and/or 'finality or completeness'. Both semantic shades are reflected in the following conjunct sentence:

करी	के बारे में	पता	लग	गया	और	असली	करी
curry	**ke bāre mẽ**	**patā**	**lag**	**gayā**	**aur**	**aslī**	**curry**
curry	about	address	strike	went	and	genuine	curry

चखने	का	मौका	भी	मिल	जायेगा।
cak^{h}ne	**kā**	**maukā**	**b^{h}ī**	**mil**	**jāyegā**
taste	of	opportunity	also	get	go-will

The verbs पता लगना **patā lagnā** 'to come to know' and **milnā** मिलना 'to get' are subjected to the compound verb construction, and the helping verb जाना **jānā** 'to go' loses its literal meaning.

The 'opportunity to . . .' x का मौका मिलना x kā maukā milnā

Note the word-for-word translation of the English expression, 'we will get the chance to taste the genuine curry'.

हमको	असली	करी	चखने	का	मौका	मिल	जायेगा।
hamko	**aslī**	**curry**	**cak^{h}ne**	**kā**	**maukā**	**mil**	**jāyegā**
we-to	genuine	curry	taste	of	opportunity	get	go-will

The expression 'to get the opportunity to do x' requires the experiential subject; therefore, the subject हम **ham** 'we' is followed by the postposition को **ko**. Since the Hindi verb never agrees with the subject that is followed by a postposition, the verb in the above sentence agrees with मौका **maukā** 'opportunity', which is masculine singular. Also, the genitive का **kā** agrees with मौका **maukā**.

बातचीत **bātcīt Dialogue 2** (CD 2; 30)

आग!आग! ***āg! āg! 'Fire! Fire!'***

The next week, Mr and Mrs Bill Hassett come to the Singhs' residence for dinner. They converse with each other on a wide variety of subjects. Finally, the delicious smell of the food begins to overpower their conversation. In the meanwhile, the hostess announces that the dinner is served.

बिल: वाह! वाह! शानदार खुशबू आ रही है, और इन्तज़ार करना मुश्किल है।
BILL: vāh! vāh! shāndār xushbū ā rahī hɛ, aur intazār karnā mushkil hɛ.
ज्योत्सना: आइये, तो खाना शुरू किया जाए। यह है आपकी पसन्द – तेज़ मिर्च वाली चिकन करी।
JYOTSNA: āiye, to kʰānā shuru kiyā jāye. ye hɛ, āpkī pasand – tez mirca vālī chicken curry.
(Bill takes a lot of curry while Mrs Hassett takes only a little bit. After taking the first substantial bite)
बिल: ओहहह! आग! आग!
BILL: (fanning his mouth) Ohhh . . . āg! . . . āg!
ज्योत्सना: क्यों क्या हुआ?
JYOTSNA: kyõ kyā huā?
बिल: ये तो 'करी' नहीं है! यह तो ज्वालामुखी है! ! और मैं अपना आग बुझाने का सामान भी नहीं लाया।
BILL: ye to curry nahī̃ hɛ! ye to jwālāmukʰī hɛ!! aur mɛ̃ apnā āg bujʰāne kā sāmān bʰī nahī̃ lāyā.
ज्योत्सना: आग बुझाने का सामान यह है – अगर बहुत मिर्च लग रही है तो दही लीजिए।
JYOTSNA: āg bujʰāne kā sāmān ye hɛ – agar bahut mirca lag rahī hɛ to dahī lījiye.
(After a while Bill's mouth cools down)
बिल: सच, अमरीका में तेज़ मसालेदार खाना इतना तेज़ नहीं होता।
BILL: sac, amrīkā (America) mẽ tez masāledār kʰānā itnā tez nahī̃ hotā.
ज्योत्सना: हाँ, यह तो हिन्दुस्तान है। यहाँ 'तेज़' का मतलब 'बहुत तेज़' है। हम लोग बहुत तेज़ खाते हैं लेकिन हिन्दुस्तान में सब लोग इतना 'तेज़' नहीं खा सकते।

JYOTSNA: hā̃, ye to hindustān hɛ. yahā̃ 'tez' kā matlab 'bahut tez' hɛ. ham log bahut tez k^{h}āte hɛ̃ lekin hindustān mẽ sab log itnā tez k^{h}ānā nahī̃ k^{h}ā sakte.

बिल: गलत-फ़हमी दूर करने के लिये शुक्रिया। मैं अब समझ गया कि 'तेज़' खतरनाक शब्द है।

BILL: galat-fahamī dūr karne ke liye shukriyā. mɛ̃ ab samaj^h gayā ki 'tez' xatarnāk shabda hɛ.

BILL: *Wow! Wow! the splendid fragrance (of food) is coming; (it) is difficult to wait any longer* (i.e. I cannot wait more).

JYOTSNA: *Please come, let's start eating* (lit. eating should be started). *This is your favourite – hot chicken curry* (lit. sharp pepper one chicken curry).

(Bill takes a lot of curry while Mrs Hassett takes a little bit. After taking the first substantial bite)

BILL: *(fanning his mouth) Oh . . . h . . . h! Fire! Fire!*

JYOTSNA: *Why? What happened?*

BILL: *This is not curry! This is a volcano!! And I did not bring my fire extinguisher.*

JYOTSNA: *This is (your) fire extinguisher – if (it) is very hot, then take some yoghurt.* (lit. if very much pepper striking (you)).

(After a while Bill's mouth cools down.)

BILL: *Truly, in the US the spicy food is not so spicy.*

JYOTSNA: *Yes, this is India. Here 'hot' means 'very hot.' We eat very hot food, but not all people can eat such hot (food) in India.*

BILL: *Thanks for dispelling (my) misconception. Now I (fully) understand that 'tez' is a dangerous word.*

शब्दावली **shabdāvalī Vocabulary**

वाह! वाह!	**vāh! vāh!**	Wow! Wow! bravo!
शानदार	**shāndār**	grand, splendid
खुशबू	**xushbū** (f.)	fragrance (lit. happy smell)
शुरू करना	**shuru karnā (+ne)**	to begin
शुरू किया जाए/जाये	**shuru kiyā jāye**	should be started
मिर्च	**mirca** (f.)	chilli peppers
ओ	**oh**	exclamation of pain/sorrow
आग	**āg** (f.)	fire
ज्वालामुखी	**jwālāmuk^{h}ī** (m.)	volcano
बुझाना	**buj^{h}ānā (+ne)**	to extinguish
सामान	**sāmān** (m.)	baggage, goods, stuff, tools
लाना	**lānā (–ne)**	to bring
दही	**dahī** (m./f.)	yoghurt

सच	**sac** (m.)	truth, true
इतना	**<itnā>**	this/so much/many
गलत	**galat**	wrong
गलतफ़हमी	**galat-fahamī** (f.)	misconception, misunderstanding
दूर	**dūr**	far, distant
दूर करना	**dūr karnā** (+ne)	to dispel, to eliminate
ख़तरा	**<xatrā>** (m.)	danger
ख़तरनाक	**xatarnāk**	dangerous
शब्द	**shabda** (m.)	word

Pronunciation

Words such as **xatrā** and **itnā** are written as ख़तरा **xatarā** and इतना **itanā**, respectively. The omitted vowel of ख़तरा **xatrā** surfaces in ख़तरनाक **xatarnāk**.

Notes

Ambiguity

The following expression from the opening line of Dialogue 2 is ambiguous:

और	इंतजार	करना	मुश्किल	है।
aur	**intazār**	**karnā**	**mushkil**	**hɛ.**
and	wait	to do	difficult	is

(It) is difficult to wait any longer *or* And, (it) is difficult to wait.

In other words, और **aur** can be interpreted either as a conjunction marker or as a modifier of इंतजार/इन्तजार **intazār**.

Passive construction

The English expression 'Let's begin eating' is paraphrased as 'Eating should be done.'

खाना	शुरु	किया	जाए/जाये।
k^{h}ānā	**shuru**	**kiyā**	**jāye.**
eating	begin	did	go-subjunctive

The verb phrase is in the passive subjunctive form. The passive construction in Hindi takes a compound verb construction in the sense that it involves a main verb and the helping verb. The only difference is that the main verb, rather than being in a stem form, is in the past form.

Passive

Main verb (past form)	*Helping verb* (जाना ***jānā*** + *tense*)		
किया **kiyā**	जाए/जाये	**jāye**	should be done
पढ़ा **paR**[h]**ā**	जाता है	**jātā hɛ**	is read
पढ़ा **paR**[h]**ā**	गया	**gayā**	was read
पढ़ा **paR**[h]**ā**	जाएगा/जायेगा	**jāyegā**	will be read
बोला **bolā**	जा रहा है	**jā rahā hɛ**	is being spoken/told

In other words, the passive is formed by using the main verb in the past form. The helping verb is always जाना **jānā** 'to go', which undergoes tense conjugation like any other helping verb in a compound verb construction.

Like English passive subjects, which are appended with 'by', Hindi passive subjects are attached to the postposition से **se** 'from, by'. Here is the list of pronominal forms with the postposition से **se**:

मैं + से = मुझसे		हम + से = हमसे	
mɛ̃ + **se** = **muj**[h]**se**	by me	**ham** + **se** = **hamse**	by us
तू + से = तुझसे		तुम + से = तुमसे	
tū + **se** = **tuj**[h]**se**	by you	**tum** + **se** = **tum se**	by you
		आप + से = आपसे	
		āp + **se** = **āpse**	by you (honorific)
वह + से = उससे		वे + से = उनसे	
vo + **se** = **usse**	by him/her	**ve** + **se** = **unse**	by them

Since the passive subject is always followed by the postposition से **se**, the passive verb can never agree with it; instead it agrees with the object, as in

मुझसे	किताब	पढ़ी	गई/गयी।
muj[h]**se**	**kitāb**	**paR**[h]**ī**	**gayī.**
me-by	book (f.)	read-past-f. sg.	passive-go + past-f. sg.

The book was read by me.

If the feminine object किताब **kitāb** 'book' is replaced by the masculine object ख़त **xat** 'letter', the passive verb form will be in the masculine singular form.

मुझसे	खत	पढ़ा	गया।
muj^{h}se	**xat**	**paR^{h}ā**	**gayā.**
me-by	letter (m.)	read-past-m. sg.	passive-go + past-f. sg.

The letter was read by me.

One important difference between Hindi and English is that both transitive and intransitive verbs can be passivized in Hindi, while only transitive verbs can be passivized in English. See the Grammar section for more details.

Omitted subject

अगर	(आपको)	बहुत	मिर्च	लग	रही	है	तो	(आप)
agar	**(āp-ko)**	**bahut**	**mirca**	**lag**	**rahī**	**hɛ**	**to**	**(āp)**
If	(you-to)	very	pepper	strike	ing	is	then	(you)

कुछ	दही	लीजिये।
kuc^{h}	**dahī**	**lījiye.**
some	yoghurt	take

The omitted subject of the first clause is experiential while it is simple nominative in the second clause.

The past participle and the passive construction

You must have discovered by now that there is no neat correspondence between the English and Hindi passives. The English passive construction can be paraphrased in one of the following three ways. First, those instances where English and Hindi both use the passive construction to express the target idea. For example, English expressions such as 'it is said' and 'it is heard' are translated by means of the Hindi passive, as in:

कहा	जाता	है।
kahā	**jātā**	**hɛ.**
say-past	passive-go-present	is

(It) is said.

सुना	जाता	है।
sunā	**jātā**	**hɛ.**
hear-past	passive-go-present	is

(It) is heard.

As mentioned in Unit 2, Hindi is a 'pro-drop' language and the English dummy 'it' is not translated.

Second, English passives are sometimes translated as past participial forms in Hindi. Consider sentence 4 in Reading practice 1 at the start of this chapter:

कागज़	पर	क्या	लिखा	है?
kāgaz	**par**	**kyā**	**likʰā**	**hɛ?**
paper	on	what	written (past. ppl.)	is

What is written on the paper?

Compare the English sentence with its corresponding Hindi sentence. The Hindi sentence does not use the passive construction. Instead, the past participial form of the verb लिखना **likʰnā** is used in the corresponding Hindi sentence.

Third, Hindi intransitive verbs are translated as passive in English.

Intransitive		*Transitive*	
बिकना **biknā**	to be sold	बेचना **becnā**	to sell
बनना **bannā**	to be made	बनाना **banānā**	to make
खुलना **kʰulnā**	to be opened	खोलना **kʰolnā**	to open

Since English does not have intransitive verbs corresponding to those in Hindi, the Hindi intransitive verbs are best translated by means of the English passive. For example, a common billboard sight in India is

यहाँ	किताबें	बिकती	हैं।
yahā̃	**kitābẽ**	**biktī**	**hɛ̃**
here	books	be sold-pres.	are

Books are sold here.

Notice that the English meaning does not correspond to the Hindi structure. In Hindi, the intransitive verb बिकना **biknā** is conjugated in the simple present tense form. Thus, the Hindi sentence is in its active form, as opposed to the passive form in English.

Negation and auxiliary deletion

The present auxiliary verb is dropped with negative sentences in the following two sentences:

अमेरिका	में	तेज़	मसालेदार	खाना	इतना	तेज़।
amerikā	**mẽ**	**tez**	**masāledār**	**k^hānā**	**itnā**	**tez**
America	in	sharp	spicy	food	so much	sharp

नहीं	होता	है।
nahī̃	**hotā**	**hɛ**
not	be-present	is[aux.]

In America the hot food is not so hot.

and

लेकिन	हिन्दुस्तान	में	सब	लोग	इतना	तेज़	खाना
lekin	**hindustān**	**mẽ**	**sab**	**log**	**itnā**	**tez**	**k^hānā**
but	India	in	all	people	so much	sharp	food

नहीं	खा	सकते	(हैं)।
nahī̃	**k^hā**	**sakte**	**(hɛ̃).**
not	eat	can-present	are

But in India not everybody can eat such hot food.

अभ्यास **ab^hyās Exercises**

Exercise 1

Match the places with the purpose for which people visit them. Then complete the sentence according to the model presented below:

Place	*Purpose*	
पुस्तकालय	किताबें	पढ़ने
pustakālaya	**kitābẽ**	**paR^hne**
library	to read	books

Sentence

लोग	पुस्तकालय	किताब	पढ़ने	जाते	हैं।
log	**pustakālaya**	**kitābẽ**	**paR^hne**	**jāte**	**hɛ̃.**

People go to the library to read books.

Do not attempt to translate the English place names into Hindi.

	Place	*Purpose*	
1	laundromat	बियर पीने	***beer*** **pīne**
2	restaurant	फिल्म देखने	***film*** **dek^hne**
3	cinema	तैरने	**tɛrne**

4 college पढ़ने **paR^{h}ne**
5 swimming pool खाना खाने **k^{h}ānā k^{h}āne**
6 bar दवाई लेने **davāī lene**
7 pharmacy कपड़े धोने **kapRe d^{h}one**

Exercise 2

Change the present participial phrase into its corresponding past participial form in the following sentences:

1 वो बैठते हुए बोला। vo bɛT^{h}te hue bolā.
2 जॉन सोते हुए हँस रहा था। John sote hue hãs rahā t^{h}ā.
3 ये शहर सोता सा लगता है। ye shɛhɛr sotā sā lagtā hɛ.
4 लड़की रोती हुई घर आयी। laRkī rotī huī g^{h}ar āyī.
5 औरत ने स्विमिंग पूल पर लेटते हुए कहा। aurat ne *swimming pool* par leTte hue kahā.

Exercise 3

Which participial forms modify/match the noun.

लिखा	lik^{h}ā	बात	bāt
सुनी	sunī	खत	xat
हँसता	hãstā	लड़का	laRkā
चलती	caltī	लोग	log
भूले	b^{h}ūle	गाड़ी	gāRī
भागती	b^{h}āgtī	बिल्ली	billī

Exercise 4

Change the following sentences into their corresponding passive form:

1 जॉन ने एक कहानी पढ़ी। John ne ek kahānī paR^{h}ī.
2 हम लोग खाना खा रहे हैं। ham log k^{h}ānā k^{h}ā rahe hɛ̃.
3 तुम क्या करोगे? tum kyā karoge?
4 मैंने चिकन करी बनाई। mɛ̃ne *chicken curry* banāyī.
5 बिल ये पढ़ेगा। Bill ye paR^{h}egā.
6 क्या आपने गाना गाया? kyā āpne gānā gāyā?

Exercise 5

Underline the appropriate form of the subject, verb etc. given within the brackets in the following sentences:

1 (हमको/हम/हमने) वहाँ जाने का मौका (मिला/मिल)।
(hamko/ham/hamne) vahā̃ jane kā maukā (milā/mile).
2 (जॉन ने/जॉन/जॉन को) हिन्दुस्तान (जाना/जाने) का मौका अकसर मिलता है।
(John ne/John ko/John) hindustān (jānā/jāne) kā maukā aksar miltā hɛ.
3 ये सुनहरा मौका (था/थी)। सुनहरा 'golden'
ye sunhɛrā maukā (t^{h}ā/t^{h}ī).
4 (आपको/आप) किताब लिखने का मौका कब (मिलेगी/मिलेगा)।
(āpko/āp) kitāb lik^{h}ne kā maukā kab (milegī/milegā).
5 इस कागज़ में क्या (लिखा/लिखी) है।
is kāgaz mẽ kyā (lik^{h}ā/lik^{h}ī) hɛ?
6 बिल्ली को मौका (मिला/मिली) और वो दूध पी गयी।
billī ko maukā (milā/milī) aur vo dud^h pī gayī.
7 ये बहुत (अच्छा मौका/अच्छे मौके) की बात है।
ye bahut (acc^{h}ā maukā/acc^{h}e mauke) kī bāt hɛ.

10 भारतीय त्यौहार b^hāratiya tyauhāra

Indian festivals

By the end of this unit you should be able to:

- use various types of relative clauses
- use complex sentences
- understand more about Hindi passives
- get cultural information about the festivals of India
- distinguish between scholarly and formal Sanskritized style and informal Persianized style

 **(CD 2; 32)**

In this unit we will describe some Indian festivals and other symbols which underlie the colourful mosaic of the culture and spirit of India. You will notice a slight shift in the style, which is more Sanskritized now. This style is preferred in formal, literary, scholarly and cultural endeavours. The Persianized style is preferred in informal and conversational situations.

पढ़ने का अभ्यास १ paR^{h}ne kā ab^{h}yās 1 Reading practice 1

दिवाली ***Dīvālī*** ***The festival of lights***

1 दिवाली शब्द संस्कृत के दीपावली शब्द से आया है।
'dīvālī' shabda sanskrit ke 'dīpāvalī' shabda se āyā hɛ.

2 दीपावली या दीवाली का अर्थ है – दीपकों की पंक्ति।
dīpāvalī yā dīvālī kā art^{h}a hɛ – dīpakõ kī paŋkti.

3 यह भारत का सबसे प्रसिद्ध त्यौहार है।
ye b^{h}ārat kā sab se prasidd^{h}a tyauhār hɛ.

4 दिवाली अक्तूबर या नवम्बर के महीने में आती है।
divālī aktūbar (*October*) yā navambar (*November*) ke mahīne mẽ ātī hɛ.

5 यह त्यौहार अच्छाई की बुराई पर और प्रकाश की अंधकार पर विजय का प्रतीक है।
ye tyauhāra acc^{h}āī kī burāī par aur prakāsha kī and^{h}kāra par vijaya kā pratīka hɛ.

6 ये राजा राम की राक्षस रावण पर विजय की ख़ुशी में मनाया जाता है।
ye rājā rām kī rākshasa rāvaN par vijaya kī xushī mẽ manāyā jātā hɛ.

7 कहा जाता है कि जब चौदह वर्ष के बनवास और रावण पर विजय पाने के बाद राजा राम अपने राज्य, अयोध्या, लौट रहे थे, तब हर घर ने ख़ुशी में दिये जलाये।
kahā jātā hɛ ki jab caudā varsha ke banvās aur rāvaN par vijay pāne ke bād rājā rāma apane rājya, Ayod^{h}yā, lauT rahe t^{h}e, tab har g^{h}ar ne xushī mẽ diye jalāye.

8 इसलिये दिवाली की रात को आज तक हर घर में दिये जलाये जाते हैं।
isliye divālī kī rāt ko āj tak har g^{h}ar mẽ diye jalāye jāte hɛ̃.

9 आप इस त्यौहार को भारत का क्रिसमस कह सकते हैं। यह त्यौहार भारत से बाहर – सिंगापुर, नेपाल, त्रिनिदाद, फ़ीजी आदि कई देशों में मनाया जाता है।
āp is tyauhār ko 'b^{h}ārata kā *Christmas*' kɛh sakte hɛ̃. ye tyauhār b^{h}ārat se bāhar – Singapore, Nepal, Trinidad, Fiji ādi kaī deshõ mẽ b^{h}ī manāyā jātā hɛ.

10 दिवाली की रात को लोग पटाख़े और फुलझड़ियाँ चलाते हैं और हर घर में लक्ष्मी पूजन होता है।
divālī kī rāt ko log paTāk^{h}e aur p^{h}ul-j^{h}aRiyā̃ calāte hɛ̃ aur har g^{h}ar mẽ 'lakshmī pūjana' hotā hɛ.

11 जैसे क्रिसमस सिर्फ़ ईसाई ही नहीं मनाते, वैसे दिवाली सिर्फ़ हिन्दुओं का त्यौहार नहीं है। आज-कल लगभग सभी धर्मों के लोग दिवाली मनाते हैं।
jɛse *Christmas* sirf īsāī hī nahī̃ manāte, vɛse divālī sirf hinduõ kā tyauhār nahī̃ hɛ. āj-kal lagb^{h}ag sab^{h}ī d^{h}armõ ke log divālī manāte hɛ̃.

1 *The word 'dīvāli' originated* (lit. came from = originate) *the Sanskrit word 'dīpāvalī'.*
2 *The meaning of 'dīpāvalī' or 'dīvālī' is 'a row of lamps.'*
3 *This is the most famous festival of India.*
4 *Divali comes in the month of October or November.*
5 *This festival is a symbol of the victory of 'good' over 'evil', and 'light' over 'darkness'.*
6 *This (festival) is celebrated in the glory* (lit. happiness) *of King Rama's victory over the demon (king) Ravana.*
7 *(It) is said that when, after fourteen years of exile and obtaining victory over Ravana, King Rama was returning to his kingdom, Ayodhya, then every house lit lamps in happiness (at his return).*
8 *Therefore, on Divali night until today, lamps are lit in every house.*
9 *You can call this festival 'the Christmas of India'. This festival is also celebrated in many countries outside India – Singapore, Nepal, Trinidad, Fiji, etc.*
10 *On Divali night, people light firecrackers and fireworks; and the goddess Lakshmi is worshipped* (lit. the worship of Lakshmi happens/occurs).
11 *(Just) as not only Christians celebrate Christmas, (similarly) Divali is not the festival of Hindus alone. Nowadays people of almost every religion celebrate Divali.*

शब्दावली **shabdāvalī Vocabulary**

दिवाली/दीवाली	**dīvālī**	the festival of lights/lamps
संस्कृत	**<sanskrita>** (f.)	Sanskrit
अर्थ	**art^{h}a** (m.)	meaning
दीपक/दिया	**dīpak/diyā** (m.)	an earthen lamp
पंक्ति	**paŋkti** (f.)	line, row
भारत	**<b^{h}ārata>** (m.)	the official name of India
प्रसिद्ध	**<prasidd^{h}a>**	famous
त्यौहार	**<tyauhāra>** (m.)	festival

अच्छाई	**acc^{h}āī** (f.)	good (n.), quality, ideal
बुराई	**burāī** (f.)	evil
प्रकाश	**<prakāsha>** (m.)	light
अन्धकार	**<and^{h}kāra>** (m.)	darkness
विजय	**<vijaya>** (f.)	victory
प्रतीक	**<pratīka>** (m.)	symbol
राजा	**rājā** (m.)	king, emperor
राम	**<rāma>** (m.)	Lord Rama (proper name)
राक्षस	**<rākshasa>** (m.)	demon
रावण	**<rāvaNa>** (m.)	the demon king, Ravana
विजय	**<vijaya>** (f.)	victory
मनाना	**manānā** (+**ne**)	to celebrate (festival, holiday), persuade
चौदह	**<caudā>**	fourteen
वर्ष	**varsha** (m.)	year
बनवास	**<banvāsa>** (m.)	exile, residence in forest
पाना	**pānā** (+**ne**)	to find, obtain
राज्य	**rājya** (m.)	kingdom
अयोध्या	**ayod^{h}yā** (f.)	Ayodhya, a place name
लौटना	**lauTnā** (–**ne**)	to return
जलाना	**jalānā** (+**ne**)	to light, to burn; to kindle
आदि	**ādi**	etc.
कई	**kaī**	several
देश	**<desha>** (m.)	country
पटाखा	**paTāxā** (m.)	a firecracker
फुलझड़ी	**p^{h}ul-j^{h}aRī** (f.)	a kind of firework that emits flower-like sparks
चलाना	**calānā** (+**ne**)	to drive, to manage (business), to light/ play firecrackers
लक्ष्मी	**lakshmī** (f.)	Lakshmi, the goddess of wealth, fortune, prosperity
पूजन	**<pūjana>** (m.)	worship
जैसे (कि)	**jɛse (ki)**	as, as if
ईसाई	**īsāī**	a Christian
वैसे	**vɛse**	like that, similarly
हिन्दु	**hindu**	a Hindu
लगभग	**<lagb^{h}aga>**	about, approximately, almost
धर्म	**<d^{h}arma>** (m.)	religion

Pronunciation

With the exception of चौदह **caudā**, all the words enclosed in angle brackets < > are written with the word-final vowel अ **a**. However, in colloquial pronunciation, the final अ **a** is dropped. Since the above passage is written in high and formal style, the use of the word-final अ **a** is indicated.

The numeral **caudā** 'fourteen' is written चौदह **caudah**.

Notes

Sanskritized vs Perso-Arabic style

Style differences in Hindi primarily involve vocabulary. High or formal literary style is often equated with borrowing from Sanskrit, and colloquial style usually borrows from Arabic and Persian. The simple substitution of the Perso-Arabic words for the corresponding Sanskrit words will yield the informal colloquial style of Hindi.

Sanskrit		*Perso-Arabic*		
अर्थ	**art^{h}a**	मतलब	**matlab**	*meaning*
भारत	**b^{h}ārata**	हिन्दुस्तान	**hindustān**	*India*
प्रसिद्ध	**prasidd^{h}a**	मशहूर	**mashhūr**	*famous*
वर्ष	**arsha**	साल	**sāl**	*year*
लगभग	**lagb^{h}aga**	करीब	**karīb**	*about, approximately*

Agentless passives

The Hindi equivalent of the English sentence 'this festival is celebrated' is:

ये	त्यौहार	मनाया	जाता	है।
ye	**tyauhār**	**manāyā**	**jātā**	**hɛ.**
this	festival (m.)	celebrate-past	passive-go-pres.	is

This festival is celebrated.

Hindi tends to omit the passive subject. The opening clause of sentence 7 of Reading practice 1 further exemplifies this point. Notice the omission of the passive subject ('by x') in the following paragraph:

कहा	जाता	है।
kahā	**jātā**	**hɛ.**
say-past	passive-go-pres.	is

(It) is said.

Generic passive subjects, such as 'by people', are understood in these sentences.

Relative clauses

The relative clause relates two clauses. The relative clause contains a relative pronoun which begins with the sound **j-** in Hindi, while in English a relative pronoun begins with the **wh-** word. For example, the English sentence 'The people who live in India celebrate Divali' is paraphrased as 'which/who people live in India, those people celebrate Divali'. So, the Hindi sentence would be

जो	लोग	भारत	में	रहते	हैं
jo	**log**	**b^{h}ārat**	**mẽ**	**rɛhɛte**	**hɛ̃**
who	people	India	in	live-present	are

वे	लोग	दिवाली	मनाते	हैं।
ve	**(log)**	**divālī**	**manāte**	**hɛ̃.**
those	people	Divali	celebrate-pres.	are

The people who live in India celebrate Divali.

The जो **jo-** clause is called the relative clause and is linked to the correlative clause. The second repeated noun (लोग **log** 'people') can be dropped, and the final result is as follows:

जो	लोग	भारत	में	रहते	हैं	वे	दिवाली	मनाते	हैं।
jo	**log**	**b^{h}ārat**	**mẽ**	**rɛhte**	**hɛ̃**	**ve**	**divālī**	**manāte**	**hɛ̃.**

The list of relative and correlative pronouns is given below:

	Simple *Singular*	*Plural*	*Oblique* *Singular*	*Plural*	
Relative	जो **jo**	जो **jo**	जिस **jis**	जिन **jin**	who/which
Correlative	वो/वह **vo**	वे **ve**	उस **us**	उन **un**	

The correlative pronouns are the same as the third person pronouns. Observe one more example of Hindi relative clauses:

जिस	त्यौहार	का	नाम	दिवाली	है,	वो	प्रसिद्ध	है।
jis	**tyauhār**	**kā**	**nām**	**dīvālī**	**hɛ,**	**vo**	**prasiddh**	**hɛ**
which-obl.	festival	of	name	Divali	is	that	famous	is

The festival whose name is Divali is famous.

Other types of relative clause found in Hindi and their markers are as follows:

	Relative	*Correlative*
Place	जहाँ **jahā̃** where, in which	वहाँ **vahā̃** there, in that place
Time	जब **jab** when	तब **tab** then
Manner	जैसे **jɛse** as, in which manner	वैसे **vɛse** in that manner
Directional	जिधर **jid^{h}ar** in which direction	उधर **udhar** in that direction
Kind	जैसा **jɛsā** as/which kind	वैसा **vɛsā** that kind
Quantity	जितना **jitnā** as much/many as	उतना **utnā** that much/many

The relative clauses of kind and quantity behave like 'green' types of adjective which agree with their following noun in number and gender.

The instance of a time relative clause can be found in sentence 7 of the Reading practice at the beginning of this unit:

जब	राजा	राम	अपने	राज्य	लौट	रहे	थे,
jab . . .	**rājā**	**rām**	**apne**	**rājya**	**lauT**	**rahe**	**t^{h}e**
when	king	Rama	own	kingdom	return	ing	was

तब	हर	घर	ने	ख़ुशी	में	दिये	जलाए/जलाये।
tab	**har**	**g^{h}ar**	**ne**	**xushī**	**mẽ**	**diye**	**jalāye.**
then	every	house	agent	happiness	in	lamps	lit

When King Rama was returning to his kingdom, then every house lit lamps in happiness.

Sentence 11 exemplifies the manner relative clause:

जैसे	क्रिसमस	सिर्फ़	ईसाई	ही	नहीं
jɛse	**Christmas**	**sirf**	**īsāī**	**hī**	**nahī̃**
as	Christmas	only	Christians	emp.part.	not

मनाते,
manāte,
celebrate-present

वैसे	दिवाली	सिर्फ़	हिन्दुओं	का	त्यौहार	नहीं	है।
vɛse	**dīvālī**	**sirf**	**hinduõ**	**kā**	**tyauhār**	**nahī̃**	**hɛ.**
in that manner	Divali	only	Hindus	of	festival	not	is

(Just) as not only Christians celebrate Christmas (similarly) Divali is not the festival of the Hindus alone.

पढ़ने का अभ्यास २ **paR^{h}ne kā ab^{h}yās 2** Reading practice 2 (CD 2; 34)

होली - एक और रंग-बिरंगा त्यौहार ***holī ek aur raŋga-biraŋgā tyauhār Holi, the festival of colours***

1 होली भारत का एक और रंग-बिरंगा त्यौहार है।
holī b^{h}ārat kā ek aur raŋga-biraŋgā tyauhār hɛ.
2 यह बसन्त ऋतु में आती है।
ye vasanta ritu mẽ ātī hɛ.
3 इस समय गाँवों में फ़सल कटने के बाद हर घर में अनाज आ जाता है।
is samaya gāvõ mẽ fasal kaTne ke bād har g^{h}ar mẽ bahut anāj ā jātā hɛ.
4 इसलिये ये त्यौहार खुश-हाली का सन्देश लाता है।
isliye ye tyauhār xush-hālī kā sandesh lātā hɛ.
5 इस दिन लोग बहुत उत्साह से एक दूसरे पर रंग फेंकते हैं।
is din log bahut utsāha se ek dūsre par raŋga fẽkte hɛ̃.
6 बच्चे पिचकारी से रंगीन पानी डालते हैं, जब कि बड़े लोग सूखे रंग से खेलते हैं, जिसको गुलाल कहते हैं।
bacce pickārī se raŋgīn pānī Dālte hɛ̃, jab ki baRe log sūk^{h}e raŋga se k^{h}elte hɛ̃ jis ko 'gulāl' kɛhte hɛ̃.
7 हालाँकि इस दिन हर तरह का रंग लगाया जाता है, लाल रंग सर्व—प्रिय है क्योंकि लाल रंग प्रेम का प्रतीक है।
hālā̃ki is din har tarā kā raŋga lagāyā jātā hɛ, lāl raŋga sarva-priya hɛ kyõki lāl raŋga 'prema' kā pratīk hɛ.
8 होली के दिन भारत में 'कारनीवल' जैसा वातावरण होता है। यह बड़ी धूम-धाम से वृंदावन में मनाया जाता है जहाँ श्रीकृष्ण पले थे।
holī ke din b^{h}ārat mẽ '*Carnival*' jɛsā vātāvaraNa hotā hɛ. ye baRī d^{h}ūm-d^{h}ām se brindāban mẽ manāyā jātā hɛ jahā̃ shrī krishn pale t^{h}e.
9 होली के बारे में कई प्राचीन कहानियाँ प्रचलित हैं जो मन की पवित्रता पर ज़ोर देती है।
holī ke bāre mẽ kaī prācīn kahāniyā̃ pracalit hɛ̃ jo mana kī pavitratā par zor detī hɛ̃.
10 इस दिन लोग बड़ी प्रसन्नता से एक-दूसरे को गले लगाते हैं और शत्रुता भूल कर शत्रु को भी मित्र बना लेते हैं।
is din log baRī prasannatā se ek-dūsre ko gale lagāte hɛ̃ aur shatrutā b^{h}ūl kar shatru ko b^{h}ī mitra banā lete hɛ̃.

1 *Holi is another colourful festival of India.*
2 *It falls during spring* (lit. it comes during the spring season).

3 *At this time after the harvest* (lit. cutting) *of the crop, every house is full of grain* (lit. in every house, a lot of grain comes).
4 *Therefore, this festival brings the message of prosperity.*
5 *On this day people throw colour on each other with great enthusiasm.*
6 *The children throw coloured water with a water-gun while the elders play with dry colour, which is called 'gulāl'.*
7 *Although on this day all kinds of colours are used, (the) red (colour) is the favourite because it is the symbol of 'love'.*
8 *On the day of Holi generally (there) is a carnival-like atmosphere in India. This (festival) is celebrated with great joy* (lit. pomp and show) *in Brindavan where Lord Krishna was brought up.*
9 *(There) are several stories prevalent about Holi which emphasize the purification of the mind.*
10 *On this day people embrace each other with great joy and, forgetting enmity* (lit. and having forgotten enmity) *(they) make even the enemy (their) friend.*

शब्दावली **shabdāvalī** **Vocabulary**

होली	**holī** (f.)	the festival of colours
रंग	**raŋga** (m.)	colour
रंग-बिरंगा	**raŋga-biraŋgā**	colourful
वसन्त	**<basanta>**	spring
ऋतु	**ritu** (f.)	season
गाँव	**gā̃v** (m.)	village
फसल	**fasal** (f.)	crop
कटना	**kaTne** (–**ne**)	to be cut
के बाद	**(ke) bād**	after
अनाज	**anāj** (m.)	grain, corn
खुश-हाली	**xush-hālī** (f.)	prosperity
सन्देश	**sandesh** (m.)	message
लाना	**lānā** (–**ne**)	to bring
उत्साह	**utsāh** (m.)	enthusiasm, joy, zeal
एक दूसरे से	**ek dūsre se**	with one another/each other
फेंकना	**p^{h}ẽknā** (+**ne**)	to throw
पिचकारी	**pickārī** (f.)	a syringe-shaped water-gun made of wood or metal
रंगीन	**raŋgīna**	colourful
पानी	**pānī** (m.)	water
डालना	**Dālnā** (+**ne**)	to put in, throw
जबकि	**jabki**	while
सूखा	**sūk^{h}ā** (m. adj.)	dry

खेलना	**k^{h}elnā** (+/–**ne**)	to play
कहते हैं	**kɛhte hɛ̃**	is called/is said
हालाँकि	**hālā̃ki**	although
लगाना	**lagānā** (+**ne**)	to attach, to stick
लाल	**lāl**	red
सर्व-प्रिय	**sarva-priya**	loved by all, the most favourite
प्रेम	**prema** (m.)	love
जैसा	**jɛsā**	as
वातावरण	**vātāvaraNa** (m.)	atomosphere, environment
धूमधाम से	**d^{h}ūm-d^{h}ām se**	with pomp and show
बृंदावन	**<brindāvan>**	the place where Lord Krishna was brought up
श्रीकृष्ण	**shrī krishna**	Lord Krishna
पलना	**palnā** (–**ne**)	to be brought up
प्राचीन	**prācīna**	ancient
प्रचलित होना	**pracalit honā** (–**ne**)	to be prevalent
मन	**mana** (m.)	mind
पवित्रता	**pavitratā** (f.)	purification, holiness
ज़ोर देना	**zor denā** (+**ne**)	to emphasize
प्रसन्नता	**prasannatā** (f.)	happiness, joy
गले लगाना	**gale lagānā**	to embrace
शत्रु	**shatru** (m.)	enemy
शत्रुता	**shatrutā** (f.)	enmity, hostility
भूलना	**b^{h}ūlnā** (+/–**ne**)	to forget
मित्र	**mitra** (m.)	friend

पढ़ने का अभ्यास ३ paR^{h}ne kā ab^{h}yās 3 Reading practice 3 (CD 2; 35)

रक्षा-बन्धन/राखी Rakshāband^{h}an or rāk^{h}ī

'The festival of love and protection'

1. रक्षाबन्धन का दूसरा नाम राखी भी है।
   rakshāband^{h}ban kā dūsrā nām rāk^{h}ī b^{h}ī hɛ.
2 यह भाई-बहन के अटूट प्रेम को याद दिलाता है।
   ye b^{h}āī-bɛhɛn ke aTūT prem ko yād dilātā hɛ.
3 इस दिन हर बहन अपने भाई को सुनहरा धागा बाँधती हैं।
   is din har bɛhɛn apne b^{h}āī ko ek sunharā d^{h}āgā bā̃d^{h}tī hɛ̃.
4 इस धागे का अर्थ है कि भाई अपने बहन को वचन देता है कि वह हमेशा उसकी रक्षा करेगा।

is d^{h}āge kā art^{h}a hɛ ki b^{h}āī apnī bɛhɛn ko vacan detā hɛ ki vo hameshā uskī rakshā karegā.

5 यहाँ तक कि विदेशी भाई भी पुराने समय से इस वचन को पूरा करते रहे हैं।
yahā̃ tak ki videshī b^{h}āī b^{h}ī purāne samaya se is vacan ko pūrā karate rahe hɛ̃.

6 सोलहवीं शताब्दी में गुजरात के सुल्तान ने चित्तौड़ पर आक्रमण किया।
saulvī shatābdī mẽ gujarāt ke sultān ne cittauRa par ākramaNa kiyā.

7 चित्तौड़ की रानी कर्णवती ने पराजित होने से पहले दिल्ली के मुग़ल सम्राट हुमायूँ के पास राखी भेजी।
cittuRa kī rānī karNavatī ne parājit hone se pɛhɛle dillī ke mugal samrāT hūmāyū̃ ke pās rāk^{h}ī b^{h}ejī.

8 जब तक हुमायूँ अपनी अपनायी बहन को बचाने के लिये चित्तौड़ पहुँचा, तब तक रानी जौहर रचा चुकी थी।
jab tak hūmāyū̃ apnī apnāyī bɛhɛn ko bacāne ke liye cittauRa pahũcā, tab tak rānī jauhar racā cukī t^{h}ī.

9 लेकिन हुमायूँ ने फिर भी गुजरात के सुलतान को हराया और रानी कर्णवती के बेटे को, जिसको लड़ाई के समय छिपाकर चित्तौड़ से बाहर भेज दिया गया था, राज्य का उत्तराधिकारी बनाया।
lekin hūmāyū̃ ne p^{h}ir b^{h}ī gujrāt ke *sultān* ko harāya aur rānī karNavatī ke beTe ko, jisko laRāī ke samaya c^{h}ipā kar cittauRa se bāhar b^{h}ej diyā gayā t^{h}ā, rājya kā uttarād^{h}ikārī banāyā.

1 *Rakshabandan's other name is Rakhi.*
2 *This (festival) reminds (us) of the unbreakable love between brother and sister.*
3 *On this day every sister ties (bracelets of) golden thread (on) her brother('s wrist).*
4 *The meaning of this thread is that the brother vows to his sister that he will defend and always protect her.*
5 *Even foreign brothers have been fulfilling this vow since the olden times.*
6 *In the sixteenth century the Sultan of Gujarat attacked Chittaur.*
7 *The queen of Chittaur, Karnavati sent Rakhi to the Mogul king of Delhi before her defeat.*
8 *By the time Humayun reached Chittaur to save his (now) adopted sister, the queen Karnavati had immolated herself.*
9 *Still Humayun defeated the Sultan of Gujarat and made the son of the queen Karnavati the heir of the kingdom, who (had been) sent secretly out of Chittaur at the time of battle (with the Sultan of Gujarat).*

शब्दावली **shabdāvalī Vocabulary**

रक्षा–बन्धन	**rakshā-band^{h}an** (m.)	'the festival of love and protection'
अटूट	**aTūT**	unbreakable
याद दिलाना	**yād dilānā** (+ne)	to remind
सुनहरा	**sunharā** (m. adj.)	golden
धागा	**d^{h}āgā** (m.)	(bracelets of) thread
बाँधना	**bā̃d^{h}nā** (+ne)	to tie
अर्थ	**art^{h}a** (m.)	meaning
वचन	**vacan** (m.)	promise
रक्षा करना	**rakshā karnā** (+ne)	to protect, to defend
यहाँ तक कि	**yahā̃ tak ki**	to the point, to the exent that
विदेशी	**videshī** (m.)	foreigner
पूरा	**purā** (m. adj.)	complete, whole, full
पूरा करना	**pūrā karnā** (+ne)	to complete
सोलहवीं	**<solvī̃>**	sixteenth
शताब्दी	**shatābdī** (m.)	century
गुजरात	**gujarāt**	the state of Gujarat
सुलतान	**sultān** (m.)	a Sultan, king, emperor
चित्तौड़	**cittauRa**	a very famous historical place in Rajasthan
आक्रमण करना	**ākramaNa karnā** (+ne)	to attack
रानी	**rānī** (f.)	queen
पराजित होना	**parājit honā** (–ne)	to be defeated
मुग़ल	**mugal**	the Moguls
सम्राट	**samrāT** (m.)	king, emperor
भेजना	**b^{h}ejnā** (+ne)	to send
अपनाना	**apnānā** (+ne)	to adopt
अपनायी	**apnāyī**	adopted
बचाना	**bacānā** (+ne)	to save
तब तक	**tab tak**	by then
जौहर रचाना	**jauhar racānā**	When defeat seemed certain, Rajput women immolated themselves while Rajput men used to perform a deliberate battle to the death, leaving the enemy with an empty victory. The Rajputs are from the colourful and glamorous desert state of Rajasthan in the north-west of India.
चूँकि	**cū̃ki**	because
हराना	**harānā** (+ne)	to defeat

लड़ाई	**laRāī** (f.)	fight, battle, war
छिपा कर	**c^{h}ipā kar**	secretly
राज्य	**rājya** (m.)	kingdom
उत्तराधिकारी	**uttarād^{h}ikārī** (f.)	heir, inheritor
बनाना	**banānā** (+ne)	to make

Cultural note

उपहार देना और विनम्रता **Gift-giving and politeness**

Gift-giving is a special art in India which requires linguistic finesse. Most Indians don't open their gifts in the presence of their guests. Don't come to a premature judgement about this behavior. They express their gratitude indirectly using expressions such as:

ये	तकलीफ़	आपने	क्यों	की?
ye	**taklīf**	**āpne**	**kyõ**	**kī?**
This	trouble	you-agent	why	did

Why did you go to this trouble?

Or

इसकी	तो	कोई	ज़रूरत	नहीं	थी।
iskī	**to**	**koī**	**zarurat**	**nahī̃**	**t^{h}ī.**
Its	to-part.	any	need	not	was

As regards this, there was no need.

Your answer should be:

तकलीफ़	की	क्या	बात	है?
taklīf	**kī**	**kyā**	**bāt**	**hɛ?**
trouble	of	what	matter	is

What's the trouble?

You, as a guest, can use the following expression while offering the gift:

एक	छोटी	सी	चीज़	लाया/लायी	हूँ।	आशा	है	कि
ek	**c^{h}oTī**	**sī**	**cīz**	**lāyā/lāyī**	**hū̃.**	**āshā**	**hɛ**	**ki**
one	little	-ish	thing	brought (m./f.)	am.	hope	is	that

आपको	पसन्द	आयेगी।
āpko	**pasand**	**āyegī.**
you-to	likeness	come-will

(I) brought a very small(ish) gift. (I) hope you like it.

However, nowadays educated Indians are familiar with Western culture and both open gifts in the presence of their guests and openly express their gratitude.

Observation exercise

भारतीय स्वास्तिक b^hārtīya swāstika 'The Indian swastika'

Speaking of festivals, perhaps I should point out that one should not be frightened or draw the wrong conclusions if one sees a swastika sign on the occasion of a festivity, or even posted permanently on shops or products. In India, particularly among the Hindus, Buddhists and Jains, the symbol is an integrated aspect of spiritual, social and commercial life. The Nazis' symbol was borrowed from India and was twisted in meaning. The original Indian swastika is the symbol of universal prosperity and the well-being of humanity. The original Indian swastika is shown below.

You will have noticed that in the Indian swastika, the four lines point to the four directions and there is a point of cross-section in the middle. This cross-section point symbolizes an individual. The symbol states: 'Wherever I am there should be prosperity around me in all four directions.' Thus, this symbol is created and recreated in the spirit of world peace and prosperity in India every day. Never lose sight of its intrinsic symbolic meaning. If the word 'swastika' still creates shock waves in the West, then imagine the resentment of Indians whose most spiritual and auspicious symbol has been deformed in the West, to the extent that they feel totally betrayed. In short, the Indian swastika is not *twisted* but is straight. Furthermore, it is usually accompanied by an expression beginning with शुभ **shub^h^a**, which means 'auspicious'.

अभ्यास **ab^h^yās Exercises**

Exercise 1

Match the passive statements given in the right-hand column with the three festivals given on the left:

दिवाली	divālī	शत्रुओं को भी मित्र बनाया जाता है। shatruõ ko b^h^ī mitra banāyā jātā hɛ.
होली	holī	दिये जलाये जाते हैं। diye jalāye jāte hɛ̃.
रक्षाबन्धन	rakshāband^h^an	धागा बाँधा जाता है। d^h^āgā bā̃d^h^ā jātā hɛ.
		पटाख़े चलाये जाते हैं। paTāxe calāye jāte hɛ̃.
		गुलाल लगाया जाता है। gulāl lagāyā jātā hɛ.
		रंग से खेला जाता है। raŋga se k^h^elā jātā hɛ.
		राजा राम के अपने राज्य लौटने की ख़ुशी में मनाया जाता है। rājā rām ke apne rājya lauTne kī xushī mẽ manāyā jātā hɛ.

Exercise 2

Translate into English the sentences given in the right-hand column in Exercise 1.

Exercise 3

Read the following relative clause statements and then identify the festival associated with each statement:

1 वो त्यौहार जो अक्तूबर के महीने में आता है।
vo tauhār jo aktūbar ke mahīne mẽ ātā hɛ.
2 वो त्यौहार जो भाई और बहन का है।
vo tauhār jo b^hāī aur bɛhɛn kā hɛ.
3 वो त्यौहार जिसमें बहन भाई को धागा बाँधती है।
vo tauhār jismẽ bɛhɛn b^hāī ko d^hāgā bā̃d^htī hɛ.
4 वो त्यौहार जिस दिन लोग एक दूसरे पर रंग फेंकते हैं ।
vo tauhār jis din log ek-dūsre par raŋga p^hẽkte hɛ̃.
5 वो त्यौहार जिस दिन राजा राम अयोध्या लौटे थे।
vo tauhār jis din rājā rām ayod^hyā lauTe t^he.

मूल व्याकरण
mūl vyākaraNa

Reference grammar

Nouns

Nouns are inflected for gender, number and case.

Gender

There are two genders in Hindi, masculine and feminine. The gender system is partly semantically based and partly phonologically based. The rule of thumb is that inflected nouns ending in आ **-ā** are usually assigned masculine gender whereas the nouns ending in ई **-ī** are feminine. The semantic criterion (logical sex) takes precedence over the phonological criterion. Overall, the gender is unpredictable. रास्ता **rāstā** 'path' is masculine but राह **rāh** 'path' is feminine. दाढ़ी **dāR^{h}ī** 'beard' is feminine and so is सेना **senā** 'army'. Although आदमी **ādmī** ends in ई **-ī**, it is masculine, and माता **mātā** ends in आ **-ā** but is feminine. The class of masculine nouns which *do not end* in आ **-ā** and the feminine nouns which do not end in ई **-ī** are affectionately called 'nerd' nouns.

People of the male sex take masculine gender while those of the female sex are assigned feminine gender. Therefore, nouns such as लड़का **laRkā** 'boy' and आदमी **ādmī** 'man' are masculine whereas लड़की **laRkī** 'girl' and औरत **aurat** 'woman' are feminine. The same is true of some non-human animate nouns. Nouns such as कुत्ता **kuttā** 'dog', घोड़ा **g^{h}oRā** 'horse', बंदर **bandar** 'monkey' and बैल **bɛl** 'ox' are masculine and कुतिया **kutiyā** 'bitch', घोड़ी **g^{h}oRī** 'mare', बंदरी **bandarī** 'female monkey' and गाय **gāy** 'cow' are feminine.

Nouns denoting professions are usually masculine, as भंगी **b^{h}aŋgī** 'sweeper'.

Some animate nouns (species of animals, birds, insects, etc.) exhibit unigender properties in the sense that they are either masculine or feminine. For example, मच्छर **macc^h^ar** 'mosquito', कीड़ा **kīRā** 'insect', चीता **cītā** 'leopard' and उल्लू **ullū** 'owl' are masculine in gender, and nouns such as चिड़िया **ciRiyā** 'bird', कोयल **koyal** 'cuckoo', तितली **titlī** 'butterfly', मक्खी **makk^h^ī** 'fly' and मछली **mac^h^lī** 'fish' are feminine. To specify the sex of animate nouns, words such as नर **nar** 'male' and मादा **mādā** 'female' are prefixed to create compound nouns such as मादा-मच्छर **mādā-macc^h^ar** 'female-mosquito' and नर-चिड़िया **nar-ciRiyā** 'male-bird'.

In the case of inanimate nouns, land, abstract, collective and material nouns gender is partly determined by form and partly by semantics. On many occasions both criteria fail to predict the gender. The names of the following classes of nouns are usually masculine:

trees – पीपल **pīpal** (the name of a tree), सागवान **sāgvān** 'teak', देवदार **devdār** 'cedar', चीड़ **cīR** 'pine', आम **ām** 'mango' (however, इमली **imlī** 'tamarind' is feminine);
minerals and jewels – लाल **lāl** 'ruby', सोना **sonā** 'gold', कोयला **koyalā** 'coal, हीरा **hīrā** 'diamond' (however, चाँदी **cā̃dī** 'silver' is feminine);
liquids – तेल **tel** 'oil', दूध **dūd^h^** 'milk', पानी **pānī** 'water' (however, शराब **sharāb** 'wine/liquor' is feminine);
crops – धान **d^h^ān** 'rice', बाजरा **bājrā** 'millet', मटर **maTar** 'pea';
mountains and oceans – हिमालय **himālaya** 'Himalayas', हिन्दमहासागर **hindmahāsāgar** 'Indian Ocean';
countries – हिन्दुस्तान **hindustān** 'India', पाकिस्तान **pākistān** 'Pakistan', अमरीका **amrīkā** 'America';
Gods, demons, and heavenly bodies – ब्रह्मा **brahmā** 'Brahma', सूरज **sūraj** 'sun';
days and months (Native calendar) – सोमवार **somvār** 'Monday', वैसाख **vaisāk^h^** 'Vaisakh';
body parts – सिर **sir** 'head', कान **kān** 'ear', हाथ **hāt^h^** 'hand' (however, आँख **ā̃kh** 'eye', जबान **zabān** 'tongue' are feminine); and
abstract nouns – प्रेम **prem** 'love', गुस्सा **gussā** 'anger', सुख **suk^h^** 'comfort' (however, some abstract nouns, including a synonym of प्रेम **prem** 'love', i.e. मोहब्बत **mohabbat**, are feminine).

Number

Like English, Hindi has two ways of indicating numbers: singular and plural. However, there are some differences between the Hindi and the English way of looking at the singularity or pluralrity of objects. Words such as पजामा **pajāmā** 'pyjamas', बाल **bāl** 'hair' and कैंची **kẽcī** 'scissors' are singular in Hindi but plural in English. Similarly, चावल **cāval** 'rice' is singular in English but is both singular and plural in Hindi.

Masculine nouns which end in आ **-ā** change to **-e** in their plural form. The other group (the 'nerd group') of masculine nouns that do not end in आ **-ā** remain unchanged. Therefore, they adopt they following patterns:

Masculine nouns

Pattern I: ending in **ā** → **e**

बेटा	**beTā**	son	बेटे	**beTe**	sons
लड़का	**laRkā**	boy	लड़के	**laRke**	boys

Exceptions: राजा **rājā** 'king', पिता **pitā** 'father' – remain unchanged.

Pattern II ('nerd nouns'): not ending in **ā** → remain unchanged

आदमी	**ādmī**	man	आदमी	**ādmī**	men
गुरु	**guru**	teacher	गुरु	**guru**	teachers

Feminine nouns

Similarly, feminine nouns also exhibit patterns. Singular feminine nouns ending in **-ī** (including those ending in **i** or **iyā**) change to **iyā̃** in their plural forms, while those feminine nouns not ending in **-ī** add **ẽ** in the plural.

Pattern I: ending in ī → iyā̃

बेटी	**beTī**	daughter	बेटियाँ	**beTiyā̃**	daughters
लड़की	**laRkī**	girl	लड़कियाँ	**laRkiyā̃**	girls
चिड़िया	**ciRiyā**	bird	चिड़ियाँ	**ciRiyā̃**	birds

Pattern II ('nerd nouns'): not ending in ī → add ẽ

किताब	**kitāb**	book	किताबें	**kitābẽ**	books
माता	**mātā**	mother	माताएँ	**mātāẽ**	mothers
बहू	**bahū**	bride	बहुएँ	**bahuẽ**	brides

Note that feminine nouns ending in a long **ū** shorten the vowel before the plural ending.

Direct and oblique case

Some nouns or noun phrases reflect 'peer pressure' under the influence of a postposition, i.e. they change their shape when they appear before a postposition. The form of the noun which occurs before a postposition is called the *oblique* case. The regular non-oblique forms are called *direct* forms, as shown above.

Masculine singular nouns which follow pattern I change under the influence of postpositions. The word-final vowel आ **ā** changes to **e** in the oblique case. However, all plural nouns change and end in **õ** before postpositions. The following examples illustrate these rules.

Masculine nouns

Pattern I: ending in -ā

	Direct			*Oblique case (before postpositions)*		
Singular	बेटा	**beTā**	son	बेटेको	**beTe ko**	to the son
				(i.e. **ā** → **e**)		
Plural	बेटे	**beTe**	sons	बेटोंसे	**beTõ se**	by the sons
				(i.e. **e** → **õ**)		

Pattern II ('nerd nouns'): not ending in ā

	Direct			*Oblique case (before postpositions)*		
Singular	आदमी	**ādmī**	man	आदमी में	**ādmī mẽ**	in the man
				(i.e. no change)		
Plural	आदमी	**ādmī**	man	आदमियों में	**ādmiyõ mẽ**	in the men
				(i.e. **õ** added; slight change in the vowel **ī** which becomes **i**, and the semivowel **y** intervenes.)		

Feminine nouns

Pattern I: ending in ī

	Direct	*Oblique case (before postpositions)*	
Singular	बेटी **beTī** daughter	बेटी पर **beTī par** (i.e. no change)	on the daughter
Plural	बेटियाँ **beTiyā̃** daughters	बेटियों पर **bɛTiyõ par** (i.e. **ā̃** changes to **õ**)	on the daughters

Pattern II ('nerd nouns'): nouns not ending in ī

	Direct			*Oblique case (before postpositions)*		
Singular	किताब	**kitāb**	book	किताब में	**kitāb mẽ** (i.e. no change)	in the book
Plural	किताबें	**kitābẽ**	book	किताबों में	**kitābõ mẽ** (i.e. **ẽ** changes to **õ**)	in the books

Articles

Hindi has no equivalents to the English articles 'a', 'an' and 'the'. This gap is filled by means of indirect devices such as the use of the numeral एक **ek** for the indefinite article, and the use of the postposition को **ko** with an object to fulfill the function of the definite article.

Pronouns

Although the case system of pronouns is essentially the same as that of nouns, pronouns have more case forms in the oblique case than nouns, as exemplified below by the difference in pronominal form with different postpositions.

Personal: singular

Direct	*Oblique*			
	General Oblique	*Oblique +* को ***ko*** *(e.g. me)*	*Oblique +* का ***kā*** *(e.g. my) possessives*	*Oblique +* ने ***ne*** *(agentive past)*
मैं **mɛ̃** I	मुझ **mujʰ**	मुझको = मुझे **mujʰko = mujʰe** me	मेरा **merā** my	मैंने **mɛ̃ne** I
तू **tū** you	तुझ **tujʰ**	तुझको = तुझे **tujʰko = tujʰe** (to) you	तेरा **terā** your	तूने **tūne** you
वह/वो **vo** he/she	उस **us**	उसको = उसे **usko = use** (to) him/her	उसका **uskā** his/her	उसने **usne** he/she
यह/ये **ye** this	इस **is**	इसको = इसे **isko = ise**	इसका **iskā**	इसने **isne**

Personal: plural

Direct	*Oblique*			
	General Oblique	*Oblique +* को ***ko***	*Oblique +* का ***kā*** *(e.g. our) possessives*	*Oblique +* ने ***ne*** *(agentive past)*
हम **ham** we	हम **ham**	हमको = हमें **hamko = hamẽ** (to) us	हमारा **hamārā** our	हमने **hamne** we
तुम **tum** you (familiar)	तुम **tum**	तुमको = तुम्हें **tumko = tumhẽ** (to) you	तुम्हारा **tumhārā** your	तुमने **tumne** you
आप **āp** you (honorific)	आप **āp**	आपको **āpko** (to) you	आपका **āpkā** your	आपने **āpne** you
वे **ve** they	उन **un**	उनको = उन्हें **unko = unhẽ** (to) them	उनका **unkā** their	उन्होंने **unhõne** they
ये **ye** these	इन **in**	इनको = इन्हें **inko = unhẽ**	इनका **inkā**	इन्होंने **inhõne**

Other Pronouns: singular

Direct	*Oblique*			
	General Oblique	*Oblique + को **ko***	*Oblique + का **kā*** *possessives*	*Oblique + ने **ne*** *(agentive past)*
कौन **kaun** who?	किस **kis**	किसको = किसे **kisko = kise** (to) whom?	किसका **kiskā** whose?	किसने **kisne** who?
जो **jo** who (relative clause)	जिस **jis**	जिसको = जिसे **jisko = jise** (to) whom	जिसका **jiskā** whose	जिसने **jisne** who
क्या **kyā** what	किस **kis**	किसको = किसे **kisko = kise**	किसका **kiskā**	–
कोई **koī** someone	किसी **kisī**	किसीको **kisīko** (to) someone	किसीका **kisīkā** someone's	किसीने **kisīne** someone

Other pronouns: plural

Direct	*Oblique*			
	General oblique	*Oblique + को **ko***	*Oblique + का **kā*** *possessives*	*Oblique + ने **ne*** *(agentive past)*
कौन **kaun** who?	किन **kin**	किनको = किन्हें **kinko = kinhẽ** (to) whom?	किनका **kinkā** whose?	किन्होंने **kinhõne** who?
जो **jo** who (relative clause)	जिन **jin** who	जिनको = जिन्हें **jinko = jinhẽ** (to) whom	जिनका **jinkā** whose	जिन्होंने **jinhone** who

Adjectives

Adjectives can be classified into two groups: हरा **harā** 'green' (inflecting adjectives) and लाल **lāl** 'red' (non-inflecting adjectives). Like masculine nouns, green adjectives end in आ -**ā**. They change their form, or agree, with the following nouns in terms of number and gender and show the signs of 'peer pressure' before a postposition. Red adjectives which do not end in आ -**ā** remain invariable. The following endings are used with the green adjectives when they are inflected for number, gender and case.

Pattern I: the हरा harā 'green' adjectives (inflecting)

	Direct case		*Oblique case*	
	Singular	*Plural*	*Singular*	*Plural*
Masculine	-ā	-e	-e	-e
Feminine	-ī	-ī	-ī	-ī

Example:

Direct		*Oblique*	
अच्छा लड़का **acc^hā laRkā**	good boy	अच्छे लड़के से **acc^he laRke se**	by a/the good boy
अच्छे लड़के **acc^he laRke**	good boys	अच्छे लड़कों से **acc^he laRkõ se**	by good boys
अच्छी लड़की **acc^hī laRkī**	good girl	अच्छी लड़की से **acc^hī laRkī se**	by a/the good girl
अच्छी लड़कियाँ **acc^hī laRkiyā̃**	good girls	अच्छी लड़कियों से **acc^hī laRkiyõ se**	by good girls

Pattern II: the red (लाल lāl) adjectives (non-inflecting)

Direct		*Oblique*	
सुन्दर लड़का **sundar laRkā**	handsome boy	सुन्दर लड़के से **sundar laRke se**	by a/the handsome boy
सुन्दर लड़के **sundar laRke**	handsome boys	सुन्दर लड़कों से **sundar laRkõ se**	by handsome boys
सुन्दर लड़की **sundar laRkī**	beautiful girl	सुन्दर लड़की से **sundar laRkī se**	by a/the beautiful girl
सुन्दर लड़कियाँ **sundar laRkiyā̃**	beautiful girls	सुन्दर लड़कियों से **sundar laRkiyõ se**	by beautiful girls

Possessive pronouns (listed under oblique pronouns + का **kā**), the *reflexive pronoun* अपना **apnā** 'self' and *participles* behave like green adjectives; therefore, they are inflected in number, gender and case.

Postpositions

The Hindi equivalent of English prepositions such as 'to', 'in', 'at', 'on', etc. are called postpositions because they follow nouns and pronouns rather than precede them as in English.

Simple postpositions

Simple postpositions consist of one word. Here is the list of some important simple postpositions.

का	**kā**	of (i.e. possessive marker)
को	**ko**	to; also object marker
तक	**tak**	up to, as far as
ने	**ne**	agent marker for transitive verbs in simple past, present perfect and past perfect tenses
पर	**par**	on, at
में	**mẽ**	in
से	**se**	from, by, object marker for some verbs.
वाला	**vālā**	-er (and wide range of meanings)

Two postpositions, का **kā** and वाला **vālā**, also change like green adjectives; all others act like red adjectives.

Compound postpositions

Compound postpositions consist of more than one word. They behave exactly the same way as the simple postposition, i.e. they are the source of peer pressure and thus require nouns or pronouns to be in the oblique case. Examples of some of the most frequent compound postpositions are given below:

के **ke**-type			की **kī**-type		
के बारे में	**ke bāre mẽ**	about	की तरफ	**kī taraf**	towards
के आगे	**ke āge**	in front of	की जगह	**kī jagah**	instead of

के सामने	**ke sāmne**	facing	की तरह	**kī tarā**	like
के पहले	**ke pɛhle**	before	की बजाय	**kī bajāy**	instead of
के बाद	**ke bād**	after			
के नीचे	**ke nīce**	below			
के ऊपर	**ke ūpar**	above			

Notice that most compound postpositions begin with either के **ke** or की **kī** but *never* with का **kā**.

Question words

In English, the question words such as 'who', 'when' and 'why' begin 'wh-' (exception 'how'); Hindi question words begin with the क **k-** sound. Some of the most common question words are listed below:

Pronouns

क्या	**kyā**	what	*see* pronouns for oblique forms
कौन	**kaun**	who	*see* pronouns for oblique forms
कौन-सा	**kaun-sā**	which	कौन **kaun** remains invariable but सा **sā** changes like the green adjectives

Possessive pronouns

See oblique + का **kā** forms of क्या **kyā** and कौन **kaun** in the section on pronouns.

Adverbs

कब	**kab**	when
कहाँ	**kahā̃**	where
क्यों	**kyõ**	why
कैसा	**kɛsā**	how, of what kind
कितना	**kitnā**	how much, how many

The last two adverbs, कैसा **kɛsā** and कितना **kitnā**, are changeable and behave like the green adjectives.

Question words and word order

In Hindi it is not usual to move question words such as 'what', 'how' and 'where' to the beginning of the sentence. The question words usually stay in their original position, i.e. somewhere in the middle of the sentence. The only exception is the yes–no question, where the Hindi question क्या **kyā** is placed at the beginning of the sentence.

Verbs

The concept of time is quite different in Hindi from the 'unilinear' concept of time found in English. In other words, time is not viewed as smoothly flowing from the past through the present into the future. It is possible to find instances of the present or future within the past. For example, the English expression 'he said that he was going' will turn out to be 'he said that he is going' in Hindi. Similarly, the concept of habituality is also different in Hindi. It is possible to say in English 'I always went there'; however, in Hindi one has to use the past habitual instead of the English simple past to indicate a habitual act. Therefore, the translational equivalent of the English sentence 'I always go there' will be 'I always used to go there' in Hindi.

Infinitive, gerundive or verbal nouns

ना **nā** is suffixed to the verbal stem to form the infinitive (or gerundive or verbal noun) form of the verb. ना **nā** follows the stem in Hindi rather than preceding it.

Simple infinitive

Stem		*Stem* + *ना* ***nā***		
पी	**pī**	पीना	**pīnā**	to drink, drinking
कर	**kar**	करना	**karnā**	to do, doing
जा	**jā**	जाना	**jānā**	to go, going

The infinitive marker आ **ā** becomes ए **e** in the oblique case (e.g. पीने से **pīne se** 'by drinking').

Causative verbs

Intransitive, transitive and detransitive verbs are made causative by a very productive process of suffixation. Two suffixes, आ **-ā** (called the 'first causative' suffix) and वा **-vā** (the 'second causative' suffix) are attached to the stem of a verb, and are placed before the infinitive marker ना **-nā**. The process of causativization brings about some changes in some stems (as in दे **de** 'to give'). Here are examples of some causative verb types:

Type 1

No changes occur in the verbal stem.

Intransitive	*Transitive*	*Causative*
उड़ना **uRnā** to fly	उड़ाना **uRānā** to fly x	उड़वाना **uRvānā** to cause y to fly x
पकना **paknā** to be cooked	पकाना **pakānā** to cook x	पकवाना **pakvnā** to cause y to cook x

Type 2

The stem-vowel of the intransitive verb undergoes either a raising or a shortening process (shown in *italics*) in its corresponding transitive and causative forms.

Intransitive	*Transitive*	*Causative*
जागना **j*ā*gnā** to wake	जगाना **j*a*gānā** to awaken x	जगवाना **j*a*gvānā** to cause y to awaken x
लेटना **l*e*Tnā** to lie down	लिटाना **l*i*Tānā** to lay down	लिटवाना **l*i*Tvānā** to cause y to lay down x
झूलना **j^h*ū*lnā** to swing	झुलाना **j^h*u*lānā** to swing x	झुलवाना **j^h*u*lvānā** to cause y to swing x

Type 3

The stem-vowel of the transitive verb undergoes either a raising or a shortening process in its corresponding intransitive and causative forms.

In cases where the stem is disyllabic, it is the second vowel that undergoes such changes. The distinction between the causative marker वा **-vā** and its corresponding transitive marker आ **-ā** is neutralized; the two causal suffixes occur in free variation.

Type 3a

Intransitive	*Transitive*	*Transitive (with आ* ***-ā****)/causative*
मरना **m*a*rnā**	मारना **m*ā*rnā**	मराना/मरवाना **m*a*rānā/m*a*rvānā**
to die	to kill	to cause y to kill x
पिसना **p*i*snā**	पीसना **p*ī*snā**	पिसाना/पिसवाना **p*i*sānā/p*i*svānā**
to be ground	to grind x	to cause y to grind x
पुजना **p*ū*jnā**	पूजना **p*ū*jnā**	पुजाना/पुजवाना **p*u*jānā/p*u*jvānā**
to be worshipped	to worship x	to cause y to worship x
खुलना **k^h*u*lnā**	खोलना **k^h*o*lnā**	खुलाना/खुलवाना **k^h*u*lānā/k^h*u*lvānā**
to be/become opened	to open x	to cause y to open x

Type 3b

Transitive verbs show one of the following tendencies: a new semantic distinction between the derived and the base transitive forms is created, as shown by the gloss in set A; or derived transitive and causative verbs undergo one level of causativization, as is the case with the set B.

Set A

Transitive	*Transitive (with आ* ***-ā****)*	*Causative*
पढ़ना **paR^{h}nā**	पढ़ाना **paR^{h}ānā**	पढ़वाना **paR^{h}vānā**
to read	to teach	to cause y to teach x
बोलना **b*o*lnā**	बुलाना **b*u*lānā**	बुलवाना **b*u*lvānā**
to speak	to call	to cause y to call x

Set B

The causative marker वा **-vā** occurs in free variation with ला **-lā**. The verbal stem undergoes vowel changes, as in

Transitive			*Transitive (with आ -ā)/causative*		
देना	**d*e*nā**	to give	दिवाना/दिलाना	**d*i*vānā/d*i*lānā**	to cause y to give x
धोना	**d^h*o*nā**	to wash	धुवाना/धुलाना	**d^h*u*vānā/d^h*u*lānā**	to cause y to wash x

Type 4

Some verbs show both consonantal and vowel changes in their corresponding transitive forms. The consonantal alternations are as follows: the intransitive stem-final क **k** becomes च **c**, and the intransitive stem-final ट **T** becomes retroflex ड़ **R**.

Intransitive		*Transitive*		*Causative*	
बिकना	**b*i*knā**	बेचना	**becnā**	बिकवाना	**bikvānā**
to be sold		to sell x		to cause y to sell x	
टूटना	**T*ū*Tnā**	तोड़ना	**t*o*Rnā**	तुड़ाना/तुड़वाना	***tu*RāNā/*tu*RvāNā**
to be broken		to break x		to cause y to break x	

Auxiliary/copula verb

Present

The present tense auxiliary/copular verb agrees in number and person with its subject.

होना **honā** 'to be'

	Singular			*Plural*		
First person	हूँ	**hū̃**	I am	हैं	**hɛ̃**	we are
Second person	है	**hɛ**	you are	हो	**ho**	you (familiar तुम) are
				हैं	**hɛ̃**	you (honorific आप) are
Third person	है	**hɛ**	he, she, it is	हैं	**hɛ̃**	they are

Past

The past tense auxiliary/copular verb agrees in number and gender with its subject.

होना **honā** 'to be'

	Singular			*Plural*		
Masculine	था	$\mathbf{t^h\bar{a}}$	was	थे	$\mathbf{t^he}$	were
Feminine	थी	$\mathbf{t^h\bar{\imath}}$	was	थीं	$\mathbf{t^h\tilde{\bar{\imath}}}$	were

Another conjugation of होना **honā** is as follows:

	Singular			*Plural*	
Masculine	हुआ	**huā**	happened	हुए	**hue**
Feminine	हुई	**huī**		हुईं	**huī̃**

Future

The future tense auxiliary/copular verb agrees in number, gender and person with its subject.

होना **honā**: masculine

	Singular	*Plural*
First person	हूँगा **hū̃gā** I will be	होंगे **hõge** we will be
Second person	होगा **hogā** you will be	होगे **hoge** you (familiar) will be होंगे **hõge** you (आप **āp**, honorific) will be
Third person	होगा **hogā** he/she/it will be	होंगे **hõge** they will be

होना **honā**: feminine

For the feminine forms, replace the word-final vowel of the masculine forms with ई **ī**.

Subjunctive

For the subjunctive forms of होना **honā**, simply drop the final syllable (i.e. गा **gā**, गे **ge**, गी **gī**) from the future tense forms.

Main Verb

Simple present/imperfective/present habitual

The simple present is formed by adding the following suffixes to the main verbal stem:

	Singular		*Plural*	
Masculine	-ता	**-tā**	-ते	**-te**
Feminine	-ती	**-tī**	-ती	**-tī**

The main verb is followed by the present auxiliary forms.

Example: verb stem लिख **lik^{h}** 'to write'

Masculine

Singular		*Plural*	
मैं लिखता हूँ I write	**mẽ lik^{h}tā hū̃**	हम लिखते हैं we write	**ham lik^{h}te hẽ**
तू लिखता है you write	**tū lik^{h}tā hɛ**	तुम लिखते हो you (familiar) write	**tum lik^{h}te ho**
		आप लिखते हैं you (honorific) write	**āp lik^{h}te hẽ**
वह लिखता है he writes	**vo lik^{h}tā hɛ**	वे लिखते हैं they write	**ve lik^{h}te hẽ**

Feminine

Replace ता **-tā** and ते **-te** in the masculine paradigm with ती **-tī**.

Past habitual

The past habitual is derived by substituting the past auxiliary forms for the present auxiliary forms in the simple present tense.

Examples: verb stem लिख **lik^h** 'to write'

Masculine

Singular	*Plural*
मैं लिखता था **mɛ̃ lik^htā t^hā** I used to write	हम लिखते थे **ham lik^hte t^he** we used to write
तू लिखता था **tū lik^htā t^hā** you used to write	तुम लिखते थे **tum lik^hte t^he** you (familiar) used to write आप लिखते थे **āp lik^hte t^he** you (honorific) used to write
वह लिखता था **vo lik^htā t^hā** he used to write	वे लिखते थे **ve lik^hte t^he** they used to write

Feminine

Replace ता **-tā** and ते **-te** in the masculine paradigm with ती **-tī**. Also substitute the auxiliaries थी **t^hī** and थीं **t^hī̃** for था **t^hā** and थे **t^he**, respectively.

Simple past/perfective

The simple past is formed by adding the following suffixes to the verb stem. No auxiliary verb follows the main verb.

	Singular	*Plural*
Masculine	आ **-ā**	ए **-e**
Feminine	ई **-ī**	ईं **-ī̃**

Example: verb stem बैठ **bɛT^h** 'sit'

Masculine

Singular	*Plural*
मैं बैठा **mɛ̃ bɛT^hā** I sat	हम बैठे **ham bɛT^he** we sat
तू बैठा **tū bɛT^hā** you sat	तुम बैठे **tum bɛT^he** you (familiar) sat आप बैठे **āp bɛT^he** you (honorific) sat
वह बैठा **vo bɛT^hā** he sat	वे बैठे **ve bɛT^he** they sat

Feminine
The verb-final आ **ā** and ए **e** are replaced by ई **ī** and ईं **ī̃**, respectively.

Transitive verb and the agentive postposition ने ne

Transitive verbs take the agentive postposition ने **ne** with the subject and the verb agreeing with the object instead of the subject. Observe the paradigm of the simple past tense with the transitive verb लिख **lik^h** 'to write'.

Example: verb stem लिख lik^h 'to write'

Masculine

Singular	*Plural*
मैंने चिट्ठी लिखी **mẽne ciTT^{h}ī lik^{h}ī** I wrote a letter	हमने चिट्ठी लिखी **hamne ciTT^{h}ī lik^{h}ī** we wrote a letter
तूने चिट्ठी लिखी **tūne ciTT^{h}ī lik^{h}ī** you wrote a letter	तुमने चिट्ठी लिखी **tumne ciTT^{h}ī lik^{h}ī** you (familiar) wrote a letter आपने चिट्ठी लिखी **āpne ciTT^{h}ī lik^{h}ī** you (honorific) write a letter
उसने चिट्ठी लिखी **usne ciTT^{h}ī lik^{h}ī** he wrote a letter	उन्होंने चिट्ठी लिखी **unhõne ciTT^{h}ī lik^{h}ī** they wrote a letter

The verb agrees with चिट्ठी **ciTT^{h}ī** 'letter', which is a feminine singular noun. Therefore the verb stays the same regardless of the change in the subject.

Important transitive verbs which do *not* take the ने **ne** postposition are: मिलना **milnā** 'to meet', लाना **lānā** 'to bring' and बोलना **bolnā** 'to speak.'

Default agreement
The rule of thumb is that the verb does not agree with a constituent which is followed by a postposition. For example, if the object marker को **ko** is used with चिट्ठी **ciTT^{h}ī**, the verb will agree with neither the subject nor the object. In such situations, the verb will stay in the *masculine singular* form.

Present perfect

Present perfect verbs are formed by adding the present tense auxiliary forms to the simple past tense. Transitive verbs take the ने **ne** postposition with their subjects.

Example: verb stem बैठ **bɛTʰ** 'to sit'

Masculine

Singular	*Plural*
मैं बैठा हूँ **mɛ̃ bɛTʰā hū̃** I have sat (down)	हम बैठे हैं **ham bɛTʰe hɛ̃** we have sat (down)
तू बैठा है **tū bɛTʰā hɛ** you have sat (down)	तुम बैठे हो **tum bɛTʰe ho** you (familiar) have sat (down) आप बैठे हैं **āp bɛTʰe hɛ̃** you (honorific) have sat (down)
वह बैठा है **vo beTʰā hɛ** he has sat (down)	वे बैठे हैं **ve bɛTʰe hɛ̃** they have sat (down)

Past perfect

Past perfect verbs are formed by adding the past tense auxiliary forms to the simple past tense. Transitive verbs take the ने **ne** postposition with their subjects.

Example: verb stem बैठ **bɛTʰ** 'to sit'

Masculine

Singular	*Plural*
मैं बैठा था **mɛ̃ bɛTʰā tʰā** I had sat (down)	हम बैठे थे **ham bɛTʰe tʰe** we had sat (down)
तू बैठा था। **tū bɛTʰā tʰa** You had sat (down)	तुम बैठे थे **tum bɛTʰe tʰe** you (familiar) had sat (down) आप बैठे थे **āp bɛTʰe tʰe** you (honorific) had sat (down)
वह बैठा था **vo beTʰā tʰā** he had sat (down)	वे बैठे थे **ve bɛTʰe tʰe** they had sat (down)

Future

The following person-number-gender suffixes with a stem form the future tense.

Pronouns	*Singular*				*Plural*			
	Masculine		*Feminine*		*Masculine*		*Feminine*	
First person	ऊँगा	**-ũgā**	ऊँगी	**-ũgī̃**	एँगे	**-ẽge**	एँगी	**-ẽgī**
Second person	एगा	**-egā**	एगी	**-egī**	ओगे	**-oge**	ओगी	**-ogī**
					एँगे	**-ẽge**	एँगी	**-ẽgī**
Third person	एगा	**-egā**	एगी	**-egī**	एँगे	**-ẽge**	एँगी	**-ẽgī**

Example: verb stem लिख **lik^h** 'to write'

Masculine

Singular	*Plural*
मैं लिखूँगा **mẽ lik^{h}ũgā** I will write	हम लिखेंगे **ham lik^{h}ẽge** we will write
तू लिखेगा **tū lik^{h}egā** you will write	तुम लिखोगे **tum lik^{h}oge** You (familiar) will write
	आप लिखेंगे **āp lik^{h}ẽge** you (honorific) will write
वह लिखेगा **vo lik^{h}egā** he will write	वे लिखेंगे **ve lik^{h}ẽge** they will write

Feminine

Replace the last syllable गा **-gā** and गे **-ge** in the masculine paradigm with गी **-gī**.

Subjunctive/optative

The subjunctive (also called optative and hortative) is used to express suggestion, possibility, doubt, uncertainty, apprehension, wish, desire, encouragement, demand, requirement or potential. Subjunctive forms are not coded for gender. Drop the गा **gā**, गे **ge** and गी **gī** endings from the future form, and the remainder will constitute the subjunctive form.

Imperative

The imperative is formed by adding the following endings to the stem:

Intimate/impolite	*Familiar*	*Polite*	*Extra polite*	*Future*	
no suffix	ओ **-o**	इए/इये **-iye**	इएगा **-iyegā**	ना **-nā**	(=infinitive)

Examples

intimate/impolite	तू जा	**tū jā**	Go
familiar	तुम जाओ	**tum jāo**	Go
polite	आप जाइए	**āp jāiye**	(Please) go
extra polite	आप जाइएगा	**āp jāiyegā**	(Please) go
future (non-immediate)	आप जाना	**āp/tum jānā**	(Please) go (sometime in future)

Negative particles and the imperative

नहीं **nahī̃** is not used with imperatives.
मत **mat** is usually used with intimate, familiar and future imperatives.
न **na** is usually used with polite, extra polite and future imperatives.

Present progressive/continuous

The progressive aspect is expressed by means of the independent word रह **rah**, which is homophonous with the stem of the verb रहना **rahnā** 'to live'. The progressive marker agrees with the number and gender of the subject; therefore it can be realized in one of the following three forms:

Progressive marker: रह **rah** '-ing'

Singular *Masculine*	*Feminine*	*Plural* *Masculine*	*Feminine*
रहा **rahā**	रही **rahī**	रहे **rahe**	रहीं **rahī̃**

Examples: verb stem लिख **likʰ** 'to write'

Masculine

Singular		*Plural*	
मैं लिख रहा हूँ	**mɛ̃ likʰ rahā hū̃**	हम लिख रहे हैं	**ham likʰ rahe hɛ̃**
I am writing		we are writing	
तू लिख रहा है	**tū likʰ rahā hɛ**	तुम लिख रहे हो	**tum likʰ rahe ho**
you are writing		you (familiar) are writing	
		आप लिख रहे हैं	**āp likʰ rahe hɛ̃**
		you (honorific) are writing	
वह लिख रहा है	**vo likʰ rahā hɛ**	वे लिख रहे हैं	**ve likʰ rahe hɛ̃**
he is writing		they are writing	

Feminine

Replace रहा **rahā** and रहे **rahe** in the masculine paradigm with रही **rahī**.

Past progressive/continuous

The present auxiliary verb in the present progressive construction is replaced by the past auxiliary verb (था **tʰā** 'was'; थे **tʰe** 'were'; feminine थी **tʰī**, थीं **tʰī̃**) in the past progressive forms.

Irregular verbs

Here is a list of five Hindi irregular verbs in tense forms such as past, imperative and future:

जाना	करना	लेना	देना	पीना
jānā	**karnā**	**lenā**	**denā**	**pīnā**
to go	to do	to take	to give	to drink

Simple past

गया	किया	लिया	दिया	पिया
gayā	**kiyā**	**liyā**	**diyā**	**piyā**
went (m. sg.)	did (m. sg.)	took (m. sg.)	gave (m. sg.)	drank (m. sg.)
गये	किये	लिये	दिये	पिये
gaye (m. pl.)	**kiye** (m. pl.)	**liye** (m. pl.)	**diye** (m. pl.)	**piye** (m. pl.)
गयी	की	ली	दी	पी
gayī (f. sg.)	**kī** (f. sg.)	**lī** (f. sg.)	**dī** (f. sg.)	**pī** (f. sg.)
गयीं	कीं	लीं	दीं	पीं
gayī̃ (f. pl.)	**kī̃** (f. pl.)	**lī̃** (f. pl.)	**dī̃** (f. pl.)	**pī̃** (f. pl.)

Imperative

(polite)	कीजिए/कीजिये **kījiye**	लीजिए/लीजिये **lījiye**	दीजिए/दीजिये **dījiye**	पीजिए/पीजिये **pījiye**
(familiar)	regular	लो **lo**	दो **do**	पियो **piyo**

Future

लेना **lenā** to take	लूँगा **lū̃gā** I will take लेंगे **lẽge** will take (m. pl.)	लोगे **loge** you (तुम) will take	लेगा **legā** will take (m. sg.)
देना **denā** to give	दूँगा **dū̃gā** I will give देंगे **dẽge** will give (m. pl.)	दोगे **doge** you (तुम) will give	देगा **degā** will give (m. sg.)

Participles

Present/imperfective participle

The present participial marker is **-t-** which immediately follows the verbal stem and is, in turn, followed by number and gender markers, as shown below:

Masculine *Singular*	*Plural*	*Feminine* *Singular*	*Plural*
stem + ता stem-**t-ā**	stem + ते stem-**t-e**	stem + ती stem-**t-ī**	stem + ती stem-**t-ī**

The present participle may be used as either adjective or adverb. The optional past participial form of the verb होना **honā** 'to be' may immediately follow the present participial form. The forms of the optional element are as follows:

Masculine *Singular*	*Plural*	*Feminine* *Singular*	*Plural*
हुआ **huā**	हुए **hue**	हुई **huī**	हुईं **huī̃**

Examples

चलता (हुआ) लड़का	**caltā (huā) laRkā**	walking boy
चलती (हुई) लड़की	**caltī (huī) laRkī**	walking girl

The present participial form and the optional 'to be' form agree in number and gender with the following head noun. The retention of the optional form makes the participial phrase emphatic in nature. The present participle indicates an *ongoing action.*

Past/perfective participle

The past participial form is derived by adding the following suffixes, declined for number and gender, to the verbal stem. Like the present participle, the optional past participial form of the verb होना **honā** 'to be' may immediately follow the past participial form.

Masculine *Singular*	*Plural*	*Feminine* *Singular*	*Plural*
stem + ा stem-**ā**	stem + े stem-**e**	stem + ी stem-**ī**	stem + ी stem-**ī**

The past participle may be used as either adjective or adverb. The past participial form and the optional 'to be' form agree in number and gender with the following head noun. The retention of the optional form makes the participial phrase emphatic in nature. The past participle indicates a *state*, as in

बैठी (हुआ) लड़का	**bɛTʰā (huā) laRkā**	a seated boy
बैठी (हुई) लड़की	**bɛTʰī (huī) laRkī**	a seated girl

The irregular past participle is formed the same way as the past tense form.

Absolutive/conjunctive participle

The absolutive/conjunctive participle is formed by adding the invariable कर **kar** to the verbal stem, as in

Stem			*Conjunctive participle*		
लिख	**lik^h**	write	लिख कर	**lik^h kar**	having written
आ	**ā**	come	आ कर	**ā kar**	having come
पी	**pī**	drink	पी कर	**pī kar**	having drunk

ते ही **-te hī** participle 'as soon as'

This participle is formed by adding the invariable ते ही **-te hī** 'as soon as' to the verbal stem.

Stem			*'as soon as' participle*		
लिख	**lik^h**	write	लिखते ही	**lik^{h}te hī**	as soon as (s/he) wrote
आ	**ā**	come	आते ही	**āte hī**	as soon as (s/he) came
पी	**pī**	drink	पीते ही	**pīte hī**	as soon as (s/he) drank

Agentive participle

The agentive participle is formed by adding the marker वाला **vālā** to the oblique infinitive form of the verb. वाला **vālā** agrees in number and gender with the following noun.

Masculine				*Feminine*			
Singular		*Plural*		*Singular*		*Plural*	
वाला	**vālā**	वाले	**vāle**	वाली	**vālī**	वाली	**vālī**

Examples

Stem	*Oblique infinitive*	*Agentive participle*	
लिख	लिखने	लिखने वाला लड़का	
lik^h	**lik^{h}ne**	**lik^{h}ne vālā laRkā**	the boy who writes.
write		लिखने वाले लड़के	
		lik^{h}ane vāle laRke	the boys who write.
		लिखने वाली लड़की	
		lik^{h}ne vālī laRkī	the girl who writes
		लिखने वाली लड़कियाँ	
		lik^{h}ne vālī laRkiyā̃	the girls who write

अभ्यास: कुंजी
$ab^{h}y\bar{a}s$: kuñjī

Key to exercises

हिन्दी लेखन और उच्चारण hindī $lek^{h}an$ aur uccāraN
Hindi writing system and pronunciation

Exercise 1

1 C 2 A 3 C 4 B 5 B

Exercise 2

1 A, D 2 B, D 3 A, B 4 B, C 5 B, D

Exercise 3

1	टाक	Tāk	i.e. 1 B
2	ठक	$T^{h}ak$	i.e. 2 B
3	डाग	Dāg	i.e. 3 B
4	धक	$d^{h}ak$	i.e. 4 A
5	पड़	paR	i.e. 5 B
6	सर	sar	i.e. 6 A
7	कढ़ी	$kaR^{h}\bar{\imath}$	i.e. 7 B
8	ठीक	$T^{h}\bar{\imath}k$	i.e. 8 B

Exercise 4

1	काल	kāl	i.e. 1 A
2	दिन	din	i.e. 2 A
3	मिल	mil	i.e. 3 A
4	चूक	cūk	i.e. 4 B
5	मैल	mɛl	i.e. 5 B

6 सेर ser i.e. 6 A
7 बिन bin i.e. 7 A
8 बल bal i.e. 8 B

पहला पाठ - लिपि pɛhlā pāT^h – lipi Script unit 1

Exercise 1

1 aman 2 asal 3 jalan 4 kalam 5 kamal 6 garam
7 jab 8 kab 9 tab 10 sab

Exercise 2

ka, ya, t^{h}a, ta, g^{h}a, d^{h}a, b^{h}a, ma, va, ba

Exercise 3

1 ख, र, व 2 ठ, त, ठ, थ 3 द, ड, ध, ढ 4 प, फ, ब, य 5 र, ड़, ढ़

Exercise 4

1 कट 2 गल 3 चल 4 नमक 5 सबक 6 परख 7 सदर
8 चलन 9 मन 10 पल 11 गरम

दूसरा पाठ - लिपि dūsrā pāT^h – lipi Script unit 2

Exercise 1

1 b^{h}ārī 2 baRā 3 kitanā 4 kālā 5 b^{h}ārat
6 gāRī 7 kinārā 8 gīt 9 gāyab 10 cāval
11 cāhnā 12 ciRiyāg^{h}ar 13 zarā 14 jīvan 15 jāpān
16 cor 17 mor 18 p^{h}al 19 b^{h}ūt 20 caut^{h}āu
21 Daul 22 pulis 23 hāt^{h}ī 24 sitār 25 shām

(Note: व is transcribed as v above.)

Exercise 2

1 जबकि 2 की 3 बाज़ार 4 राजा 5 रानी 6 पहचान 7 नई 8 बनारस
9 कानपुर 10 माता 11 पिता 12 कभी 13 मिलन 14 ज़मीन 15 कार 16 महीना
17 साल 18 दिन 19 चार 20 सात 21 सवेरा 22 चाय 23 पानी 24 पति
25 भालू 26 रात 27 दोपहर 28 खोल 29 सौ 30 सोना

Exercise 3

1 रिचर्ड 2 बिल 3 सेयरा 4 जैनिफर 5 डॉन

Exercise 4

रुपया डर
रूखा नाम
कर थान
कि घर
और डाल

तीसरा पाठ – लिपि **tīsrā pāT^h – lipi Script unit 3**

Exercises 1–2

1 थाना वहीं है।
2 आप मेरी मदद कर सकते हैं?
3 मैं वहाँ कैसे जाऊँ?
4 ये मेरी गलती नहीं।
5 यहाँ खतरा है।
6 बचाओ!
7 यह बहुत ज़रूरी है।
8 डाक-खाना कहाँ है?
9 किस खिड़की पर जाऊँ?
10 टिकट कितना लगेगा?
11 ई-मेल अमरीका भेजना चाहता हूँ।
12 मुझे चिन्ता/फ़िक है।

Exercise 3

1 आइए 2 आओ 3 खाइए 4 खा लो 5 माइक

Exercise 4

1 hā vs hā̃ 2 hū vs hū̃ 3 hɛ vs hɛ̃ 4 me vs mẽ

चौथा पाठ – लिपि **caut^{h}ā pāT^h – lipi Script unit 4**

Exercise 1

1 पूछ-ताछ का दफ़्तर।
2 मैं रास्ता भूल गयी हूँ।

3 मैं रास्ता भूल गया हूँ।
4 तंग मत करो।
5 मैं कुंजी ढूंढ रहा हूँ।
6 नहीं मिल रही।
7 चिट्ठी हवाई डाक से भेजिये।
8 क्या आप ये सामान सीधे बम्बई भेज सकते हैं?
9 समान के लिये रसीद दीजिये।
10 मेरा सामान नहीं आया।

Exercise 2

1 ham ek haftā dillī mẽ rahẽge.
2 mɛ̃ yahā̃ c^{h}uTTī par hū̃.
3 ham yahā̃ kām se āye hɛ̃.
4 ye merā pāsporT hɛ.
5 kyā is sāmān par DyūTī lagegī?
6 ye cīzẽ mere apne istemāl ke liye hɛ̃.
7 mere pās DyūTī vālā sāmān nahī̃ hɛ.
8 mere pās kuc^h gifTs hɛ̃.
9 is mẽ sirf kapRe aur kitābẽ hɛ̃.
10 is ke alāvā koī aur cīz nahī̃ hɛ.

Exercise 4

nokiyā fon kī duniyā mẽ āpkā svāgat hɛ.

hindī mẽ TɛkT mɛsej b^{h}ejie.

pāvar kuñjī nevī kuñjī
haTāẽ kuñjī skrāl kuñjī
nambar kuñjiyā̃

पाँचवाँ पाठ - लिपि **pā̃cvā̃ pāT^h – lipi Script unit 5**

Exercise 1

1 ā # i # ye
2 aur # tẽ
3 paR^h # tā
4 su # no
5 na # mas # te
6 mi # lẽ # ge
7 sun # kar
8 ād # mī

Exercise 3

mausam	dillī	mumbaī	kolkatā
tāpmān	das digrī sī	padrah digrī sī	solah digrī sī
barsāt	bārish	bādal	d^hūp
havā	tez	halkī	mand

पाठ १ pāT^h ek Unit 1

Exercise 1

1 नमस्ते। 2 ठीक है। 3 सलाम। 4 अल्लाह का शुक्र है। 5 अच्छा, नमस्ते। 6 सत् स्री अकाल है। 7 मेहरबानी है or अल्लाह का शुक्र है। 8 नमस्ते जी। 9 हुकम नहीं, विनती है।

1 namaste 2 T^hīk hɛ. 3 salām 4 allāha kā shukra hɛ. 5 (acc^{h}ā), namaste. 6 sat srī akāl jī. 7 meharbānī hɛ *or* (allāh kā) shukra hɛ. 8 namaste jī. 9 hukam nahī̃, vintī hɛ.

Exercise 2

1 नमस्ते।	नमस्ते।
2 क्या हाल है?	ठीक है
3 आप के मिज़ाज कैसे हैं?	अल्लाह का शुक्र है।
4 खुदा हाफ़िज़	खुदा हाफ़िज़।
5 सब ख़ैरियत है?	मेहरबानी है।
6 सलाम।	सलाम

1 namaste.	namaste.
2 kyā hāl hɛ?	T^hīk hɛ.
3 āp ke mizāj kaise hɛ̃?	allāh kā shukr hɛ.
4 xudā hāfiz	xudā hāfiz.
5 sab xɛriyat hɛ?	meharbānī hɛ.
6 salām	salām.

Exercise 3

Conversation 1

A: सलाम ।
B: सलाम।

B: सब ख़ैरियत है?
A: मेहरबानी है, और आपके मिज़ाज कैसे हैं?
B: अल्लाह का शुक्र है।

A: salām.
B: salām.
B: sab xɛriyat hɛ?
A: meharbānī hɛ, aur āp ke mizāj kɛse hɛ̃?
B: allāh kā shukr hɛ.

Conversation 2

A: सत् स्री अकाल जी।
B: सत् स्री अकाल जी।
B: क्या हाल है?
A: ठीक है, और आप?
B: मैं भी ठीक हूँ।
A: अच्छा, सत् स्री अकाल।
B: सत् स्री अकाल।

A: sat srī akāl jī.
B: sat srī akāl jī.
B: kyā hāl hɛ?
A: T^{h}īk hɛ, aur āp?
B: mɛ̃ b^{h}ī T^{h}īk hũ.
A: acc^{h}ā, sat srī akāl.
B: sat srī akāl.

Exercise 4

1 सवाल: क्या हाल है?
जवाब: ठीक है।
सवाल: और आप?
जवाब: मैं भी ठीक हूँ।
2 सवाल: आप कैसे हैं?
जवाब: ठीक हूँ।

1 Question: kyā hāl hɛ?
Answer: T^{h}īk hɛ.
Question: aur āp?
Answer: mɛ̃ b^{h}ī T^{h}īk hũ.
2 Question: āp kɛse hɛ̃?
Answer: T^{h}īk hũ.

Exercise 5

	Long sentences	*Short sentences*
1	और आप कैसे हैं?	कैसे हैं?
2	मैं भी ठीक हूँ।	ठीक हूँ।
3	आपकी मेहरबानी है।	मेहरबानी है।
4	आपके मिज़ाज कैसे हैं?	मिज़ाज कैसे हैं?

1	aur āp kɛse hɛ̃?	kɛse hɛ̃?
2	mɛ̃ b^hī T^hīk hũ.	T^hīk hũ.
3	āpkī meharbānī hɛ.	meharbānī hɛ̃.
4	āpke mizāj kɛse hɛ̃?	mizāj kɛse hɛ̃?

Exercise 6

Most probably both are Hindus. हिन्दू हैं। hirdū hɛ̃

पाठ २ **pāT^h do Unit 2**

Exercise 1

मैं दिल्ली का हूँ। मेरे चार भाई हैं। मेरा छोटा भाई शिकागो में काम करता है। मेरे दो बड़े भाई इंग्लैड़ में रहते हैं। मेरा नाम अमर है। मैं स्कूल जाता हूँ। मेरी दो बहनें भी हैं।मेरे पिता जी भी काम करते हैं। आप कहाँ रहते हैं? आपके कितने भाई-बहनें हैं। आपकी माता जी क्या काम करती हैं।

mɛ̃ dillī kā hũ̄. mere cār b^hāi hɛ̃. merā c^hoTā b^hāī *Chicago* mɛ̃ kām kartā hɛ. mere do baRe b^hāī *England* mẽ rɛhte hɛ̃. merā nām amar hɛ. mɛ̃ *school* jātā hũ̄. merī do bɛhɛnẽ b^hī hɛ̃. mere pitā jī b^hī kām karte hɛ̃. āp kahā̃ rɛhte hɛ̃? āpke kitne b^h āī-bɛhɛnẽ hɛ̃. āpkī mātā jī kyā kām kartī hɛ̃?

Exercise 2

acc^{h}a	burā	अच्छा	बुरा
baRā	c^hoTā	बड़ा	छोटा
bɛhɛn	b^haī	बहन	भाई
laRkā	laRkī	लड़का	लड़की
ādmī	aurat	आदमी	औरत
hā̃	nahī̃	हाँ	नहीं

Exercise 3

banāras	se	बनारस से
shɛhɛr	mẽ	शहर में
das	bɛhɛnẽ	दस बहनें
cār	b^{h}āī	चार भाई
do	ādmī	दो आदमी
kitne	b^{h}āī	कितने भाई
pīlī	sāRī	पीली साड़ी

Exercise 4

kahiye	कहिए
xushī	खुशी
baRī xushī huī	बड़ी खुशी हुई
pūrā nām	पूरा नाम
dūsrā	दूसरा
kitne b^{h}āī	कितने भाई
milẽge	मिलेंगे

Exercise 5

a d g a ⓑ a d z x ⓢ ⓤ ⓝ ⓘ ⓨ ⓔ z y x u f g
l l k j ⓐ z x c v b n m a s ⓟ q w e r t y
z x c v Ⓡ a d g a r t y f g h ⓐ s g h j o
r t y f ⓘ b g t ⓧ ⓤ ⓢ ⓗ ⓘ ⓘ z q ⓣ s k x p
c v b n ⓘ w s x e d v r a t g h t ⓐ h z c
q a z w c w s v f r y h n m h u i k ⓐ u c

Exercise 6

Voices of two women: Abhilasha Pande and Meenu Bharati
Setting: A crowded shop

अभिलाषा:	(*bumps into Meenu*) माफ़ कीजिये।
मीनू:	माफ़ी की बात नहीं। बहुत भीड़ है।
अभिलाषा:	सच।
मीनू:	मेरा नाम मीनू भारती है।
अभिलाषा:	और मेरा नाम अभिलाषा पाँडे है।
मीनू:	मैं यहाँ रोज़ आती हूँ।
अभिलाषा:	आप दिल्ली की हैं ना?
मीनू:	जी हाँ।

ABHILASHA: (*bumps into Meenu*) māf kījiye.
MEENU: māf kī bāt nahī̃. bahut b^{h}īR hɛ.
ABHILASHA: sac.
MEENU: mera nām Meenu Bharati hɛ.
ABHILASHA: aur merā nām Abhilasha Pande hɛ.
MEENU: mɛ̃ yahā̃ roz ātī hū̃.
ABHILASHA: āp dillī kī hɛ̃ nā?
MEENU: jī hā̃.

पाठ ३ **pāT^{h} tīn Unit 3**

Exercise 1

1 मुझको जयपुर की टिकट चाहिये/मुझको जयपुर के लिये टिकट चाहिये। *variation*: चाहिये = चाहिए
2 क्या आपको दवाई चाहिये?
3 मुझको दो घर चाहिये।
4 मुझको *गराज* में कार चाहिये।
5 आपको यह सुन्दर साड़ी चाहिये।

1 muj^{h}ko jaipur kī TikaT cāhiye/muj^{h}ko jaipur ke liye TikaT cāhiye.
2 kyā āpko davāī cāhiye?
3 muj^{h}ko do g^{h}ar cāhiye.
4 muj^{h}ko *garage* mẽ kār cāhiye.
5 āpko ye sundar sāRī cāhiye.

Exercise 2

1 मेरी एक बहन है। 2 मेरे दो भाई हैं। 3 मेरे पास एक कम्प्यूटर है। 4 मेरा हाल ठीक है। 5 मुझको सिर-दर्द है। 6 मुझको काम चाहिये। 7 मेरा लड़का घर लेता है।

1 merī ek bɛhɛn hɛ. 2 mere do b^{h}āī hɛ̃. 3 mere pās ek kampyuTar hɛ. 4 merā hāl T^{h}īk hɛ. 5 muj^{h}ko sir-dard hɛ. 6 ~~muj^{h}ko~~ kām cāhiye. 7 merā laRkā g^{h}ar letā hɛ.

Exercise 3

मुझको	बुख़ार है।
मेरे पास	रुपये हैं।

आपके	घर में कितने आदमी हैं?
मेरा शहर	बहुत सुन्दर है।
इह फ्लाईट	आपके लिये है।
इसका दाम	क्या है?

mujʰko	buxār hɛ.
mere pās	rupiye hɛ̃.
āpke	ghar mẽ kinte ādmī hɛ̃?
merā shɛhɛr	bahut sundar hɛ.
ye *flight*	āpke liye hɛ.
is kā dām	kyā hɛ?

Exercise 4

WAITER: नमस्ते।
YOU: नमस्ते।
WAITER: आप कैसे हैं?
YOU: (मैं) ठीक हूँ।
WAITER: आपको मैन्यू चाहिये?
YOU: नहीं, लंच के लिये स्पैशल क्या है?
WAITER: *लंच-स्पेशल* शाकाहारी *(i.e. vegetarian)* है।
YOU: शाकाहारी-*स्पेशल* ठीक है। वह क्या है? *or* *वैजीटेरियन-स्पेशल* ठीक है। यह क्या है?
WAITER: दाल, रोटी, रायता, सब्ज़ी और चावल।
YOU: मुझको दाल ज़रा मसालेदार चाहिये।
WAITER: ठीक है।

WAITER: namaste.
YOU: namaste.
WAITER: āp kɛse hɛ̃?
YOU: (mɛ̃) Tʰīk hū̃.
WAITER: āpko *menu* cāhiye?
YOU: nahī̃, lunch ke liye *special* kyā hɛ?
WAITER: *lunch-special* shākāhārī (*i.e. vegetarian*) hɛ.
YOU: shākāhārī-*special* Tʰīk hɛ. vo kyā hɛ? *or vegetarian-special* Tʰīk hɛ. ye kyā hɛ?
WAITER: dāl, roTī, rāytā, sabzī aur cāval.
YOU: mujʰko dāl zarā masāledār cāhiye.
WAITER: Tʰīk hɛ.

पाठ ४ Unit 4

Exercise 1

मुझको पढ़ना पसन्द है। मुझको क्या पसन्द है? मुझको क्या-क्या पसन्द है। मुझको गाने का शौक है। मुझको तैरने का शौक है। मुझको खाने का शौक है।

mujʰko paRʰnā pasand hɛ. mujʰko kyā pasand hɛ? mujʰko kyā-kyā pasand hɛ? mujʰko gāne kā shauk hɛ. mujʰko tɛrne kā shauk hɛ. mujʰko kʰāne kā shauk hɛ.

By substituting आपको **āpko** for मुझको **mujʰko**, you can generate six more sentences.

Exercise 2

1 जवाब: गाने के अलावा जॉन को नाचना पसन्द है।
2 जवाब: जूडी को कहानियाँ और कविताएँ लिखने के / का शौक हैं/ है ।
3 जवाब: रमेश को मुर्गा खाना नापसन्द है।
रमेश को माँसाहारी (*or चिकन*) खाना नापसन्द है।
रमेश को कविताएँ नापसन्द हैं।
रमेश को देशी-संगीत (*or कन्ट्री* संगीत) नापसन्द है।
4 जवाब: रमेश को समोसा खाना पसन्द है।
रमेश को शाकाहारी (*or वैजीटेरियन*) खाना पसन्द है।
रमेश को कहानियाँ पसन्द हैं।
रमेश को भारतीय संगीत पसन्द है।
रमेश को भारतीय (*or* हिन्दुस्तानी) संगीत पसन्द है।

1 gāne ke alāvā John ko nācnā pasand hɛ.
2 Judy ko kahāniyā̃ aur kavitāẽ likʰne kā shauk hɛ. *or*
Judy ko kahāniyā̃ aur kavitāẽ likʰne ke shauk hɛ̃.
3 Ramesh ko murgā (or chicken) kʰānā nāpasand hɛ.
Ramesh ko *non-vegetarian* (or mā̃sāhārī) kʰānā nāpasand hɛ.
Ramesh ko kavitāẽ nāpasand hɛ̃.
Ramesh ko deshī saŋgīt (or country music) nāpasand hɛ.
4 Ramesh ko samosā kʰānā pasand hɛ.
Ramesh ko shākāhārī (or *vegetarian*) kʰānā pasand hɛ.
Ramesh ko kahāniyā̃ pasand hɛ̃.
Ramesh ko bʰārtīya (or *hindustānī/Indian*) saŋgīt pasand hɛ.

Exercise 3

1 John likes to eat/eating. John likes food.
2 John likes to sing/singing. John likes (the) song.

Exercise 4 (examples)

x करने से मना करना। उन का कहना (कि) कमरा साफ़ करो।

x karne se manā karnā (to prohibit from doing x); unkā kɛhnā: kamrā sāf karo (their saying: clean your room).

Exercise 5

मुझको तैरने का शौक है। मुझको तैरना पसन्द है। मुझको तैरना अच्छा लगता है।
Variation: मुझको = मुझे

muj^hko tɛrne kā shauk hɛ. muj^hko tɛrnā pasand hɛ. muj^hko tɛrnā acc^hā lagtā hɛ.

Exercise 6

1	cats	बिल्लियाँ
2	dogs	कुत्ते
3	spicy foods	मसालेदार खाना
4	cricket (game)	क्रिकेट
5	b^haratnāTayam	भरतनाट्यम्
6	rock music	रॉक संगीत

पाठ ५ Unit 5

(If you are female, the final vowel of the verb forms given in italics needs to be replaced by the vowel ई **ī**.)

मेरा नाम x है।
(number) दिन आगरा रहूँ *गा*।
दिल्ली और आगरा जाऊँ *गा*।
यह दिल्ली (x शहर) का पता है।
fill out the address.
(number) दिनों के बाद।
(or x (number) तारीख़ को)।
जी नहीं।
merā nām x hɛ.
(number) din rahū̃*gā*.
dillī aur āgrā jāū̃*gā*.
ye dillī (x city) kā patā hɛ:
(fill out the addresss)

(number) dinõ ke bād.
(or x (number) tārīx ko).
jī nahī̃.

Exercise 2

मैं आपके लिये क्या कर सकता हूँ? हम आगरा जाना चाहते हैं? आगरा कितनी दूर है? बहुत दूर नहीं, लेकिन आप कब जा रहे हैं? हम कल जाएँगे। गाड़ी सुबह दिल्ली से चलती है। आप गाड़ी से जाना चाहते हैं?

mɛ̃ āpke liye kyā kar saktā hū̃? ham āgrā jānā cāhte hɛ̃. āgrā kitnī dūr hɛ? bahut dūr nahī̃, lekin āp kab jā rahe hɛ̃? ham kal jāẽge. gāRī subā dillī se caltī hɛ. āp gāRī se jānā cāhte hɛ̃?

Exercise 3

प्रिय राकेश

तुम्हारा ख़त मिला। पढ़ कर ख़ुशी हुई। तुम कब आ रहे हो? कल मैं शिकागो जा रहा हूँ। शिकागो बहुत बड़ा शहर है। मैं शिकागो हवाई जहाज़से जाऊँगा। लेकिन मैं हवाई जहाज़ से नहीं जाना चाहता हूँ। गाड़ी मुझे हवाई जहाज़ से ज़्यादा पसन्द है। बाकी सब ठीक है।

तुम्हारा दोस्त,
राजीव।

Priya Rakesh:

tumhārā xat milā. paR^{h} kar xushī huī. tum kab ā rahe ho? kal mɛ̃ *Chicago* jā rahā hū̃. *Chicago* bahut baRā shɛhɛr hɛ. mɛ̃ *Chicago* hawāī jahāz (airplane) se jāū̃gā. lekin mɛ̃ hawāī jahāz se nahī̃ jānā cāhtā hū̃. gāRī muj^{h}e hawāī jahāz se zyāda pasand hɛ. bākī sab T^{h}īk hɛ.

tumhārā dost,
Rājīv

Exercise 4

आप कहाँ जा रही हैं? आप यहाँ कितने दिन रहेंगी? आप किस का काम कर रही हैं? क्या आपको चाय बहुत पसन्द है? आपके कितने भाई हैं?

āp kahā̃ jā rahī hɛ̃. āp yahā̃ kitne din rahẽgī? āp kiskā kām kar rahī hɛ̃? kyā āpko cāy bahut pasand hɛ? āpke kitne b^{h}aī hɛ̃?

Exercise 5

अगर मुझको एक मिलियन डॉलर मिलेंगे, तो मैं दुनिया का सफ़र करूँगा/ करूँगी। राजा/ रानी की तरह रहूँगा/ रहूँगी। अपने लिये एक नाव और रोल्स राय्स ख़रीदूँगा/ खरीदूँगी। अपनी पत्नी / अपने पति के लिये हीरे ख़रीदूँगा /ख़रीदूँगी। लेकिन ख़ुशी से पागल नहीं हो जाऊँगा/ जाऊँगी । कुछ देर के बाद अपनी नौकरी करने जरूर जाऊँगा/ जाऊँगी।

agar muj^{h}ko ek *million dollars* milẽge, to mɛ̃ duniyā kā safar karū̃gā/karū̃gī. rājā/rānī kī tarah rahū̃gā/rahū̃gī. apne liye ek nāv aur Rolls Royce xarīdū̃gā /xarīdū̃gī. apnī patnī/ apne pati ke liye hīre xarīdū̃gā/xarīdū̃gī. lekin xushī se pāgal nahī̃ ho jāū̃gā/jāū̃gī, kuc^h der ke bād apnī naukrī karne zarūr jāū̃gā/jāū̃gī.

Exercise 6

हम *रोबात* हैं। हम *कैलिफ़ोर्निया* से हैं। हम हिन्दी बोल सकते हैं। हम हिन्दी समझ भी सकते हैं।हम हिन्दी गाने गा सकते हैं । हमारी *मैमोरी* बहुत बड़ी है। हम हर सवाल पूछ सकते हैं और हर जवाब दे सकते हैं। यानी हर काम कर सकते हैं।हम हमेशा काम कर सकते हैं।हम कभी नहीं थकते हैं। हमारे पास हर सवाल का जवाब है। लेकिन मसालेदार खाना नहीं खा सकते (हैं)।

ham *Robot* hɛ̃. ham *California* se hɛ̃. ham hindī bol sakte hɛ̃. ham hindī samaj^h b^{h}ī sakte hɛ̃. ham hindī gāne gā sakte hɛ̃. hamārī *memory* bahut baRī hɛ. ham har savāl pūc^h sakte hɛ̃ aur har javāb de sakte hɛ̃. yānī har kām kar sakte hɛ̃. ham hameshā kām kar sakte hɛ̃. ham kab^{h}ī nahī̃ t^{h}akte hɛ̃. hamāre pās har savāl kā javāb hɛ. lekin masāledār k^{h}ānā nahī̃ k^{h}ā sakte.

Exercise 7

1 स्मिथ मि॰ *अमरीका* अगले महीने जाएँगे (जायेंगे)।
2 वे *ब्रिटिश एयरवेज़* से *न्यू यॉर्क* जाएँगे (जायेंगे)।
3 जी नहीं।
4 क्योंकि वे अपने बच्चों को *डिज़्नी वर्ड* दिखाना चाहते हैं।
5 वे *डिज़्नी वर्ड* सात दिन (or एक हफ़्ता) रहेंगे।

1 Smith jī *America* agle mahīne jāẽge.
2 ve *British Airways* se New York jāẽge.
3 jī nahī̃.
4 kyõki ve apne baccõ ko *Disney World* dik^{h}ānā cāhte hɛ̃.
5 ve *Disney World* sāt din (*or* ek haftā) rahẽge.

पाठ ६ Unit 6

Exercise 1

मेरे दोस्त, वे दिन कितने अच्छे थे! मैंने सोचा वे दिन हमेशा रहेंगे। वे दिन बचपन के दिन थे। मैं हमेशा खेलता था और नाचता था । हर चीज़ सुन्दर थी। हर दिन नया था और हर रात का अन्दाज़ था। अब वे दिन नहीं रहे।

mere dost, ve din kitne acc^{h}e t^{h}e! mɛ̃ne socā ve din hameshā rahẽge. ve bacpan ke din t^{h}e. mɛ̃ hameshā k^{h}eltā thā aur nāctā t^{h}ā. har cīz sundar t^{h}ī. har din nayā t^{h}ā aur har rāt kā andāz t^{h}ā. ab ve din nahī̃ din rahe.

Exercise 2

1 मैं वहाँ गयी।
2 उसने मुझको बताया।
3 हम घर आये।
4 तुम घर देर से पहुँचे।
5 उन्होंने पुलिस को रिपोर्ट की।
6 आपको यह किताब कब मिली।

1 mɛ̃ vahā̃ gayī.
2 usne muj^{h}ko batāyā.
3 ham g^{h}ar āye.
4 tum g^{h}ar der se pahũce.
5 unhõne *police* ko *report* kī.
6 āpko ye kitāb kab milī.

Exercise 3

1 आपके माता-पिता का जन्म कहाँ हुआ?
2 आपके माता-पिता का जन्म कब हुआ?
3 क्या उनका परिवार अमीर था या ग़रीब था?
4 उनकी शादी कब हुई?
5 उनकी उमर कितनी थी जब उनकी शादी हुई?
6 उनकी *अरैंज्ड मैरिज* हुई या *लव मैरिज*?
7 क्या आपकी माँ आपके पिता से छोटी हैं?

1 āpke mātā-pitā kā janma kahā̃ huā?
2 āpke mātā-pitā kā janma kab huā?
3 kyā unkā parivār amīr t^{h}ā yā garīb t^{h}ā?

4 unkī shādī kab huī?
5 unkī umar kitnī t^{h}ī jab unkī shādī huī?
6 unkī *arranged marriage* huī yā *love marriage*?
7 kyā āpkī mā̃ āp ke pitā se choTī hɛ̃?

Exercise 4

1 कल किसका जन्म दिन था?
2 किसके परिवार ने एक पार्टी की?
3 वह *पार्टी* कब हुई?
4 जान को किसके बारे में मालूम नहीं था?
5 यह कैसी *पार्टी* थी?
6 जॉन का जन्म दिन कब था?

1 kal kiskā janma din t^{h}ā?
2 kiske parivār ne ek party kī?
3 vo *party* kab huī?
4 John ko kiske bāre mẽ mālūm nahī̃ t^{h}ā?
5 ye kɛsī party t^{h}ī?
6 John kā janma din kab t^{h}ā?

Exercise 5

1 सच	2 झूठ	3 झूठ	4 झूठ	5 सच	6 सच	7 सच
1 sac	2 j^{h}ūT	3 j^{h}ūT	4 j^{h}ūT	5 sac	6 sac	7 sac

1 पुराने ज़माने में आदमी घर में काम नहीं करते थे।
2 आज-कल सारा परिवार टीवी देखता है।
3 आज-कल आदमी और औरतें खाना बनाते हैं।

1 purāne zamāne mẽ ādmī g^{h}ar mẽ kām nahī̃ karte t^{h}e.
2 āj-kal sārā parivār *TV* dek^{h}tā hɛ.
3 āj-kal ādmī aur auratẽ k^{h}ānā banāte hɛ̃.

पाठ ७ Unit 7

Exercise 1

1 <u>मुझको</u> सितार आती है।
2 क्या <u>आप</u> तैर सकते हैं?
3 <u>उसको</u> कहाँ जाना पड़ता है।

4 उन्होंने संगीत कब सीखा?
5 वह *सेल्ज़मैन* है। उसको बाहर जाना पड़ता है।
6 जॉन को बहुत काम है। इसलिये उसको कुछ फुरसत नहीं है।

1 muj^{h}ko sitār ātī hɛ.
2 kyā āp tɛr sakte hɛ̃?
3 usko kahā̃ jānā hɛ?
4 unhõne saŋgīt kab sīk^{h}ā?
5 vo *salesman* hɛ. usko bāhar jānā paRtā hɛ.
6 John ko bahut kām hɛ. isliye usko kuc^{h} fursat nahī̃ hɛ.

Exercise 2

1 बिल को जल्दी है क्योंकि उसकी गाड़ी दस मिनट में जाने वाली है।
2 ड्राइवर जल्दी करो, मेरे दोस्त की फ़्लाइट आने वाली है।
3 सरदी का मौसम था, जल्दी बरफ़ गिरने वाली थी।
4 पार्टी के लिये मेहमान पहुँचने वाले हैं।
5 शाम का समय था, अन्धेरा होने वाला था।
6 आप कभी हिन्दुस्तान गये हैं?

1 Bill ko jaldī hɛ kyõki uskī gāRī das minute mẽ jāne vālī hɛ.
2 *Driver* jaldī karo, mere dost kī *flight* āne vālī hɛ.
3 sardī kā mausam t^{h}ā, jaldī barf girne vālī t^{h}ī.
4 *party* ke liye mɛhmān pahũcne vāle hɛ̃.
5 s^{h}ām kā samay t^{h}ā, and^{h}rā hone vālā t^{h}ā.
6 āp kab^{h}ī hindustān gaye hɛ̃?

Exercise 3

1 अध्यापक उसको पढ़ाना है।
2 *डॉक्टर* उसको मरीज़ को देखना है।
3 गायक उसको गाना है।
4 *ड्राइवर* उसको कार चलानी है।
5 धोबी उसको कपड़े धोने हैं।
6 लेखक उसको लिखना है।

1 ad^{h}yāpak usko paR^{h}ānā hɛ.
2 *Doctor* usko marīz ko dek^{h}nā hɛ.
3 gāyak usko gānā hɛ.
4 *Driver* usko kār calānī hɛ.
5 d^{h}obī usko kapRe d^{h}one hɛ̃.
6 lek^{h}ak usko lik^{h}nā hɛ.

Exercise 4

1 क्या आप मेरे लिए *रिकोमैंडेशन लैटर* लिख देंगे?
2 रात आयी और अंधेरा हो गया था।
3 मैं हिन्दी नहीं पढ़ सकता, आप ये खत पढ़ दीजिये ।
4 वो थोड़ा थोड़ा तैर सकता/लेता है।
5 उसको बहुत अच्छा नाचना आता है।
6 मैं आपकी बात बिल्कुल भूल गया।

1 kyā āp mere liye *recommendation letter* likh dẽge?
2 rāt āyī aur andʰerā ho gayā tʰā.
3 mɛ̃ hindī nahī̃ paRʰ saktā, āp ye xat paRʰ dījiye.
4 vo tʰoRā tʰoRā tɛr saktā/letā hɛ.
5 usko bahut accʰā nācnā ātā hɛ.
6 mɛ̃ āp kī bāt bilkul bʰūl gayā.

Exercise 5

बचपन में मुझे दूध पीना पड़ता था। बचपन में *डॉक्टर* के पास जाना पड़ता था। बचपन में मुझे दवाई पीनी पड़ती थी। बचपन में मुझे टीका लगवाना पड़ता था। बचपन में मुझे माता-पिता के साथ चीज़ें खरीदने जाना पड़ता था।

bacpan mẽ mujʰe dūdʰ pinā paRtā tʰā. bacpan mẽ mujʰe *doctor* ke pās jānā paRtā tʰā. bacpan mẽ mujʰe davāī pīnī paRtī tʰī. bacpan mẽ mujʰe Tikā lagvānā paRtā tʰā. bacpan mẽ mujʰe mātā-pitā ke sāth cīzẽ xarīdne jānā paRtā tʰā.

Exercise 6

1 झूठ	2 सच	3 झूठ	4 झूठ	5 सच	6 झूठ	7 सच
1 jʰ	2 s	3 jʰ	4 jʰ	5 s	6 jʰ	7 s

पाठ ८ Unit 8

Exercise 1

आइये, तशरीफ़ रखिये। तकलीफ़ की बात क्या है? शायद आपको दफ़्तर में काम ज़्यादा हो। वह आपका इन्तजार कर रही थी। आदाब अर्ज़ है।

āiye, tashrīf rakʰiye. taklīf kī bāt kyā hɛ? shāyad āpko daftar mẽ kām zyādā ho. vo āpkā intazār kar rahī tʰī. ādāb arz hɛ.

Exercise 2

1 माफ़ कीजिये, मैं चैक भेजना भूल गया।
2 मैंने खाना खा लिया।
3 आपका बुखार बढ़ गया।
4 आपने कुछ ज़वाब नहीं दिया।
5 आप मेरी सलाह मान लीजिये।

1 māf kījiye, mɛ̃ *cheque* b^{h}ejnā b^{h}ūl gayā.
2 mɛ̃ne k^{h}ānā k^{h}ā liyā.
3 āpkā buxār baR^{h} gayā.
4 āpne kuc^{h} javāb nahī̃ diyā.
5 āp merī salāh mān lījiye.

Exercise 3

1 अध्यापक छात्रों को पढ़ाता है।
2 डॉक्टर टीका लगाता है।
3 *कैशियर* *चैक कैश* करता है।
4 दर्ज़ी कपड़े बनाता है।
5 खानसामा खाना बनाता है।
6 *ड्राइवर* कार चलाता है।
7 सिविल इंजिनियर इमारतें बनवाता है।

1 ad^{h}yāpak c^{h}ātrõ ko paR^{h}ātā hɛ.
2 DākTar (doctor) Tīkā lagātā hɛ.
3 *cashier* *cheque cash* kartā hɛ.
4 darzī kapRe banātā hɛ.
5 k^{h}ānsāmā k^{h}ānā banātā hɛ.
6 *driver* kār calātā hɛ.
7 *civil engineer* imāratẽ banvātā hɛ.

Exercise 4

1 श्याम ने हिल्डा से अपनी कार चलवायी।
2 श्याम हिल्डा से अपना ख़त लिखवायेगा।
3 श्याम हिल्डा से अपना घर बनवा रहा है।
4 श्याम हिल्डा से अपनी कहानी सुनवा रहा है।
5 श्याम हिल्डा से अपनी लड़की को पढ़वाता है।

1 Shyam: shyām ne hilDā se apnī kār calvāyī.
2 Shyam: shyām hilDā se apnā xat lik^{h}vāyegā.
3 Shyam: shyām hilDā se apnā g^{h}ar banvā rahā hɛ.

4 Shyam: shyām hilDā se apnī kahānī sunvā rahā t^{h}ā.
5 Shyam: shyām hilDā se apnī laRkī ko paR^{h}vātā hɛ.

Exercise 5

1 हँसना: मुझे वह हँसती लड़की बहुत पसन्द है।
2 खेलना: खेलते बच्चे बहुत सुन्दर लग रहे थे।
3 गाना: गाती चिड़िया उड़ रही थी।
4 सितार बजाना: सितार बजाता आदमी बहुत अच्छा है।
5 तैरना: तैरती मछलियों को देखो।
6 रोना: डॉक्टर ने रोते बच्चे को टीका लगाया।

1 hãsnā: muj^{h}e vo hãstī laRkī bahut pasand hɛ.
2 k^{h}elnā: k^{h}elte bacce bahut sundar lag rahe t^{h}e.
3 gānā: gātī ciRiyā uR rahī t^{h}ī.
4 sitār bajānā: sitār bajātā ādmī bahut acc^{h}ā hɛ.
5 tɛrnā: tɛrtī mac^{h}aliyõ ko dek^{h}o.
6 ronā: *Doctor* ne rote bacce ko Tīkā lagāyā.

Exercise 6

मैं *रेलवे स्टेशन* परअपने दोस्त का इंतज़ार कर रहा था। थोड़ी देर बाद गाड़ी आयी और मेरा दोस्त गाड़ी से उतरा। हम बहुत खुश हो कर मिले। इस बार पाँच साल के बाद हमारी मुलाकात हुई। थोड़ी देर बाद मैंने कहा, 'इस बार बहुत देर के बाद यहाँ आये हो'।उसने जवाब दिया, 'अच्छी बात थी कि अगर गाड़ी देर से न आती, तो मैं आज भी न आता'।

mɛ̃ *railway station* par apne dost kā intzār kar rahā t^{h}ā. t^{h}oRī der bād gāR^{h}ī āyī aur merā dost gāR^{h}ī se utrā. ham bahut xush ho kar mile. is bār pā̃c sāl ke bād hamārī mulākāt huī. t^{h}oRī der bād mɛ̃ne kahā, 'is bār bahut der ke bād yahā̃ āye ho'. usne javāb diyā, 'acc^{h}ī bāt t^{h}ī ki agar gāRhī der se na ātī, to mɛ̃ āj b^{h}ī na ātā'.

पाठ ९ Unit 9

1 लोग *लाँड्रीमेट* कपड़े धोने जाते हैं।
2 लोग *रैस्टोरैंट* खाना खाने जाते हैं।
3 लोग *मूवी थिएटर* फिल्म देखने जाते हैं।
4 लोग *कॉलिज* पढ़ने जाते हैं।
5 लोग *स्विमिंग पूल* तैरने जाते हैं।
6 लोग *बार बियर* पीने जाते हैं।
7 लोग *फार्मेसी* दवाई लेने जाते हैं।

1 log *laundrymat* kapRe d^h^one jāte hɛ̃.
2 log *restaurant* k^h^ānā k^h^āne jāte hɛ̃.
3 log *movie* theatre film dek^h^ne jāte hɛ̃.
4 log *college* paR^h^ne jāte hɛ̃.
5 log *swimming pool* tɛrne jāte hɛ̃.
6 log *bār beer* pīne jāte hɛ̃.
7 log *pharmacy* davāī lene jāte hɛ̃.

Exercise 2

1 वह बैठे हुए बोला।
2 जॉन सोये हुए हँस रहा था।
3 यह शहर सोया सा लगता है।
4 लड़की रोयी हुई घर आयी ।
5 औरत ने *स्विमिंग पूल* पर लेटे हुए कहा।

1 vo bɛT^h^e hue bolā.
2 John so(y)e hue has rahā t^h^ā.
3 ye shɛhɛr sotyā sā lagtā hɛ.
4 laRkī royī huī g^h^ar āyī.
5 aurat ne *swimming pool* par leTe hue kahā.

Exercise 3

सुनी	बात
लिखा	खत
हँसता	लड़का
चलती	गाड़ी
भूले	लोग
भागते	बिल्ली

sunī	bāt
lik^h^ā	xat
hãstā	laRkā
caltī	gāRī
b^h^ūle	log
b^h^āgtī	billī

Exercise 4

1 जॉन से एक कहानी पढ़ी गयी।
2 हम लोगों से खाना खाया जा रहा है।

3 तुमसे क्या किया जायेगा?
4 मुझसे *चिकन करी* बनायी गयी।
5 बिल से यह पढ़ा जायेगा।
6 क्या आपसे गाना गाया गया?

1 John se ek kahānī paR^{h}ī gayī.
2 ham logõ se k^{h}ānā k^{h}āyā jā rahā hɛ.
3 tumse kyā kiyā jāyegā?
4 muj^h se *chicken curry* banāyī gayī.
5 Bill sẽ ye paR^{h}ā jāyegā.
6 kyā āpse gānā gāyā gayā?

Exercise 5

1 हमको वहाँ जाने का मौका मिला।
2 जॉन को हिन्दुस्तान जाने का मौका अक्सर मिलता है।
3 यह सुनहरा मौका था।
4 आपको किताब लिखने का मौका कब मिलेगा?
5 इस कागज़ में क्या लिखा है?
6 बिल्ली को मौका मिला और वह दूध पी गयी।
7 यह बहुत अच्छे मौके की बात है।

1 hamko vahā̃ jāne kā maukā milā.
2 John ko hindustān jāne kā maukā aksar miltā hɛ.
3 ye sunhɛra maukā t^{h}ā.
4 āpko kitāb lik^{h}ne kā maukā kab milegā?
5 is kāgaz mẽ kyā lik^{h}ā hɛ?
6 billī ko maukā milā aur vo dud^h pī gayī.
7 ye bahut acc^{h}e mauke kī bāt hɛ.

पाठ १० Unit 10

Exercise 1

दीवाली	दिये जलाये जाते हैं।
	पटाख़े चलाये जाते हैं।
	राजा राम के अपने राज्य लौटने की ख़ुशी में मनाया जाता है।
होली	शत्रुओं को भी मित्र बनाया जाता है।
	गुलाल लगाया जाता है।
	रंग से खेला जाता है।
रक्षाबन्धन	धागा बाँधा जाता है।

dīvālī	diye jalāye jāte hɛ̃.
	paTāxe calāye jāte hɛ̃.
	rājā rām ke apne rājya lauTane kī xushī mẽ manāyā jātā hɛ.
holī	shatruõ ko b^{h}ī mitra banayā jātā hɛ.
	gulāl lagāyā jātā hɛ.
	raŋga se k^{h}elā jātā hɛ.
rakshāband^{h}an	d^{h}āgā bā̃dhā jātā hɛ.

Exercise 2

1 Enemies are also made friends.
2 Lamps are lit.
3 The thread is tied.
4 Fire crackers are lit.
5 Gulal is used.
6 (It) is played with colour.
7 (It) is celebrated in the happiness of the return of King Rama to his kingdom.

Exercise 3

1	दीवाली	dīvālī
2	रक्षाबन्धन	rakshāband^{h}an
3	रक्षाबन्धन	rakshāband^{h}an
4	होली	holī
5	दीवाली	dīvālī

शब्दकोष क्रम
shabadkosh kram
Dictionary order

The dictionary order of Devanagari script is given below, working vertically down the columns. The nasalized vowels precede the oral vowels. The conjunct forms of a consonant (non-syllabic) follow all the syllabic forms. Thus, आँ **ā̃** precedes आ **ā**, whereas the non-syllabic form क् **k** follows कौ **kau**. The Sanskrit letters क्ष **ksha**, त्र **tra** and ज्ञ **gya** follow क् **k**, त् **t** and ज् **j**, respectively.

अ	a	क/क़	ka/qa	ठ	T^{h}a	ब	ba
आ	ā	ख/ख़	k^{h}a/xa	ड/ड़	Da/Ra	भ	b^{h}a
इ	i	ग/ग़	ga/Ga	ढ/ढ़	D^{h}a/R^{h}a	म	ma
ई	ī	घ	g^{h}a	ण	Na	य	ya
उ	u	ङ	ŋa	त	ta	र	ra
ऊ	ū	च	ca	थ	t^{h}a	ल	la
ऋ	ri	छ	c^{h}a	द	da	व	wa/va
ए	e	ज/ज़	ja/za	ध	d^{h}a	श	sha
ऐ	ɛ	झ	j^{h}a	न	na	ष	SHa
ओ	o	ञ	ña	प	pa	स	sa
औ	au	ट	Ta	फ/फ़	p^{h}a/fa	ह	ha

मूल शब्दावली
aŋgrezī-hindī shabdāvalī

English–Hindi glossary

Some basic vocabulary useful for everyday communication is given below. The vocabulary is presented in the following groups:

- body, health and ailments
- colours
- family and relatives
- food and drink
- numbers
- time
- important verbs

The gender of the nouns is specified as masculine (m.) and feminine (f.). Adjectives are given in their base masculine singular form. Since the plural forms of the nouns are predictable from the gender, only the singular forms are listed. Verbs are specified for the agentive (+/–ने **ne**; in perfective tenses) and experiential subjects (+को **ko**) if they fail to select the regular nominative subjects. Also, if the object of a verb takes a specific postposition instead of the regular को **ko** postposition, it is specified in the following way:

wait इंतज़ार करना **x kā intzār karnā** 'to wait for x'

This shows that the verb इंतज़ार करना **intzār karnā** 'to wait' takes the का **kā** 'of' postposition instead of को **ko** or the equivalent of the English 'for'. Verbs are listed in the infinitive form.

Body, health and ailments

Parts of the body and appearance

ankle — एड़ी — **eRī** (f.)
back — पीठ — **pīT**^{h} (f.)
bald — गंजा — **ganjā** (m.)
beard — दाढ़ी — **dāR**^{h}**ī** (f.)
blood — लहू, ख़ून — **lahū** (m.), **xūn** (m.)
body — शरीर, जिस्म — **sharīr** (m.), **jisma** (m.)
chest — छाती — **c**^{h}**ātī** (f.)
ear — कान — **kān** (m.)
elbow — कोहनी — **kohnī** (f.)
eye — आँख — **ā̃k**^{h} (f.)
face — चेहरा, मुँह — **cehrā** (m.), **mũh** (m.)
finger — उंगली — **uŋglī** (f.)
foot — पैर — **pɛr** (m.)
forehead — माथा — **māt**^{h}**ā** (m.)
hair — बाल — **bāl** (m.)
hand — हाथ — **hāt**^{h} (m.)
head — सिर — **sir** (m.)
heart — दिल — **dil** (m.)
kidney — गुर्दा — **gurdā** (m.)
knee — घुटना — **g**^{h}**uTnā** (m.)
leg — लात, टाँग — **lāt** (f.), **Tā̃g** (f.)
lip — होंठ — **hõT**^{h} (m.)
moustache — मूँछ — **mū̃c**^{h} (f.)
mouth — मुँह — **mũh** (m.)
neck — गला — **gardan** (f.)
nose — नाक — **nāk** (f.)
shoulder — कंधा — **kand**^{h}**ā** (m.)
stomach — पेट — **peT** (m.)
throat — गला — **galā** (m.)
thumb — अंगूठा — **aŋgūT**^{h}**ā** (m.)
toe — पैर की उंगली — **pɛr kī uŋglī** (f.)
tongue — जीभ, ज़बान — **jīb**^{h} (f.), **zabān** (f.)

Health and ailments

ache, pain — दर्द — **dard** (m.)
ailment, sickness — बीमारी/बिमारी — **bīmārī/bimārī** (f.)

appetite, hunger	भूख	**b^{h}ūk^{h}** (f.)
blind	अन्धा	**and^{h}ā** (m.)
blister	छाला	**c^{h}ālā** (m.)
boil	फोड़ा	**p^{h}oRā** (m.)
breath	साँस	**sā̃s** (f.)
burning sensation	जलन	**jalan** (f.)
cholera	हैज़ा	**hɛzā** (m.)
common cold	जुकाम	**zukām** (m.)
cough	खाँसी	**k^{h}ā̃sī** (f.)
deaf	बहरा	**bɛhrā** (m.)
defecation	टट्टी आना	**TaTTī ānā (+ko)**
dumb	गूँगा	**gū̃gā** (m.)
dysentry	पेचिश	**pecish** (f.)
feeling breathless	साँस चढ़ना	**sā̃s caR^{h}nā (+kā)**
feeling dizzy	सिर चकराना	**sir cakrānā (+kā)**
health	स्वास्थ्य, सेहत	**svast^{h}ya** (m.), **sehat** (f.)
healthy	स्वस्थ, तन्दुरुस्त	**svāst^{h}a, tandrust**
ill	बीमार/बिमार	**bīmār** (m.)
indigestion	बद-हज़मी	**bad-hazmī** (f.)
injury	चोट	**coT** (f.)
itch	खुजली	**k^{h}ujlī** (f.)
lame	लंगड़ा	**laŋgRā** (m.)
malaria	मलेरिया	**maleriyā** (m.)
rash	दाद	**dād** (m.)
sneeze	छींक	**c^{h}ī̃k** (f.)
sprain	मोच	**moc** (f.)
swelling	सूजन	**sūjan** (f.)
temperature	बुख़ार	**buxār** (m.)
thirst	प्यास	**pyās** (f.)
typhoid	मियादी बुख़ार	**miyādī buxār** (m.)
tuberculosis	तपेदिक, क्षय	**tapedik** (m.), **shaya** (m.)
ulcer	नासूर	**nāsūr** (m.)
unconscious	बेहोश	**behosh**

Colours

black	काला	**kālā**
blue	नीला	**nīlā**
brown	भूरा	**b^{h}ūrā**
colour	रंग	**raŋga** (m.)
green	हरा	**harā**

orange	सन्तरी	**santrī**
pink	गुलाबी	**gulābī**
purple (dark)	बैंगनी	**bɛ̃gnī**
purple (light)	जामनी	**jāmnī**
red	लाल	**lāl**
sky blue	आसमानी	**āsmānī**
saffron	केसरी	**kesarī**
white	सफेद	**safed**
white (skin)	गोरा	**gorā**
yellow	पीला	**pīlā**

Family and relatives

aunt		
father's sister	बुआ	**buā**
father's older brother's wife	ताई	**tāī**
father's younger brother's wife	चाची	**cācī**
mother's brother's wife	मामी	**māmī**
mother's sister	मौसी	**mausī**
	ख़ाला	**xālā** (Muslim)
brother	भाई	**b^hāī**
brother-in-law		
husband's older brother	जेठ	**jeT^h**
husband's sister's husband	ननदोई	**nandoī**
husband's younger brother	देवर	**devar**
wife's brother	साला	**sālā**
wife's sister's husband	साँढू	**sā̃D^hū**
child	बच्चा, बच्ची	**baccā** (m.), **baccī** (f.)
daughter	बेटी	**beTī**
daughter-in-law	बहू	**bahū**
father	पिता	**pitā** (Hindu-Sikh)
	अब्बा	**abbā** (Muslim)
father-in-law	ससुर	**sasur**
granddaughter		
daughter's daughter	दोहती	**dohtī**
son's daughter	पोती	**potī**
grandfather		
father's father	दादा	**dādā**
mother's father	नाना	**nānā**

grandmother		
father's mother	दादी	**dādī**
mother's mother	नानी	**nānī**
grandson		
daughter's son	दोहता	**dohtā**
son's son	पोता	**potā**
husband	पति	**pati** (Hindu, Sikh)
	ख़ाविन्द	**xāvind** (Muslim)
mother	माता, माँ	**mātā, mā̃** (Hindu, Sikh)
	अम्मी	**ammī** (Muslim)
mother-in-law	सास	**sās**
nephew		
brother's son	भतीजा	**b^{h}atījā**
sister's son	भाँजा	**b^{h}ā̃jā**
niece		
brother's daughter	भतीजी	**b^{h}atījī**
sister's daughter	भाँजी	**b^{h}ā̃jī**
relative	रिश्तेदार	**rishtedār**
sister	बहन	**bɛhɛn**
sister-in-law		
brother's wife	भाभी	**b^{h}āb^{h}ī**
wife's sister	साली	**sālī**
husband's sister	ननद	**nanad**
son	बेटा	**beTā**
son-in-law	जवाई	**javāī**
uncle		
father's older brother	ताऊ	**tāū**
father's sister's husband	फूफा	**p^{h}ūp^{h}ā**
father's younger brother	चाचा	**cācā**
mother's brother	मामा	**māmā**
mother's sister's husband	मौसा	**mausā** (Hindu, Sikh)
	ख़ालू	**xālū** (Muslim)
wife	पत्नी	**patnī** (Hindu, Sikh)
	बीबी	**bībī** (Muslim)
	घरवाली	**g^{h}arvālī**

Food and drink

Foodgrains and flours

black beans	लोभिया	**lob^{h}iyā** (m.)
chickpea flour	बेसन	**besan** (m.)

chick peas	छोले	**cʰole** (m. pl.)
corn	मकई	**makaī** (f.)
flour	आटा	**āTā** (m.)
flour (refined)	मैदा	**mɛdā** (m.)
lentils	दाल	**dāl** (f.)
kidney beans	राजमाँह	**rājmā̃h** (f.)
moog beans/lentils	मूँग दाल	**mū̃g dāl** (f.)
rice	चावल	**cāval** (m.)
wheat	गेहूँ	**gehū̃** (m.)

Fruits and nuts

almond	बादाम	**bādām** (m.)
apple	सेब	**sev** (m.)
apricot	खुमानी	**xumāni** (f.)
banana	केला	**kelā** (m.)
cashew nuts	काजू	**kājū** (m.)
fruit; dry fruit	फल; मेवा	**pʰal** (m.); **mevā** (m.)
grapes	अंगूर	**aŋgūr** (m.)
guava	अमरूद	**amrūd** (m.)
lemon	नींबू/नीम्बू	**nīmbū** (m.)
mango	आम	**ām** (m.)
melon	खरबूजा	**kʰarbūjā** (m.)
orange	संतरा/सन्तरा	**santrā** (m.)
peach	आड़ू	**āRū** (m.)
peanuts	मूँगफली	**mū̃gpʰalī** (f.)
pear	नाशपती	**nāshpātī** (f.)
pistachio	पिस्ता	**pistā** (m.)
plum	आलूबुख़ारा	**ālūbuxārā** (m.)
tangerine	नारंगी	**nāraŋgī** (f.)
walnut	अखरोट	**akʰroT** (m.)
watermelon	तरबूज	**tarbūj** (m.)

Vegetables

beetroot	चुकन्दर	**cukandar** (m.)
bittergourd	करेला	**karelā** (m.)
cabbage	बन्दगोभी	**bandgobʰī** (f.)
courgette	तोरी	**torī** (f.)
cucumber	खीरा	**kʰīrā** (m.)

fenugreek	मेथी	**met^{h}ī** (f.)
garlic	लहसुन	**lɛhsun** (m.)
ginger (fresh)	अदरक	**adrak** (f.)
mustard	सरसों	**sarsõ** (m.)
okra	भिंडी	**b^{h}iNDī** (f.)
onion	प्याज़	**pyāz** (m.)
peas	मटर	**maTar** (m.)
potatoes	आलू	**ālū** (m.)
pumpkin	कद्दू	**kaddū** (m.)
radish	मूली	**mūlī** (f.)
spinach	पालक	**pālak** (f.)
tomato	टमाटर	**TamāTar** (m.)
vegetable	सब्ज़ी	**sabzī** (f.)

Herbs and spices

aniseed	सौंफ	**sãũf** (m.)
asafoetida	हींग	**hĩg** (f.)
bay leaves	तेज़ पत्ता	**tez pattā** (m.)
black cardamom	बड़ी इलायची	**baRī ilāyacī** (f.)
black pepper (black)	काली मिर्च	**kālī mirca** (f.)
cardamom	इलायची	**ilāyacī** (f.)
chilli	मिर्च, लाल मिर्च	**mirca** (f.), **lāl mirca** (f.)
cinnamon	दालचीनी	**dālcīnī** (f.)
cloves	लौंग	**lãũg** (m.)
coriander	धनिया	**d^{h}aniyā** (m.)
cumin	जीरा	**jīrā** (m.)
curry powder	करी पाउडर	**karī pāuDar** (m.)
ginger (dry)	सौंठ	**sãũT^{h}** (f.)
mango powder	अमचूर	**amcūr** (m.)
mint	पौदीना	**paudīnā** (m.)
mixed spices	गरम मसाला	**garam masālā** (m.)
mustard seeds	राई	**rāī** (f.)
nutmeg	जायफल	**jāyp^{h}al** (m.)
saffron	केसर	**kesar** (m.)
salt	नमक	**namak** (m.)
spices	मसाला/मसाले	**masālā/masāle** (m.)
tamarind	इमली	**imlī** (f.)
turmeric	हल्दी	**haldī** (f.)

Food items (dishes), etc.

alcoholic drinks	शराब	**sharāb** (f.)
betel leaf	पान	**pān** (m.)
betel nut	सुपारी	**supārī** (f.)
bread (Indian)	रोटी, चपाती	**roTī** (f.), **capatī** (f.)
	फुल्का, नान,	**p^hulkā** (m.), **nān** (m.)
	पूरी, पराठा	**pūrī** (f.), **parāT^hā** (m.)
	कुल्चा, भटूरा	**kulcā** (m.), **b^haTūrā** (m.)
bread (Western)	डबल रोटी	**Dabal roTī** (f.)
butter	मक्खन	**makk^han** (m.)
buttermilk	लस्सी	**lassī** (f.)
cheese	पनीर	**panīr** (m.)
coffee	काफ़ी	**kāfī** (f.)
curry (Indian)	कढ़ी	**kaR^hī** (f.)
egg	अंडा	**aNDā** (m.)
food	खाना	**k^hānā** (m.)
non-vegetarian	माँसाहारी	**mā̃sāhārī**
vegetarian	शाकाहारी	**shākāhārī**
juice	रस	**ras** (m.)
lentils	दाल	**dāl** (f.)
meat	माँस, गोश्त	**mā̃s** (m.), **goshta** (m.)
milk	दूध	**dūd^h** (m.)
oil	तेल	**tel** (m.)
purified butter	घी	**g^hī** (m.)
sugar (white)	चीनी	**cīnī** (f.)
sugar (brown)	शक्कर	**shakkar** (f.)
sweets	मिठाई	**miT^hāī** (f.)
tea	चाय	**cāy** (f.)
tobacco	तम्बाकू	**tambākū** (m.)
vinegar	सिरका	**sirkā** (m.)
water	पानी	**pānī** (m.), **jal** (m.)
yoghurt	दही	**dahī** (m./f.)

Cooking processes

baking (oven cooking)	तन्दूरी	**tandūrī**
boiling	उबालना	**ubālnā** (+ne)
cooking	पकाना	**pakānā** (+ne)
cutting	काटना	**kāTnā** (+ne)
frying	तलना	**talnā** (+ne)

grilling	सेंकना	**sẽknā** (+**ne**)
grinding	पिसना	**pīsnā** (+**ne**)
kneading	गूँदना	**gū̃dnā** (+**ne**)
mixing	मिलाना	**milānā** (+**ne**)
peeling	छीलना	**c^{h}īlnā** (+**ne**)
roasting	भूनना	**b^{h}ūnnā** (+**ne**)
rolling	बेलना	**belnā** (+**ne**)
seasoning	तड़का लगाना	**taRkā lagānā** (+**ne**)
sieving	छानना	**c^{h}ānnā** (+**ne**)
slicing	चीरना	**cīrnā** (+**ne**)

Tastes

bitter	कड़वा	**kaRvā**
delicious/tasty	मज़ेदार	**mazedār**
savoury/salty	नमकीन	**namkīn**
sour	खट्टा	**k^{h}aTTā**
spicy	मसालेदार, मिर्चदार	**masāledār, mircavālā**
	चटपटा	**caTpaTā**
sweet	मीठा	**mīT^{h}ā**
taste	स्वाद	**svād**
tasteless	फीका, बेस्वाद	**p^{h}īkā, besvād**

Numbers

Cardinal

1 एक	**ek**	14 चौदह	**caudah**
2 दो	**do**	15 पन्द्रह	**pandrah**
3 तीन	**tīn**	16 सोलह	**solah**
4 चार	**cār**	17 सत्तरह, सत्रह	**sattrāh**
5 पाँच	**pā̃c**	18 अठारह	**aThārah**
6 छह	**che**	19 उन्नीस	**unnīs**
7 सात	**sāt**	20 बीस	**bīs**
8 आठ	**āT^{h}**	21 इक्कीस	**ikkīs**
9 नौ	**nau**	22 बाईस	**bāīs**
10 दस	**das**	23 तेईस	**teīs**
11 ग्यारह	**gyārah**	24 चौबीस	**caubīs**
12 बारह	**bārah**	25 पच्चीस	**pacc^{h}īs**
13 तेरह	**terah**	26 छब्बीस	**c^{h}abbīs**

27 सत्ताईस **sattāīs**
28 अठाईस **aT^{h}āīs**
29 उनतीस **untīs**
30 तीस **tīs**
31 इकत्तीस **ikattīs**
32 बत्तीस **battīs**
33 तैंतीस **tẽtīs**
34 चौंतीस **cãũtīs**
35 पैंतीस **pẽtīs**
36 छत्तीस **c^{h}attīs**
37 सैंतीस **sẽtīs**
38 अड़तीस **aRatīs**
39 उनतालीस **untālīs**
40 चालीस **cālīs**
41 इकतालीस **iktālīs**
42 ब्यालीस **byālīs**
43 तैंतालीस **tẽtālīs**
44 चौवालीस **cauvālīs**
45 पैंतालीस **pẽtālīs**
46 छियालीस **c^{h}iyālīs**
47 सैंतालीस **sẽtālīs**
48 अड़तालीस **aRtālīs**
49 उनचास **uncās**
50 पचास **pacās**
51 इक्यावन **ikyāvan**
52 बावन **bāvan**
53 तिरपन **tirpan**
54 चौवन **cauvan**
55 पचपन **pacpan**
56 छप्पन **c^{h}appan**
57 सत्तावन **sattāvan**
58 अट्ठावन **aTT^{h}āvan**
59 उनसठ **unsaT^h**
60 साठ **sāT^h**
61 इकसठ **iksaT^h**
62 बासठ **bāsaT^h**
63 तिरेसठ **tiresaT^h**
64 चौंसठ **cãũsaT^h**
65 पैंसठ **pẽsaT^h**
66 छियासठ **c^{h}iyāsaT^h**
67 सरसठ **sarsaT^h**
68 अड़सठ **aRsaT^h**
69 उनहत्तर **unhattar**
70 सत्तर **sattar**
71 इकहत्तर **ikhattar**
72 बहत्तर **bahattar**
73 तिहत्तर **tihattar**
74 चौहत्तर **cauhattar**
75 पचहत्तर **pac^{h}attar**
76 छिहत्तर **c^{h}ihattar**
77 सतहत्तर **satahatta**
78 अठहत्तर **aT^{h}hattar**
79 उनासी **unāsī**
80 अस्सी **assī**
81 इकासी **ikāsī**
82 बयासी **bayāsī**
83 तिरासी **tirāsī**
84 चौरासी **caurāsī**
85 पच्चासी **paccāsī**
86 छियासी **c^{h}iyāsī**
87 सत्तासी **sattāsī**
88 अट्ठासी **aTT^{h}āsī**
89 नवासी **navāsī**
90 नब्बे **nabbe**
91 इक्यानवे **ikyānve**
92 बयानवे **bayānve**
93 तिरानवे **tirānve**
94 चौरानवे **caurānve**
95 पचानवे **pacānve**
96 छियानवे **c^{h}iyānve**
97 सतानवे **satānve**
98 अठानवे **aTT^{h}ānve**
99 निन्यानवे **ninyānve**
100 सौ **sau**

0 शून्य, सिफ़र **shūnya, sifar**
150 एक सौ पचास **ek sau pacās**
1,000 हज़ार **hazār**
10,000 दस हज़ार **das hazār**

100,000 (a hundred thousand)	एक लाख	**ek lāk^h**
1,000,000 (a million)	दस लाख	**das lāk^h**
10,000,000 (ten million)	एक करोड़	**ek karoR**
1,000,000,000 (a billion)	दस करोड़	**das karoR**
10,000,000,000 (ten billion)	अरब	**arab**
100,000,000,000 (a hundred billion)	दस खरब	**das arab**
1,000,000,000,000 (a trillion)	खरब	**k^{h}arab**

Ordinal

first	पहला	**pɛhlā**
second	दूसरा	**dūsrā**
third	तीसरा	**tīsrā**
fourth	चौथा	**cauthā**
fifth	पाँचवाँ	**pā̃cvā̃**

(Afterwards just add the suffix वाँ **-vā̃** to the cardinal numbers.)

Fractions

$^1/_4$ (a quarter)	(एक) चौथाई	**ek chaut^{h}āī**
$^1/_2$ (a half)	आधा	**ād^{h}ā**
$^3/_4$ (three-quarters)	पौना	**paunā**
$1^1/_4$ (one and a quarter)	सवा	**savā (ek)**
$1^1/_2$ (one and a half)	डेढ़	**DeR^h**
$1^3/_4$ (one and three-quarters)	पौने दो	**paune do** (i.e. the next number)
$2^1/_4$	सवा दो	**savā do**
$2^1/_2$	ढाई	**D^{h}āī** (the numeral two is incorporated in the word)
$2^3/_4$	पौने तीन	**paune tīn** (i.e. the next number)
$3^1/_4$	सवा तीन	**savā tīn**
$3^1/_2$	साढ़े तीन	**sāR^{h}e tīn**
$3^3/_4$	पौने चार	**paune cār**

Then follow the pattern given below to derive the other fractional numbers.

number + $^1/_4$	**savā** + number
number + $^1/_2$	**sāR^{h}e** + number
number + $^3/_4$	**paune** + *next* number

Decimal point

decimal	दशमलव	**dashamlav**
(*Example*: 1.5	एक दशमलव पाँच	**ek dashamlav pā̃c**)

Percentages

Percentage	प्रतिशत, फीसदी	**pratishat, fīsdī**
(*Example*: 50%	पचास प्रतिशत	**pacās pratishat**)

Time

Hours

o'clock	बजे	**baje**
1:15	सवा (एक)	**savā** (ek)
1:30	डेढ़	**DeR^h**
1:45	पौने दो	**paune do** (i.e. the next number)
2:15	सवा दो	**savā do**
2:30	ढाई	**D^{h}āī** (the numeral two is incorporated in the word)
2:45	पौने तीन	**paune tīn** (i.e. the next number)
3:15	सवा तीन	**savā tīn**
3:30	साढ़े तीन	**sāR^{h}e tīn**
3:45	पौने चार	**paune cār**

Examples

कितने	बजे	हैं?		वक्त	क्या	है?
kitne	**baje**	**hɛ̃?**	*or*	**vakta**	**kyā**	**hɛ?**
how many	o'clock	are		time	what	is

What time is it?

एक बजा है।	**ek bajā hɛ.**	It is 1 o'clock.
डेढ़ बजे हैं।	**deR^h baje hɛ̃.**	It is 1:30.
पौने तीन बजे हैं।	**paune tīn baje hɛ̃.**	It is 2:45.

9:00 am	सवेरे/सुबह के नौ	**savere/subā ke nau**
9:00 pm	रात के नौ	**rāt ke nau**
4:20	चार बजकर बीस मिनट	**cār <u>bajkar</u> bīs minaT**

6:50	सात बजने में दस मिनट	**sāt bajne mẽ das minaT**
year	साल	**sāl** (m.)
month	महीना	**mahīnā** (m.)
day	दिन	**din** (m.)
hour	घन्टा	**g^{h}anTā** (m.)
minute	मिनट	**minaT** (m.)
second	सैकिन्ड, पल	**sɛkinD** (m.), **pal** (m.)

Days of the week

Monday	सोमवार	**somvār** (Hindu-Sikh), **pīr** (Muslim)
Tuesday	मंगलवार	**maŋgalvār**
Wednesday	बुधवार	**bud^{h}vār**
Thursday	गुरूवार, बृहस्पति	**guruvār**, **brihaspativār** (Hindu–Sikh)
	जुम्मेरात	**jummerāt** (Muslim)
Friday	शुक्रवार	**shukravār** (Hindu–Sikh),
	जुम्मा	**jummā** (Muslim)
Saturday	शनिवार	**shanivār** (Hindu–Sikh),
	हफ़्ता	**haftā** (Muslim)
Sunday	रविवार, इतवार	**ravivār**, **itvār**

Months

The names of the months of the Hindu and Muslim calendar are different from the Christian calendar. However, the Christian calendar is officially used, so the Indian pronunciation of the months is given below:

January	जनवरी	**janvarī**
February	फरवरी	**farvarī**
March	मार्च	**mārca**
April	अप्रैल	**aprɛl**
May	मई	**maī**
June	जून	**jūn**
July	जुलाई	**julāī**
August	अगस्त	**agasta**
September	सितम्बर	**sitambar**
October	अक्तूबर/अक्टूबर	**aktūbar**, **akTūbar**
November	नवम्बर	**navambar**
December	दिसम्बर	**disambar**

Years

The word 'year' when used as part of a date is translated as सन् **san**. For instance, 1995 (the year) is सन् उन्नीस सौ पचानवे **san unnīs sau pacānve** but one can *not* say एक हज़ार नौ सौ पचानवे **ek hazār nau sau pacānve**.

Professions

doctor	डॉक्टर	***Doctor***
driver	ड्राइवर	***Driver***
hero	नायक	**nāyak**
heroine	नायिका	**nāyikā**
lawyer	वकील	**vakīl**
policeman	पुलिस वाला	**pulis vālā**
singer	गायक	**gāyak**
teacher	अध्यापक	**ad^{h}yāpak**
washerman	धोबी	**D^{h}obī**
writer	लेखक	**lek^{h}ak**

Important verbs

Hindi verbs are listed in the infinitive form.

Abbreviations

(intr.)	intransitive verb; does not take the ने **ne** postposition in the perfect tenses
(tr.)	transitive verb; takes the ने **ne** postposition in the perfect tenses
(+ने **ne**)	takes the ने **ne** postposition in the perfect tenses
(–ने **ne**)	does not take the ने **ne** postposition in the perfect tenses
(+/–ने **ne**)	may or may not take the ने **ne** postposition in the perfect tenses
(+को **ko**)	takes the को **ko** postposition with its subject; indicates non-volitional action

accept, agree	मानना	**mānnā** (+ने **ne**)
ache	दर्द होना	**dard honā** (+को **ko**)
afraid	डर लगना	**Dar lagnā** (+को **ko**)
agree	मानना	**mānnā** (+ने **ne**)
(be) angry	गुस्सा होना	**gussā honā**
	गुस्सा करना	**gussā karnā** (+ने **ne**)
become angry	गुस्सा आना	**gussā ānā** (+को **ko**)
appear	लगना, नज़र आना	**lagnā, nazar ānā** (+को **ko**)
be able to/can	सकना	**saknā** (–ने **ne**)
be	होना	**honā** (–ने **ne**)
beat	मारना	**mārnā** (+ने **ne**)
be born	x का जन्म होना	**x kā janma honā** (–ने **ne**)
begin, start	शुरू होना	**shuru honā** (intr.) (–ने **ne**)
	शुरू करना	**shuru karnā** (tr.) (+ने **ne**)
break	तोड़ना	**toRnā** (+ने **ne**)
bring	लाना	**lānā** (–ने **ne**)
burn	जलना, जलाना	**jalnā** (intr.), **jalānā** (tr.)
buy	ख़रीदना	**xarīdnā** (+ने **ne**)
call	बुलाना	**bulānā** (+ने **ne**)
catch	पकड़ना	**pakaRnā** (+ने **ne**)
celebrate	मनाना	**manānā** (+ने **ne**)
change	बदलना	**badalnā** (+/–ने **ne**)
choose	चुनना	**cunnā** (+ने **ne**)
climb	चढ़ना	**caR^{h}nā** (–ने **ne**)
collide	x से टकराना	**x se Takrānā** (+ने **ne**)
come	आना	**ānā** (–ने **ne**)
compare	x की y से तुलना करना	**x kī y se tulnā karnā** (+ने **ne**)
complain	x की y से शिकायत करना	**x se y kī shikāyat karnā** (+ने **ne**)
complete	पूरा करना	**pūrā karnā** (+ने **ne**)
converse	x से बात करना	**x se bāt karnā** (+ने **ne**)
cost	लगना	**x (amount) lagnā** (–ने **ne**)
count	गिनना	**ginnā** (+ने **ne**)
cover	ढकना	**D^{h}aknā** (+ने **ne**)
cry	रोना, चिल्लाना	**ronā, cillānā** (–ने **ne**)
cut	कटना, काटना	**kaTnā** (intr.), **kāTnā** (tr.)
dance	नाचना	**nācnā** (+ने **ne**)
desire	x की इच्छा होना	**x kī icc^{h}ā honā** (–ने **ne**)
die	मरना	**marnā** (–ने **ne**)
disappear	गायब होना	**gāyāb honā** (intr.) (–ने **ne**)
	गायब करना	**gāyāb karnā** (tr.) (+ने **ne**)
dislike	नापसन्द होना	**nāpasand honā** (+को **ko**)

	नापसन्द करना	**nāpasand karnā** (+ने **ne**)
do	करना	**karnā** (+ने **ne**)
drink	पीना	**pīnā** (+ने **ne**)
drink (alcohol)	शराब पीना	**sharāb pīnā** (+ने **ne**)
drive	(कार) चलाना	**[kār] calānā** (+ने **ne**)
earn	कमाना	**kamānā** (+ने **ne**)
enjoy	मज़ा होना	**mazā honā** (intr.) (–ने **ne**)
	मज़ा करना	**mazā karnā** (tr.) (+ने **ne**)
	मज़ा लेना	**mazā lenā** (tr.) (+ने **ne**)
eat/dine	खाना खाना	**k^{h}ānā k^{h}ānā** (+ने **ne**)
eat breakfast	नाश्ता करना	**nāshtā karnā** (+ने **ne**)
enter	घुसना	**g^{h}usnā** (–ने **ne**)
fall	गिरना	**girnā** (–ने **ne**)
feed	खिलाना	**k^{h}ilānā** (+ने **ne**)
feel sick	x की तबीयत ख़राब होना	**x kī tabīyat xarāb honā** (–ने **ne**)
feel happy	खुश होना	**xush honā** (–ने **ne**)
feel sad	उदास होना	**udās honā** (–ने **ne**)
fight	लड़ना	**laRnā** (–ने **ne**)
finish	खत्म होना	**xatam honā** (intr.) (–ने **ne**)
	खत्म करना	**xatam karnā** (tr.) (+ने **ne**)
fix, recover, repair	ठीक होना	**T^{h}īk honā** (intr.) (–ने **ne**)
	ठीक करना	**T^{h}īk karnā** (tr.) (+ने **ne**)
fly	उड़ना, उड़ाना	**uRnā** (intr.), **uRānā** (tr.)
forgive, pardon	माफ करना	**māf karnā** (+ने **ne**)
get down, descend	उतरना	**utarnā** (–ने **ne**)
give	देना	**denā** (+ने **ne**)
go	जाना	**jānā** (–ने **ne**)
go back	वापस जाना	**vāpas jānā** (–ने **ne**)
grind	पीसना	**pīsnā** (+ने **ne**)
hate	x से नफ़रत करना	**x se nafrat karnā** (+ने **ne**)
hear	सुनना	**sunnā** (+ने **ne**)
	सुनाई देना	**sunāī denā** (+को **ko**)
hire	किराये पर लेना	**kirāye par lenā** (+ने **ne**)
hope	x की आशा होना	**x kī āshā honā** (–ने **ne**)
(get) hot	गरमी पड़ना	**garmī paRnā** (–ने **ne**)
(get) hurt	चोट लगना	**coT lagnā** (+को **ko**)
inquire	पूछताछ करना	**pūc^{h}tāc^h karnā** (+ने **ne**)
invite	x के घर आना	**x ke g^{h}ar ānā** (–ने **ne**)
	x को न्यौता देना	**x ko nyautā denā** (+ने **ne**)
jump	कूदना	**kūdnā** (–ने **ne**)
kill	मारना	**mārnā** (+ने **ne**)

knock at	खटखटाना	**k^{h}aTk^{h}aTānā** (+ने **ne**)
know	जानना	**jānnā** (+ने **ne**)
	मालूम होना	**mālūm honā** (+को **ko**)
	पता होना	**patā honā** (+को **ko**)
(come to) know	पता लगना	**patā lagnā** (+को **ko**)
laugh	हँसना	**hãsnā** (–ने **ne**)
learn	सीखना	**sīk^{h}nā** (+ने **ne**)
like	पसन्द होना	**pasand honā** (+**ko**)
	पसन्द करना	**pasand karnā** (+ने **ne**)
	अच्छा लगना	**acc^{h}ā lagnā** (+को **ko**)
love	x से प्रेम होना	**x se prem honā** (+को **ko**)
	x से प्रेम करना	**x se prem karnā** (+ने **ne**)
live	रहना	**rɛhnā** (–ने **ne**)
look	देखना	**dek^{h}nā** (+ने **ne**)
make	बनाना	**banānā** (+ने **ne**)
meet	मिलना	**milnā** (–ने **ne**)
melt	पिघलना	**pig^{h}alnā** (–ने **ne**)
mix	मिलाना	**milānā** (+ने **ne**)
need, want	चाहिये, चाहना,	**cā^{h}iye** (+को **ko**), **cāhnā** (+ने **ne**)
	x की ज़रूरत होना	**x kī zarūrat honā** (+को **ko**)
(be) nervous	घबराना	**g^{h}abrānā** (–ने **ne**)
object	x पर ऐतराज़ करना	**x par ɛtrāz karnā** (+ने **ne**)
open	खुलना, खोलना	**k^{h}ulnā** (intr.), **k^{h}olnā** (tr.)
order (someone;	आज्ञा देना,	**āgyā denā** (+ने **ne**)
but not something)	हुक्म करना	**huxam karnā** (+ने **ne**)
peel	छीलना	**c^{h}īlnā** (+ने **ne**)
permit	इजाज़त देना	**ijāzat denā** (+ने **ne**)
persuade	मनाना	**manānā** (+ने **ne**)
place	रखना	**rak^{h}nā** (+ने **ne**)
play	खेलना	**k^{h}elnā** (+ने **ne**)
play (instrument)	बजाना	**bajānā** (+ने **ne**)
praise	x की तारीफ़ करना	**x kī tārīf karnā** (+**ne**)
prepare	तैयार होना	**taiyār honā** (intr.) (–ने **ne**)
	तैयार करना	**taiyār karnā** (tr.) (+ने **ne**)
pour	डालना	**Dālnā** (+ने **ne**)
press	दबाना	**dabānā** (+ने **ne**)
push	धकेलना	**d^{h}akelnā** (+ने **ne**)
put off	टालना	**Tālnā** (+ने **ne**)
put	रखना, डालना	**rak^{h}nā** (+ने **ne**), **Dālnā** (+ने **ne**)
quarrel	लड़ना	**laRnā** (–ने **ne**)
rain	बारिश होना	**bārish honā** (–ने **ne**)
reach	पहुँचना	**pahũcnā** (–ने **ne**)

read	पढ़ना	**paR^{h}nā** (+ने **ne**)
recognize	पहचानना	**pɛhcānnā** (+ने **ne**)
refuse, prohibit	x से मना करना	**x se manā karnā** (+ने **ne**)
remember	याद होना	**yād honā** (intr. +को **ko**)
remember, memorize	याद करना	**yād karnā** (+ने **ne**)
respect	x की इज़्ज़त करना	**x kī izzat karnā** (+ने **ne**)
rest	आराम करना	**ārām karnā** (+ने **ne**)
return, come back	वापस आना, लौटना	**vāpas ānā** (–ने **ne**) **lauTnā** (–ने **ne**)
return (something)	वापस करना लौटाना	**vāpas karnā** (+ने **ne**) **lauTānā** (+ने **ne**)
ripe	पकना	**paknā** (–ने ne)
rise	उठना, चढ़ना	**uT^{h}nā** (–ने **ne**), **caR^{h}nā** (–ने **ne**)
run	दौड़ना, भागना	**dauRnā** (–ने **ne**), **b^{h}āgnā** (–ने **ne**)
say	कहना	**kɛhnā** (+ने **ne**)
seem	लगना	**lagnā** (+को **ko**)
sell	बेचना	**becnā** (+ने **ne**)
send	भेजना	**b^{h}ejnā** (+ने **ne**)
show	दिखाना	**dik^{h}ānā** (+ने **ne**)
(take) shower	नहाना	**nahānā** (+/–ने **ne**)
sing	गाना	**gānā** (+ने **ne**)
sit	बैठना	**bɛT^{h}nā** (–ने **ne**)
sleep	सोना	**sonā** (–ने **ne**)
slip	फिसलना	**p^{h}isalnā** (–ने **ne**)
sneeze	छींकना	**c^{h}ĩknā** (+/–ने **ne**)
snow	बर्फ़ गिरना	**barf girnā** (–ने **ne**)
speak	बोलना	**bolnā** (+/–ने **ne**)
spend (money)	खर्च करना	**xarca karnā** (+ने **ne**)
spend (time)	बिताना, काटना	**bitānā** (+ने **ne**), **kāTnā** (+ने **ne**)
spill	गिराना	**girānā** (+ने **ne**)
spread	बिछाना	**bic^{h}ānā** (+ने **ne**)
stand	खड़ा होना	**k^{h}aRā honā** (–ने **ne**)
stay	रहना, ठहरना	**rɛhnā** (–ने **ne**), **T^{h}ɛhɛrnā** (–ने **ne**)
steal	चोरी करना	**corī karnā** (+ने **ne**)
stop	रुकना, रोकना	**ruknā** (intr.), **roknā** (tr.)
study	पढ़ना	**paR^{h}nā** (+/–ने **ne**)
(be) surprised	हैरान होना	**hɛrān honā** (–ने **ne**)
swim	तैरना	**tɛrnā** (–ने **ne**)
take care of	देख-भाल करना	**dek^h-b^{h}āl karnā** (+ने **ne**)
take	लेना	**lenā** (+ने **ne**)
taste	चखना	**cak^{h}nā** (+ने **ne**)

teach	पढ़ाना	**paR^{h}ānā** (+ने **ne**)
telephone	टैलीफ़ोन करना	**Tɛlīfon karnā** (+ने **ne**)
tell, mention	बताना	**batānā** (+ने **ne**)
think	x का ख़्याल होना	**x kā xyāl honā** (–ने **ne**)
	सोचना	**socnā** (+ने **ne**)
throw	फेंकना	**p^{h}ẽknā** (+ने **ne**)
tired	थकना	**t^{h}aknā** (–ने **ne**)
touch	छूना	**c^{h}ūnā** (+ने **ne**)
try	x की कोशिश करना	**x kī koshish karnā** (+ने **ne**)
turn	मुड़ना, मोड़ना	**muRnā** (intr.) **moRnā** (tr.)
turn over	पलटना	**palaTnā** (+ने **ne**)
understand	समझना	**samaj^{h}nā** (+/–ने **ne**)
use	x का इस्तेमाल करना	**x kā istemāl karnā** (+ने **ne**)
uproot	उखाड़ना	**uk^{h}āRnā** (+ने **ne**)
wait	x का इंताज़ार करना	**x kā intzār karnā** (+ने **ne**)
wake up	उठना	**uT^{h}nā** (–ने **ne**)
walk	चलना	**calnā** (–ने **ne**)
want, need	चाहिये, चाहना	**cāhiye** (+को **ko**), **cāhnā** (+ने **ne**)
wash	धोना	**d^{h}onā** (+ने **ne**)
waste	गवाँना	**gavā̃nā** (+ने **ne**)
wear	पहनना	**pɛhɛnnā** (+ने **ne**)
weep	रोना	**ronā** (–ने **ne**)
win	जीतना	**jītnā** (+/–ने **ne**)
worry	x की चिन्ता करना	**x kī cintā karnā** (+ने **ne**)
worship	x की पूजा करना	**x kī pūjā karnā** (+ने **ne**)
write	लिखना	**lik^{h}nā** (+ने **ne**)

Web resource

The following link is useful for translating English words into Hindi:

http://shabdkosh.com/

हिन्दी-अंग्रेज़ी शब्दावली
hindī-aŋgrezī shabdāvalī
Hindi–English glossary

The Hindi vocabulary used in the dialogues and reading practice pieces is presented below in roman alphabetical order. However, it should be pointed out that the vowel symbol **ɛ** follows **y**, whereas the nasalized vowels (with ~) and short vowels precede their corresponding oral long vowels, respectively.

अभी	**ab^{h}ī**	right now
अभी भी	**ab^{h}ī b^{h}ī**	even now
अच्छा	**acc^{h}ā**	good, Okay
अच्छाई	**acc^{h}āī** (f.)	good (n.), quality, ideal
अच्छा लगना	**acc^{h}ā lagnā** (+**ko**)	to like
अफ़सोस	**afsos** (m.)	sorrow (m.)
अगला	**aglā**	next
अकाल पड़ना	**akāl paRnā** (–**ne**)	famine to occur
अकेला	**akelā**	alone
अकसर	**aksar**	often, usually
अमीर	**amīr**	rich
अनाज	**anāj** (m.)	grain, corn
अन्दाज	**andāz** (m.)	style
अन्धकार	**and^{h}kāra** (m.)	darkness
अंग्रेज़	**aŋgrez** (m.)	the English
अंग्रेज़ी	**aŋgrezī** (f.)	the English language
अपना	**apnā**	one's own
अपनाना	**apnānā** (+**ne**)	to adopt

अर्थ	**art^{h}a** (m.)	meaning
अर्ज़	**arz** (f.)	request
असल में	**asal mẽ**	in fact, in reality
असली	**aslī**	real, genuine
अटूट	**aTūT**	unbreakable
और	**aur**	and, more, other, else
और भी	**aur b^{h}ī**	even more
औरत	**aurat** (f.)	woman
अयोध्या	**ayod^{h}yā** (f.)	Ayodhya (place name)
आँख	**ā̃k^h**	eye
आदाब	**ādāb**	salutation, greetings
आदि	**ādi**	etc.
आदत	**ādat**	habit
आदमी	**ādmī**	man
आग	**āg**	fire
आज–कल	**āj-kal**	nowadays
आक्रमण करना	**ākramaNa karnā** (+ne)	to attack
आम	**ām**	mango (n.); common (adj.), general
आना	**ānā** (–ne)	to come
आने वाला	**āne vālā**	about to come
आप	**āp**	you (honorific)
आपके	**āpke**	your
आपको	**āpko**	to you
आराम	**ārām** (m.)	comfort, rest
आराम करना	**ārām karnā** (+ne)	to rest
आटा	**āTā** (m.)	flour
बचाना	**bacānā** (+ne)	to save
बच्चा	**baccā** (m.)	child
बचपन	**bacpan** (m.)	childhood
बहुत	**bahut**	very
बहुत खूब	**bahut xūb**	great! splendid!
बजे	**baje**	o'clock
बनाना	**banānā** (+ne)	to make
बनारस	**banāras**	Banaras (one of the oldest cities of India)
बन्द	**banda**	closed
बन्द होना	**banda honā** (–ne)	to be closed
बन्द करना	**banda karnā** (+ne)	to close
बनना	**bannā** (–ne)	to be made

बनवास	**banvāsa** (m.)	exile, residence in forest
बड़ा	**baRā**	big
बढ़ना	**baR^{h}nā** (–**ne**)	to increase, advance
बताना	**batānā** (+**ne**)	to tell
बाँधना	**bā̃d^{h}nā** (+**ne**)	to tie
बाहर	**bāhar**	outside, out
बार	**bār** (f.)	time
बारह	**bārah**	twelve
बात	**bāt** (f.)	matter, conversation, topic
बेचना	**becnā** (+**ne**)	to sell
बेकार	**bekār**	useless
बेटा	**beTā** (m.)	son
बेटी	**beTī** (f.)	daughter
भई	**b^{h}aī**	hey, well (excl.)
भरना	**b^{h}arna** (+**ne**)	to fill
भागना	**b^{h}āgnā** (–**ne**)	to run
भागते	**b^{h}āgte** (present participle)	running
भाई	**b^{h}āī** (m.)	brother/brothers
भारत	**b^{h}ārat** (m.)	India
भारतीय	**b^{h}āratīya**	Indian
भेज देना	**b^{h}ej denā** (+**ne**)	to send (compound verb)
भेजना	**b^{h}ejnā** (+**ne**)	to send
भेंट	**b^{h}ẽT**	gift
भी	**b^{h}ī**	also
भूलना	**b^{h}ūlnā** (+/–**ne**)	to forget
भूत	**b^{h}ūt** (m.)	ghost, past
बिजली	**bijlī** (f.)	electricity, lightning
बिमारी/बीमारी	**bimārī** (f.)	illness
बिना	**binā**	without
बिंदी	**bindī** (f.)	dot
बीबी	**bībī** (f.)	wife
बीमा	**bīmā** (m.)	insurance
बोलना	**bolanā** (+/–**ne**)	to speak
बृन्दावन	**brindāvan**	Brindavan (the place where Lord Krishna was brought up)
बुझाना	**buj^{h}ānā** (+**ne**)	to extinguish
बुरा	**burā**	bad
बुराई	**burāī** (f.)	evil
बुखार	**buxār** (m.)	fever
बहन	**bɛhɛn** (f.)	sister
बैरा	**bɛrā** (m.)	waiter

चखना	**cak^{h}nā** (+ne)	to taste
चलाना	**calānā** (+ne)	to drive, to manage (business), to light /play firecrackers
चलना	**calnā** (–ne)	walk
चौदह	**caudā**	fourteen
चाँद	**cā̃d** (m.)	moon
चाँदनी	**cā̃dnī**	moonlit
चाहिये/चाहिए	**cāhiye** (+ko)	desire, want
चाहना	**cāhnā** (+ne)	to want
चार	**cār**	four
चाय	**cāy** (f.)	tea
छाता	**c^{h}ātā** (m.)	umbrella
छिपा कर	**c^{h}ipā kar**	secretly
छोड़ना	**c^{h}oRnā** (+ne)	to leave
छोटा	**c^{h}oTā**	small
चीन	**cīn** (m.)	China
चीनी	**cīnī**	Chinese, sugar
चिल्लाना	**cillānā** (–ne)	to scream
चित्तौड़	**cittauRa** (m.)	Chitaur (a very famous historical place in Rajasthan)
चोर	**cor** (m.)	thief
चोरी करना	**corī karnā** (+ne)	to steal
करी/कढ़ी	**curry** (f.)	curry
चूँकि	**cū̃ki**	because

दफ़्तर/दफतर	**daftar** (m.)	office
दही	**dahī** (m./f.)	yoghurt
दर्द	**dard** (m.)	pain, ache
दरवाज़ा	**darvāzā** (m.)	door
दस	**das**	ten
दस्त	**dasta** (m.)	diarrhoea
दौड़ना	**dauRnā** (–ne)	to run
दवाई	**davāī/davā** (f.)	medicine
डॉक्टर	**DākTar** (m.)	doctor
डालना	**Dālnā** (+ne)	to put in, throw, pour
दाम	**dām** (m.)	price
देखना	**dek^{h}nā** (+ne)	to see, to look at, to notice
देर	**der** (f.)	delay, time (period of, slot of)
देश	**desh** (m.)	country
धन्यवाद	**d^{h}anyavād**	thanks
धर्म	**d^{h}arma** (m.)	religion
धागा	**d^{h}āgā** (m.)	(bracelets of) thread

धूम-धाम से	**d^{h}ūm-d^{h}ām se**	with pomp and show
दिखाना	**dik^{h}ānā** (+**ne**)	to show
दिल्ली	**dillī** (f.)	Delhi (the capital city)
दिमाग़	**dimāg** (m.)	brain
दिन	**din** (m.)	day
दो	**do**	two
दोनों	**donõ**	both
दीपक/दिया	**dīpak/diyā** (m.)	an earthen lamp
दीवाली	**dīvālī**	the festival of lights/lamps
दोस्त	**dost** (m.)	friend
दुनिया	**duniyā** (f.)	world
दूर	**dūr**	far, distant
दूर करना	**dūr karnā** (+**ne**)	to dispel, to eliminate
दूसरा	**dūsrā**	second, other, another
एक	**ek**	one
एक दो	**ek-do**	one or two
एक दूसरे से	**ek dūsre se**	with one another, each other
एक-सा	**ek-sā**	alike
फ़रिश्ता	**farishtā** (m.)	angel
फ़र्क	**farka** (m.)	difference
फ़र्ज़	**farz** (m.)	duty
फसल	**fasal** (f.)	crop
फ़ुरसत	**furasat** (f.)	free time, spare time, leisure
गलत	**galat**	wrong
गलत-फ़हमी	**galat-fahamī** (f.)	misconception, misunderstanding
गले लगाना	**gale lagānā** (+**ne**)	to embrace
गये/गए	**gaye**	went
गाँव	**gā̃v** (m.)	village
गाँव वाला	**gā̃v vālā** (m.)	villager
गाना	**gānā** (m.), v. (+**ne**)	song (n.), to sing (v.)
गाड़ी	**gāRī** (f.)	train, vehicle, cart
घन्टा/घंटा	**g^{h}anTā** (m.)	hour
घर	**g^{h}ar** (m.)	house
घोड़ा	**g^{h}oRā** (m.)	horse
घोड़ी	**g^{h}oRī** (f.)	mare
गिनना	**ginnā** (+**ne**)	to count
गोली	**golī** (f.)	tablet, pill; bullet
गुजरात	**gujarāt** (m.)	the State of Gujarat
गुमना	**gumnā** (–**ne**)	to be lost

गुस्सा	**gussā** (m.)	anger
गुठली	**guTʰlī** (f.)	stone (of a fruit)
ग्यारह	**gyārah**	eleven
हमारे यहाँ	**hamāre yahā̃**	at our place (house, country, etc.)
हमेशा	**hameshā**	always
हराना	**harānā** (+ne)	to defeat
हवा	**havā** (f.)	air, wind
हवाई अड्डा	**havāī aDDā** (m.)	airport
हज़ार	**hazār**	thousand
हाँ	**hā̃**	yes
हाल	**hāl** (m.)	condition
हालाँकि	**hālā̃ki**	although
हाथ	**hātʰ** (m.)	hand
हिन्दु/हिन्दू	**hindu/hindū**	a Hindu
हिन्दुस्तान	**hindustān** (m.)	India
हिन्दुस्तानी	**hindustānī**	Indian
हो	**ho**	are (you; तुम)
होली	**holī** (f.)	the festival of colours
होना	**honā** (–ne)	to be
हुकम	**hukam** (m.)	order
हूँ	**hū̃**	am
हैं	**hɛ̃**	are
है	**hɛ**	is
इंतजार/इन्तज़ार	**intzār** (m./f.)	wait
इंतजार करना	**intzār karnā** (+ne)	to wait
इसलिये	**isliye**	therefore, so, thus, because of this
इतना	**itnā** (m. adj.)	so much/many, this much/many
इतने में	**itne mẽ**	in the meantime
ईसाई	**īsāī**	a Christian
जब	**jab** (relative pronoun)	when
जब कि	**jab ki**	while
जहाज़	**jahāz** (m.)	a ship, vessel, plane
जलाना	**jalānā** (+ne)	to light, to burn; to kindle
जल्दी	**jaldī** (f.)	quickly, hurry
जन्म	**janma** (m.)	birth
जवाब	**javāb** (m.)	answer
जवाब देना	**javāb denā** (+ne)	to answer, reply
जाना	**jānā** (–ne)	to go
जाने वाले	**jāne vāle**	going, about to go

जाने दो	**jāne do**	let (someone) go
जानवर	**jānvar** (m.)	animal
जेब	**jeb** (f.)	pocket
जेब काटना	**jeb kāTnā (+ne)**	to pick-pocket
जी	**jī**	honorific word
जीवन	**jīvan** (m.)	life
जैसा	**jɛsā**	as
जैसे कि	**jɛse** (**ki**)	as, as if
ज्वालामुखी	**jwālāmuk^{h}ī** (m.)	volcano
कब	**kab**	when
कभी	**kab^{h}ī**	ever
कभी-कभी	**kab^{h}ī kab^{h}ī**	sometimes
कभी नहीं	**kab^{h}ī nahī̃**	never
कहाँ	**kahā̃**	where
कहानी	**kahānī** (f.)	story
कई	**kaī**	several
कल	**kal**	yesterday, tomorrow
कम	**kam**	less
कमरा	**kamrā** (m.)	room
करीब	**karīb**	about, approximately
करना	**karnā** (+**ne**)	to do
कथा	**kat^{h}ā** (f.)	story
कटना	**kaTnā** (–**ne**)	to be cut
कौन	**kaun**	who
कौन सा	**kaun sā**	which one
का	**kā**	of
काफी	**kāfī**	enough, sufficient
कागज़	**kāgaz** (m.)	paper
काम होना	**kām honā** (+**ko**)	to have work
काटना	**kāTnā** (+**ne**)	to cut
के बाद	**(ke) bād**	after, later
के बारे में	**ke bāre mẽ**	about, concerning
के बिना	**(ke) binā**	without
के लिये	**ke liye**	for
के साथ	**ke sāt^h**	with, together
के अलावा	**ke alāvā**	besides, in addition to
खाना	**k^{h}ānā** (m.), v (+**ne**)	food (n.), to eat (v.)
खलनायक	**k^{h}alnāyak** (m.)	villain
खेलना	**k^{h}elnā** (+/–**ne**)	to play
खिड़की	**k^{h}iRkī** (f.)	window
खोलना	**k^{h}olnā** (+**ne**)	to open

कीजिए/कीजिये	**kījie**	please do
किस	**kis**	which
किसी	**kisī**	someone
किस्मत	**kismat** (f.)	fortune, fate
किताब	**kitāb** (f.)	book
कितना	**kitnā**	how much/many?
कोई	**koī**	some, any, someone, anyone
कुछ	**kuc^h**	some
कुल	**kul**	total
कुरसी	**kursī** (f.)	chair
क्या	**kyā**	what
क्या	**kyā!**	what! I do not believe it!
क्यों	**kyõ**	why
क्योंकि	**kyõki**	because
कहना	**kɛhnā (+ne)**	to say
कहते हैं	**kɛhte hɛ̃**	is called, is said
कैसे	**kɛse**	how

लाल	**lāl**	red
लाना	**lānā** (**–ne**)	to bring
लगाना	**lagānā** (**+ne**)	to attach, to stick, to fix, apply
लगभग	**lagb^{h}ag**	about, approximately, almost
लगना	**lagnā** (**+ko**)	to seem, to be applied, to appear
लगना	**lagnā** (**–ne**)	to cost, to take (time)
लक्ष्मी	**lakshmī** (f.)	Lakshmi, the goddess of wealth, fortune, prosperity
लंदन	**landan**	London
लड़ाई	**laRāī** (f.)	fight, battle, war
लड़का	**laRkā** (m.)	boy
लड़की	**laRkī** (f.)	girl
लौटना	**lauTanā** (**–ne**)	to return, to come
लेकिन	**lekin**	but
लेना	**lenā** (**+ne**)	to take
लिखना	**lik^{h}nā** (**+ne**)	to write
लोग	**log** (m.)	people
लोक कथा	**lok kat^{h}ā** (f.)	folk tale

मछली	**mac^{h}lī** (f.)	fish
महा	**mahā**	great
महाभारत	**mahāb^{h}ārat** (f.)	one of the two greatest epics from Sanskrit
महीना	**mahīnā** (m.)	month

मन	**man** (m.)	mind
मनपसन्द	**man-pasand** (f.)	favourite
मनाना	**manānā** (+ne)	to celebrate (festival, holiday), to persuade
मर्द	**mard** (m.)	man
मरीज़	**marīz** (m.)	patient
मरना	**marnā** (–ne)	to die
मसाला	**masālā** (m.)	spice
मसालेदार	**masāledār**	spicy
मत	**mat**	not
मतलब	**matlab** (m.)	meaning
मौका	**maukā** (m.)	opportunity
मज़ा करना	**mazā karnā** (+ne)	to enjoy
माँस	**mā̃s** (m.)	meat
मालूम होना	**mālūm honā** (+ko)	to know, to be known
माता	**mātā** (f.)	mother
में	**mẽ**	in, during
मेहरबानी	**meharbānī** (f.)	kindness
मिलना	**milnā** (–ne)	to meet, to be available
मिलना	**milnā** (+ko)	to find, to receive, to get
मिर्च	**mirca** (f.)	chilli peppers
मित्र	**mitra** (m.)	friend
मिज़ाज	**mizāj** (m.)	temperament, nature
मुगल	**mugal**	the Moguls
मुझे	**muj^he**	(to) me
मुलाकात	**mulākāt** (f.)	meeting
मुलाकात होना	**mulākāt honā** (–ne)	to meet
मुश्किल	**mushkil**	difficult, difficulty (f.)
मैं	**mɛ̃**	I
महँगा	**mɛhɛ̃gā**	expensive
महल	**mɛhɛl** (m.)	palace
न . . . न	**na . . . na**	neither . . . nor
न?	**na?**	isn't it?
नहीं	**nahī̃**	not
नहीं तो	**nahī̃ to**	otherwise
नकल	**nakal** (f.)	copy, fake, imitation
नमक	**namak** (m.)	salt
नमस्ते	**namaste**	Hindu greeting and replies to the greeting (may be used by other religions too)
नया	**nayā**	new

नज़र **nazar** (f.) vision
नाम **nām** (m.) name
नापसन्द **nāpasand** (f.) dislike
नाश्ता **nāshtā** (m.) breakfast
ने **ne** agent marker in the perfective tenses

ओह **oh** exclamation of pain/sorrow

पहुँचना **pahũcnā** (–**ne**) to reach, arrive
पकड़ना **pakaRnā** (+**ne**) to catch
पलना **palnā** (–**ne**) to be brought up
पंक्ति/पंक्ति **paŋkti** (f.) line, row
पर **par** on, at
पराजित होना **parājit honā** (–**ne**) to be defeated
परेशान **pareshān** troubled
परहेज़ **parhez** (m.) abstinence
परहेज़ करना **parhez karnā** (+**ne**) to abstain, avoid
पढ़ना **paR^{h}nā** (–**ne**) to study
पढ़ना **paR^{h}nā** (+**ne**) to read
परिवार **parivār** (m.) family
पड़ना **paRnā** (–**ne**) to fall, to lie down,
पसन्द **pasand** (f.) choice, liking
पश्चिम **pashcim** (m.) west
पश्चिमी **pashcimī** western
पता **patā** (m.) address
पता लगना **patā lagnā** (+**ko**) to come to know
पटाखा **paTāxā** (m.) a firecracker
पत्रा **patrā** (m.) astrological chart
पवित्रता **pavitratā** (f.) purification, holiness
पाना **pānā** (+**ne**) to find, obtain
पानी **pānī** (m.) water
पास **pās** near
फल **p^{h}al** (m.) fruit
फेंकना **p^{h}ěknā** (+**ne**) to throw
फिर **p^{h}ir** again, then
फुलझड़ी **p^{h}ul-j^{h}aRī** (f.) a kind of firework which emits flower-like sparks
पिचकारी **pickārī** (f.) a syringe-shaped water-gun made of wood or metal
पीला **pīlā** yellow
पीना **pīnā** (+**ne**) to drink
प्रचलित होना **pracalit honā** (–**ne**) to be prevalent

प्राचीन	**prācīn**	ancient
प्रकाश	**prakāsha** (m.)	light
प्रसन्नता	**prasanntā** (f.)	happiness, joy
प्रसिद्ध	**prasidd^{h}a**	famous
प्रतीक	**pratīka** (m.)	symbol
प्रेम	**prema** (m.)	love
पुलिस वाला	**pulis vālā** (m.)	policeman
पुराना	**purānā**	old (inanimate)
पुस्तकालय	**pustakālaya**	library
पूछना	**pūc^{h}nā** (–**ne**)	to ask
पूजन	**pūjana** (n.)	worship
पूरा	**pūrā**	complete, whole, full
पूरा करना	**pūrā karnā** (+**ne**)	to complete
प्यार	**pyār** (m.)	love
पहला	**pɛhlā**	first
पहले	**pɛhle**	(at) first, ago, previously
पैसा	**pɛsā** (m.)	money (one hundredth of a rupee)
रक्षा-बन्धन	**rakshā-band^{h}ban** (m.)	the festival of love
रक्षा करना	**rakshā karnā** (+**ne**)	to protect, to defend
रंग	**raŋga** (m.)	colour
रंग बिरंगा	**raŋga-biraŋgā**	colourful
रंगीन	**raŋgīn**	colourful
राजा	**rājā** (m.)	king, emperor
राज्य	**rājya** (m.)	kingdom
राक्षस	**rākshasa** (m.)	demon
राम	**rāma** (m.)	Lord Rama (proper name)
रानी	**rānī** (f.)	queen
रात	**rāt** (f.)	night
रावण	**rāvaNa** (m.)	the demon king, Ravana
रेशम	**resham** (m.)	silk
रेशमी	**reshmī**	silken
ऋतु	**ritu** (f.)	season
रिवाज	**rivāj** (m.)	custom
रुकना	**ruknā** (–**ne**)	to stop
रुपया	**rupayā** (m.)	rupees (Indian currency)
रहना	**rɛhnā** (–**ne**)	live
सब	**sab**	all
सब्ज़ी	**sabzī** (f.)	vegetable
सच	**sac** (m.)	truth, true
सच	**sac!**	truth! It can't be true!

सकना	**saknā** (–**ne**)	can, be able to
सलाह	**salāh** (f.)	advice
सलाह लेना	**salāh lenā** (+**ne**)	to seek/take advice
सलाह मानना	**salāh mānnā** (+**ne**)	to accept/take advice
सलाम	**salām** (m.)	Muslim greeting and reply to the greeting
समझना	**samaj^{h}nā** (+/–**ne**)	to understand
समय	**samaya** (m.)	time
सम्राट	**samrāT** (m.)	king, emperor
संदेश	**sandesh** (m.)	message
संगीत	**saŋgīt** (m.)	music
संस्कृत	**sanskrita** (f.)	Sanskrit
सर्व-प्रिय	**sarva-priya**	loved by all, the most favourite
सौ	**sau**	hundred
सवाल	**savāl** (m.)	question
सवेरा	**saverā** (m.)	morning
साहिब	**sāhib** (m.)	sir
साल	**sāl** (m.)	year
सामान	**sāmān** (m.)	baggage, goods, stuff, tools
साड़ी	**sāRī** (f.)	saree
सात बजे	**sāt baje**	seven o'clock
से	**se**	from, with, by, than
सेवा	**sevā** (f.)	service
शादी	**shādī** (f.)	marriage
शादी-शुदा	**shādī-shudā**	married
शाम	**shām** (f.)	evening
शानदार	**shāndār**	splendid, great
शायद	**shāyad**	perhaps
शब्द	**shabda** (m.)	word
शरीर	**sharīr** (m.)	body
शताब्दी	**shatābdī** (m.)	century
शत्रु	**shatru** (m.)	enemy
शत्रुता	**shatrutā** (f.)	enmity, hostility
शौक	**shauk** (m.)	hobby, fondness, interest
श्रीकृष्ण	**shrī krishna**	Lord Krishna
शुभ	**shub^{h}a**	auspicious
शुक्रिया	**shukriyā** (m.)	thanks
शुरु करना	**shuru karnā** (+**ne**)	to begin
शहर	**shɛhɛr** (m.)	city
सीखना	**sīk^{h}nā** (+**ne**)	to learn
सिंगार	**siŋgār** (m.)	make up
सिर	**sir** (m.)	head

सिर्फ़	**sirf**	only
सोचना	**socnā** (+**ne**)	to think
सोलहवीं	**solvī̃**	sixteenth
सुबह	**subā** (f.)	morning
सुलतान	**sultān** (m.)	a Sultan, king, emperor
सुनहरा	**sunharā** (m. adj.)	golden
सुनते ही	**sunte hī**	as soon as (someone) heard
सूखा	**sūkʰā** (m. adj.)	dry
सूत	**sūt** (m.)	cotton
सूती	**sūtī**	cotton (adj.)
सैनिक	**sɛnik** (m.)	soldier
ताज	**tāj** (m.)	crown
ताजमहल	**tāj mɛhɛl** (m.)	the Taj Mahal
तब तक	**tab tak**	by then
तबीयत	**tabīyat** (f.)	health, disposition
तकलीफ	**taklīf** (f.)	trouble, bother
तकलीफ देना	**taklīf denā** (+**ne**)	to bother
तलाक	**talāk** (m.)	divorce
तर	**tar**	wet
तरी	**tarī** (f.)	liquid
तशरीफ़	**tashrīf** (f.)	(a term signifying respect)
तशरीफ लाना	**tashrīf lānā** (–**ne**)	to grace one's place, welcome, come
तशरीफ़ रखना	**tashrīf rakʰnā** (+**ne**)	to be seated
तेज़	**tez**	fast, quick, sharp, strong
था	**tʰā**	was
ठीक	**Tʰīk**	fine, okay
ठीक-ठाक	**Tʰīk-Tʰāk**	fine, hale and hearty
टीका लगाना	**Tīkā lagānā** (+**ne**)	to give an injection/a shot
तोहफा	**tohfā**	gift
थोड़ा	**tʰoRā**	little, few
तो	**to** (particle)	to, then, as regards
त्यौहार	**tyauhāra** (m.)	festival
तैरना	**tɛrnā** (–**ne**)	to swim
उम्र	**umar** (f.)	age
उपहार	**uphār**	gift
उत्साह	**utsāh** (m.)	enthusiam, joy, zeal
उत्तराधिकारी	**uttarādʰikārī** (m.)	heir, inheritor
वचन	**vacan** (m.)	promise
वह/वो	**vah/vo**	that, he, she

वही	**vahī (vah+hī)**	same, that very
वर्ष	**varsha** (m.)	year
वसन्त	**vasanta** (m.)	spring
वाह	**vāh**	ah! excellent! bravo!
वाह! वाह!	**vāh! vāh!**	wow! wow! bravo!
वापस	**vāpas**	back
वापस आना	**vāpas ānā** (–ne)	to come back
वातावरण	**vātāvaraNa** (m.)	atmosphere, environment
विदेशी	**videshī** (m.)	foreigner
विजय	**vijaya** (f.)	victory
विनती	**vintī** (f.)	request
वह कैसे	**vo kɛse**	how come?
वैसे	**vɛse**	otherwise, in addition, like that, similarly
ख़राब	**xarāb**	bad
ख़रीदना	**xarīdna** (+ne)	to buy
खतरनाक	**xatarnāk**	dangerous
ख़तरा	**xatrā** (m.)	danger
ख़्याल	**xayāl**	opinion, view
ख़ासकर	**xāskar**	especially, particularly
खुद	**xud**	oneself
खुदा हाफ़िज़	**xudā hāfiz**	goodbye
खुश–हाली	**xush-hālī** (f.)	prosperity
खुशबू	**xushbū**	fragrance (lit. happy smell)
खुशी	**xushī**	happiness
ख़ैरियत	**xɛriyat** (f.)	safety, welfare
यहाँ	**yahā̃**	here
यहाँ तक कि	**yahā̃ tak ki**	to the point, to the extent that
या	**yā**	or
याद दिलाना	**yād dilānā** (+ne)	to remind
यानी	**yānī**	that is, in other words
ज़रा	**zarā**	little, somewhat
जरूर	**zarūr**	of course, certainly
जरूरत	**zarūrat** (f.)	need, necessity
जरूरी	**zarūrī**	important, urgent, necessary
ज़ोर से	**zor se**	loudly
ज़ोर देना	**zor denā** (+ne)	to emphasize
ज़्यादा	**zyādā** (invariable)	more

Web resource

The following link is useful for translating Hindi into English:

http://shabdkosh.com/

Index

Related titles from Routledge

Colloquial Urdu

Tej K. Bhatia

Colloquial Urdu is easy to use and completely up to date! Written by experienced teachers for self-study or class use, the course offers you a step by step approach to written and spoken Urdu. No prior knowledge of the language is required.

What makes *Colloquial Urdu* your best choice in personal language learning?

- interactive – lots of exercises for regular practice
- clear – concise grammar notes
- practical – useful vocabulary and pronunciation guide
- complete – including answer key and special reference section

By the end of this rewarding course you will be able to communicate confidently and effectively in Urdu in a broad range of everyday situations.

ISBN13: 978-0-415-13540-5 (book)
ISBN13: 978-0-415-28950-4 (cds)
ISBN13: 978-0-415-44539-9 (book and cds pack)